FRENCH REFERENCE GRAMMAR

FRENCH REFERENCE GRAMMAR

FOR SCHOOLS AND COLLEGES

BY

J. E. MANSION

LATE SENIOR MODERN LANGUAGE MASTER
GEORGE WATSON'S COLLEGE
EDINBURGH

GREENWOOD PRESS, PUBLISHERS
WESTPORT, CONNECTICUT

Originally published in 1928 by D. C. Heath and Company, Boston

Reprinted by Greenwood Press, Inc.
51 Riverside Avenue, Westport, CT 06880

First Greenwood reprinting 1971
Second Greenwood reprinting 1976
Third Greenwood reprinting 1977

Library of Congress catalog card number 72-98855
ISBN 0-8371-3125-1

Printed in the United States of America

PREFACE

"Le maître ne se laissera jamais dominer par le souci du vocabulaire. Il se rappellera qu'il doit avant tout faire acquérir à ses élèves le mécanisme de la langue."—*Instructions concernant les programmes de l'enseignement secondaire.* 1908. *Langues vivantes.*

"La langue parlée par les gens cultivés doit former le fond de l'enseignement des langues vivantes. Plus tard seulement, à un stade beaucoup plus avancé, l'élève qui possède déjà assez bien cette langue parlée peut faire connaissance avec la langue littéraire." —*E. Rodhe.*

In the following pages I have endeavoured to give a presentation, sufficiently full for the use of colleges and secondary schools, of the *mechanism* of present-day French. But the constructions of a highly developed language are too complex to be embodied adequately in a few hard and fast 'rules,' and their compression within the limits of a school text-book has been rendered possible only by severe excision of all unessential matter, of all 'exceptions,' and of most of what pertains to the study of the vocabulary and of so-called 'idiom': lists of irregular nouns and adjectives, lists of adverbs, lists of verbs taking certain prepositions, etc. I have deferred to tradition so far as to include a full presentation of the numerals and of the irregular verbs, but have jettisoned the plural of *carnaval* and *régal,*[1] *et sic de similibus.*

On the other hand, I have endeavoured to state the rules of grammar fully and accurately,[2] with some indication of the

[1] I may perhaps plead in justification that in forty years I have not, that I am aware of, met the plural of these words outside of the pages of school grammars.

[2] Thus, it is inaccurate to state that the second past perfect is always, or even primarily, subordinated to a past historic; that *être suivi, précédé,* etc., always have *de* with the agent; that the noun has no article after *sans* and *ni*; that the noun subject follows the verb in a relative clause; that the passive voice is seldom used in French, etc.

It is important also to avoid writing sheer nonsense, such as is to be found in many widely used grammars: "*Ceci* et *cela* sont employés impersonnellement." "L'accent grave se place sur *a, e, u,*

limits within which they are operative; to present as *tendencies* of the language, and not as laws, many so-called rules which are in no way binding, and which are daily ignored by reputable writers; and to account for, and explain, the mechanism of French in so far as this is compatible with a non-historical treatment of the subject.

Further, I have taken to heart the precept of Rodhe, and founded this presentation of French grammar on the spoken language, and on a large collection of '*fiches*' gathered during the last ten years from nineteenth- and twentieth-century writers. To the examples given no authors' names have, except in rare cases, been attached, as they are not always given in their integrity, slight alteration to make them readily intelligible apart from their context, and much excision, having been found advantageous in a work intended for schools; but the sources of many will be at once recognized, and in particular my indebtedness to *Marie-Claire*.

The literary constructions of the language have not been ignored, but it has been my endeavour throughout to differentiate between 'normal' and 'literary' speech or writing, and also to point out at least a few of the means by which in French emotional effects are obtained. In this direction hardly anything has been done as yet, and I am conscious of the inadequacy of my own attempt; but where I am, I believe, leading the way, others will perhaps find it worth while to advance farther.

The accidence and syntax of each part of speech have been dealt with together, but it is difficult to include all the facts within this mode of presentation, and the sentence as a whole has been studied in a Second Part, which deals with such matters as word-order, the moods of the verb, the tense sequences, and the concords. This method of treatment has entailed some duplication of statements, but in dealing with facts so complex as those of language iteration is perhaps unavoidable.

While the *mechanism* of the language has thus been, it is hoped,

et il leur donne un son ouvert: *où*." "Se mettent devant le nom les adjectifs plus courts que lui: *une méchante fille*." "Le passif ne s'emploie jamais avec un verbe qui ne peut s'employer impersonnellement en français." "Adjectives of colour follow the noun: *Il a les yeux bleus*." "The subject follows the verb . . . when the verb comes first." Etc. etc.

adequately dealt with, the many peculiarities of French idiom, such as the numerous and important prepositional phrases which cannot be inferred from first principles, have been left out of account. Such facts of language properly belong to a handbook of Syntactical Idioms, for which much material has already been brought together, and which may appear in due course as a supplement to this grammar.

I need hardly give a list of works consulted; these include practically every reputable grammar published in this country, in France, in Germany, and in Scandinavia, and innumerable monographs and articles[1]—"*J'ai pris mon bien où je l'ai trouvé*"—but I must make due acknowledgment to Plattner's *Ausführliche Grammatik*, to Ch. Bally's *Traité de Stylistique française*, which should be in the hands of every language-teacher, and especially to the works of Professor Brunot. Had it not been for the example which the latter has given in studying anew, and with entire independence of tradition, the actual facts of French as he found them, I should hardly have dared to compose this little grammar, which, though written with prudence and caution, may appear to many as iconoclastic and heretical.

Of the *Tolérances* which formed the subject of a ministerial *arrêté* in 1901, no account has been taken. In so far as they recognized accomplished facts in the evolution of French, they are embodied in this grammar; where they attempted to innovate, they have remained a dead letter, and more than one of the recommendations deserved no better fate.

To the learner my presentation of many time-honoured rules may appear perplexing and less satisfactory than the 'old way.' It is no doubt both easy and soul-satisfying to learn by heart that "adjectives ending in *-able, al, ant, el, eur, eux, ible, if, ule, ile, ique,* invariably follow the noun," and only the observant and thinking student is disturbed by the fact that such rules are contradicted in every page of French.

In the study of language, however, as in that of other sciences, personal observation leads to the most satisfactory and enduring knowledge. The learner in natural science is encouraged to test facts and verify statements on his own account, and to use his text-book chiefly as a guide in his work and a source of

[1] For a fairly exhaustive review, within the dates mentioned, of the literature available, see *Bibliographie de la Syntaxe du Français* (1840–1905), par P. Horluc et G. Marinet (Paris, A. Picard et Fils, 1908).

suggestion. Let the learner in French do the same. Let him take a blank exercise-book, paragraph it to correspond with this 'text-book,' and daily enter in their proper place examples which he will himself cull from his reading, whether these examples agree with the 'text-book' or contradict it, and he will in the course of three or four years acquire the habit of observation, convictions of his own, founded on an abundant store of facts, and confidence in his knowledge. *C'est la grâce que je lui souhaite.*

J. E. M.

CONTENTS

PART II

SENTENCE CONSTRUCTION

INTRODUCTION

§ 1. We use language for two main purposes: (1) To give logical expression to facts and desires, to thoughts and judgments; (2) to give spontaneous expression to our emotions.

(1) Logical expression is deliberate and rational; in giving considered expression to our thoughts, we speak and write with care, with due regard to formal co-ordination and subordination; lucidity is our chief aim, and to achieve it we adhere strictly to such forms, concords, word sequences, and so forth, as have come to be accepted as *normal* in the language which we are using as a medium, which form the foundations of its 'grammar,' and which, used in conjunction with a *normal* vocabulary, constitute *normal* speech or writing.

Examples of 'normal' French:

La grammaire est une science qui a pour objet l'étude des règles du langage, soit écrit, soit parlé.

Dans la nature, c'est de l'eau que les végétaux et les animaux tirent la plupart des principes minéraux qui leur sont nécessaires. L'évaporation de l'eau forme les nuages, qui retombent en pluie.

Dès qu'il s'agit de rendre service, il faut songer que la vie est courte et qu'il n'y a pas un moment à perdre.

(2) The expression of our emotions, on the other hand, is spontaneous; our feelings and ideas present themselves, and find utterance, in an order which is not always logical or rational; unessential units of the sentence, and even essential words, may be omitted, and replaced by look, gesture, or tone of voice. This use of language may be described as 'emotional' or *affective.*

The following are some of the characteristics of *affective* speech in most languages, with examples in French:

Emotions find expression in exclamation rather than in logical statement. For instance, to express surprise:

Normal: Je suis surpris de vous voir.
Affective: Tiens, c'est vous!
Vous! Ah, par exemple!

Under the stress of emotion, utterance begins before the mind has clearly surveyed the whole field of the thought to which it is about to give expression, and proceeds in short spurts, a bit at a time, the result being a *dislocation* of the elements of the sentence. Examples:

Normal: Venez vite.
Affective: Venez ! vite ! *or* Vite ! venez !

In the normal 'Venez vite,' the order is fixed (adverb after verb); in affective 'Venez ! vite !' *dislocation* is revealed by the fact that we may transpose the elements of the sentence. Thus again:

Normal: Je n'ai pas le temps d'aller au café.
Affective: Du temps, pour aller au café, moi, je n'en ai pas.
Le café, je n'ai pas de temps, moi, pour y aller.
Moi ! aller au café ! je n'ai pas de temps pour ça.
Aller au café ? Je n'en ai pas le temps, moi.

Affective speech makes free use of interjections and other exclamatives.

Normal: Je pense que vous vous moquez de moi, et vous m'impatientez.
Affective: Ah çà ! dites donc, est-ce que vous vous moquez de moi ? Ah ! et puis, vous savez, vous m'embêtez, à la fin !

Normal speech is intellectual, and fond of abstract expression; affective speech uses concrete images and similes.

Normal: Ne m'irritez pas.
Affective: Ne m'échauffez par les oreilles !
Normal: Il s'enfuit.
Affective: Il prend ses jambes à son cou.

Normal speech states things as they are; affective speech indulges in gross exaggeration.

Normal: J'ai très faim.
Affective: J'ai l'estomac dans les talons.

Normal: Prenez-vous du lait dans votre thé, monsieur ? — Très peu, madame.
Affective: Du lait, monsieur ? — Une larme, madame, moins que rien !

The modes of expression of affective speech are largely a matter of vocabulary and idiom, but they also concern grammar to a considerable extent, particularly with regard to 'dislocation,' and many uses peculiar to the expression of emotion and feeling will engage our attention in the following pages.

The emotional, or affective, use of language cannot of course be clearly differentiated from its purely logical or rational use; in ordinary speech these two uses constantly overlap and commingle. Or we might say that the smooth stream of logical expression is frequently agitated by impulses and waves of emotionalism, of varying degrees of intensity, sometimes so slight as merely to cause a faint ripple on the surface, sometimes so violent as entirely to break up the normal course of logical expression. A sound knowledge of grammar helps us to detect affective uses which in a foreign language we might otherwise fail to recognize.

§ 2. Considered from another point of view, a spoken language is not one, but manifold: it varies not only with the education of the speaker, with his social status and his daily avocations, but also to a great extent with his environment. We do not speak in the same manner to an intimate friend and to a superior, on the football field and in a drawing-room. Though an elementary grammar need take cognizance only of 'educated' speech, it must enable the student to distinguish between 'careful' and 'colloquial' expression. Thus, the same man will say, speaking 'carefully':

Les cigares, je ne les aime pas;

and speaking familiarly, or 'colloquially':

Les cigares, je n'aime pas ça;

or even:

Les cigares, j'aime pas ça.

The nature of the difference between these different forms of expression must be clearly realized.

§ 3. Reference must now be made to yet another function of language. In civilized communities it becomes a means of artistic expression; it is used consciously, in poetry or in prose, to achieve artistic effects—for instance, beauty of form; its aim becomes *literary*. While much literature, and perhaps the best, has been written in language entirely normal, the literary artist frequently calls to his aid various devices, many of them affective, such as the use of unfamiliar but picturesque words, either old or new, the majestic unfolding of his thought in flowing periods, or its condensation into polished epigram; but apart from these devices he at times makes use of syntactical constructions which *do not belong to normal grammar*, and the student must learn to discriminate in the course of his reading between normal and purely literary uses.

Examples of 'literary' French:

> " Bénie soit la main qui m'étrenne ! " Ainsi marmonne avec reconnaissance le pauvre vieil aveugle à croppetons sous le porche d'une église, quand il entend tintinnabuler dans sa sébile son premier sou de la journée.—*Jean Richepin.*

The word *marmonne* is carefully chosen to suggest by its sound the toothless mumbling of old age; the author uses for *accroupi* the archaic form *à croppetons* on account of its picturesque associations with the literature of the fifteenth century; and for *sonner* the unfamiliar neologism *tintinnabuler*, because it falls pleasantly on the ear, renders happily the sound of the falling coin, and being a learned borrowing from Latin, produces a humorous effect in its homely setting. These three words are intended to tickle the ear and the mind, to *affect* us, each in a different manner; the sentence has been carefully composed with that end in view, the writing is *artistic.*

> . . . Si quelque journaliste eût demandé à ses lecteurs quel serait désormais le " prince des dilettantes," assurément, c'est sur M. Anatole France que se fût portée la presque unanimité des suffrages. . . .—*G. Michaut.*

Normal French would have *avait demandé, que se serait portée.* The uses of the past perfect subjunctive in this sentence are exclusively academic and literary; we can infer at once that the passage is taken from a university lecture or a learned preface.

> Quand on réfléchit à cette histoire de l'espèce humaine, à cette nuit profonde qui couvre en tous lieux son berceau, à ces races qui se trouvent partout en même temps et partout dans la même ignorance de leur origine, aux diversités de toute espèce qui les séparent encore plus que les distances, les montagnes et les mers, à l'étonnement dont elles sont saisies quand elles se rencontrent, à la constante hostilité qui se déclare entre elles dès qu'elles se connaissent; quand on songe à cette obscure prédestination qui les appelle

tour à tour sur la scène du monde, qui les y fait briller un moment, et qui les replonge bientôt dans l'obscurité, un sentiment d'effroi s'empare de l'âme, et l'individu se sent accablé de la mystérieuse fatalité qui semble planer sur l'espèce.—*Th. Jouffroy.*

An outstanding example of sustained and impressive thought, and of the art of leading up to a climax a well-balanced and harmonious sentence. But in normal French, *e.g.* in letter-writing, it is unnecessary, and would savour of affectation, to carry the art of composition to such a high pitch of excellence.

§ **4.** In the following pages constructions and forms not otherwise characterized may be taken to represent *normal* uses. From these we shall distinguish uses that are essentially *affective* (*dislocations,* etc.), or *colloquial,* or *literary,* using these terms in the senses explained above, but on the understanding that colloquial or literary uses are frequently affective at the same time.

Nor are the distinctions which we have outlined confined to the study of grammar ; they apply in a far greater degree to the study of vocabulary and of 'idiom,' and the student who wishes to enter thoroughly into the spirit of a language, and to cultivate a sense of style, should keep them constantly in mind.

PART I

§ **5.** The **Alphabet** is the same in French as in English.

The letters **k** and **w** are used only in foreign words.

> **la Kabylie, Kandahar, le kangourou.**
> **Waterloo, le wagon.**

§ **6.** The Alphabet is used to represent the sounds of French, as shown below:

Vowels

[iː]	**i, î, y**	rire, épître, martyr
[i]	**i, î, y**	vite, vît, cygne
[e]	**e, é, ai**	donner, été, j'ai
[ɛː]	**e, è, ê, ei, ai, aî**	terre, père, hêtre, reine, paire, chaîne
[ɛ]	**e, è, ê, ei, ai, aî**	elle, sujet, très, forêt, peine, jamais, il connaît
[aː]	**a**	rare, tard
[a]	**a, â, à, e(m), e(n)**	chat, tache, il aimât, là, femme, solennel
[ɑː]	**a, â, ea**	sable, tâche, âge, Jeanne
[ɑ]	**a, â**	pas, âgé
[ɔː]	**o, au**	fort, Laure
[ɔ]	**o, au, u(m)**	donne, Paul, j'aurai, album
[oː]	**o, ô, au**	fosse, rôle, épaule
[o]	**o, ô, au, eau**	dos, impôt, chaud, aussi, chapeau
[uː]	**ou, oû**	cour, tous [tuːs], il goûte
[u]	**ou, oû, aoû**	tout, goutte, goût, août
[yː]	**u, û, eu**	mur, mûr, ils eurent
[y]	**u, û, eu**	russe, cru, crû, j'ai eu, j'eus
[øː]	**eu, eû**	meule, jeûne
[ø]	**eu, œu**	feu, ceux, nœud, œufs
[œː]	**eu, œu**	fleur, sœur
[œ]	**eu, œu**	seul, jeune, fleurir, œuf
[ə]	**e**	le, ce, entremets, vendredi

[ɛ̃ː]	**in, ein, ain, în, im**	prince, ceindre, plaindre, vînmes, il grimpe
[ɛ̃]	**in, ein, ain, (i)en, yn, im, aim, ym**	vin, plein, main, bien, syntaxe, n'importe, faim, thym
[ɑ̃ː]	**an, en, am, em**	danse, il entre, ample, trempe
[ɑ̃]	**an, en, am, em, aon**	enfant, tambour, temps, paon
[ɔ̃ː]	**on, om**	honte, nombre, comte
[ɔ̃]	**on, om**	mon, plomb
[œ̃ː]	**um**	humble
[œ̃]	**un, eun, um**	lundi, à jeun, parfum

Diphthongs

(Formed with semi-consonants)

1. '*Ascending*'

[j]	**ie, ia, io, iou, ien, ion, ya, yeu, etc.**	pied, lierre, piano, diable, mioche, piou-piou, chrétien, ration, voyage, yeux, etc.
[w]	**oue, oua, oui, oi, oin, ouin, way, etc.**	ouest, ouate, oui, Louis, noir, je bois [bwa], le bois [bwɑ], loin, pingouin, tramway, etc.
[ɥ]	**ue, ui, ueu, etc.**	muet, huit, lui, puits, aiguille, lueur

2. '*Descending*'

[iːj]	**ille**	fille, famille
[ij]	**ill**	sillage
[ɛːj]	**eil, eill, aye**	soleil, veille, je paye
[ɛj]	**eill, ay**	ensoleillé, payer
[aːj]	**ail, aill**	travail, travaille
[aj]	**aill**	travaillons
[ɑːj]	**âill**	il bâille
[ɑj]		bâiller
[œːj]	**euil(l), œil, ueil(l)**	fauteuil, feuille, œil, orgueil, je cueille
[œj]	**euill, œill, ueill**	veuillez, œillade, cueillir

Consonants

[p]	**p, pp, b**	pain, frapper, obtenir
[b]	**b, bb**	beau, bleu, abbé

[m]	**m, mm**	mou, flamme, prisme
[f]	**f, ff, ph**	feu, effet, bref, phrase, Joseph
[v]	**v, w, f**	voir, vivre, Wagram, neuf heures
[t]	**t, tt, th, d**	table, tête, nette, moitié, théâtre, grand homme
[d]	**d, dd**	donner, addition, sud
[n]	**n, nn, mn**	né, canne, amen, automne
[s]	**s, ss, c, ç, sc, t(i), x**	sou, tasse, omnibus, cire, leçon, scène, descendre, action, six, soixante, Bruxelles
[z]	**s, z, x**	cousin, désir, les enfants, vas-y, zéro, deuxième, aux armes !
[l]	**l, ll**	lait, aile, allons, hôtel, table
[ʃ]	**ch, sch**	chose, chercher, schisme
[ʒ]	**j, g(e)**	Jean, jouer, gigot, manger, nous mangeons
[k]	**c, cc, k, ck, q, qu, ch, g**	camp, accabler, képi, bifteck, coq, quatre, écho, chrétien, suer sang et eau
[g]	**g, gg, gu, c**	gâteau, aggraver, guerre, guide, second
[ɲ]	**gn**	campagne, poignet
[r]	**r, rr, rh**	rare, être, marbre, marron, rhume
[ks]	**x, cc**	extrême, accident
[gz]	**x**	exister, Xénophon

Note.—**h** is never pronounced. A word with initial **h muette** is treated, as regards elision and 'liaison,' as if it began with a vowel. A word beginning with h aspirée is treated as if it began with a consonant, though the **h** itself is not sounded.

In a few words **h** between vowels is equivalent to a tréma : **cahier** (=caïer).

§ 7. 1. Division of Words into Syllables.

(1) Begin each syllable with a consonant if possible.

a-ni-mal, ra-me-ner, rai-son.

(2) Make the division between consonants.

lais-ser, pro-tes-tant, cin-quan-te, at-ter-rir, fil-let-te.

(3) But never separate **th, ch, pl, pr, bl, br, cl, cr, gl, gr, tr, dr, vr** (*i.e.* those consonantal groups which may occur at the beginning of a word), nor **gn** = [ɲ].

ca-tho-li-que, ca-cher, peu-ple, fai-ble, siè-cle.
ré-gler, nè-gre, vien-drai, ré-gner.

2. A syllable ending in a vowel is **open.**
A syllable ending in a consonant is **closed.**
An **e** in an **open syllable** is **mute.**

(But for the purposes of this rule the end syllable of a polysyllabic word is still considered 'open' when it ends in a plural **s** or with the verbal **s, nt.**

An **e** in a **closed syllable** is **never mute**; without bearing any accent it has the sound [ɛ] or [e].

§ 8. Accents and their Use.

´ aigu ` grave ^ circonflexe

1. In an **open syllable, e** takes the '**accent aigu**' if it is to be pronounced [e]:

é-té, es-pé-rer, les al-liés, ai-mé, ai-mée, né-gres-se, le pré, les prés.

2. **e** takes the '**accent grave**'—

(*a*) In an **open syllable,** when it is to be pronounced [ɛ], *i.e.* when it bears the stress, the end syllable being mute.

pè-re, nè-gre, j'es-pè-re, ils ai-mè-rent, col-lè-ge, cé-lè-bre.

When the open syllable does not bear the end-stress, there is no fixed rule; compare **avènement, événement; je mènerai, je céderai; pèlerin, médecin.**

(*b*) In the termination **-ès.**

progrès, succès, très, près, dès, après.

(*c*) As a distinguishing mark (not affecting the pronunciation), in

à, là (voilà, delà), çà (deçà), déjà, où.

Note.—In texts printed before 1878 the ending **-ège** was printed **-ége,** and a number of words were spelt with a tréma which now have the accent grave; *e.g.* **poète** was spelt **poëte.** These spellings are now obsolete.

3. The **accent circonflexe** is used on the five vowels **a, e, i, o, u,** and over the second letter of the groups **ai, ei, eu, oi, ou**—

(*a*) To denote the lengthening that results from the disappearance of an 's.'

hâte,	**bête,**	**île,**	**hôte,**	**maître,**	**croûte.**
haste	*beast*	*isle*	*host*	*master*	*crust*

(*b*) To denote some other contraction.

sûr, mûr, âge, âme, jeûne,
gaîment = gaiement, remercîment = remerciement.

(*c*) Merely as a sign of length.

grâce, extrême, trône, pôle, flûte, reître.

(*d*) As a distinguishing mark in

je croîs, crû, etc., **dû,** from **croître, devoir.**
(Compare **je crois, cru,** from **croire,** and **du = de le.**)

(*e*) Notice also the forms **vînmes, vîntes, tînmes, tîntes,** and **bâiller.**

Notes.—(*a*) In an initial syllable, not bearing the stress, the fall of an **s** after an **e** is indicated by **é**, not **ê**.

étude,	**échelle,**	**détruire.**
study	*scale*	*destroy*

Compare also '**j'étais**' and '**être.**'

(*b*) Initial capital letters do not as a rule take the accent, except the letter **e**. Thus:

âme, Ame; île, Ile; ôter, Oter;
but **Étude, Ère, Être.**

§ **9.** The **Apostrophe** indicates the 'elision' or fall—

1. Of **e** in **de, le, ne, que, ce, je, me, te, se.**
   l'ami d'Albert, je n'en ai qu'un, aujourd'hui, il m'invite à l'accompagner.
2. Of **a** in **la.**
   l'amie d'Henriette l'a invitée.
3. Of **i** in **si** (before **il** or **ils** only).
   s'il vient, s'ils viennent.

§ **10.** The **e** also falls in

lorsque, puisque, quoique, before **il, ils, elle, elles, on, un, une:**
lorsqu'il vient, puisqu'elle en a.

jusque, before **à, au, en, ici, où, alors:**
jusqu'ici, jusqu'à demain.

quelqu'un(e) (*but* **quelque autre, quelque étrange que ce soit**).

presqu'île (*but* **presque arrivé**).

entr'acte, entr'ouvrir, etc.

(The spelling **grand'mère, grand'tante, grand'peur,** etc., is due to a mistaken belief that the original form was '**grande mère,**' etc.)

Notes.—(*a*) Elision only takes place between words standing in close relation to each other (*i.e.* belonging to the same '*groupe de force*').

Compare: **J'y arriverai** and **Puissé-je y arriver** (in which **je** 'clings' to **puisse**, and not to **y arriver**).

Il l'a dit à son père and **Dis-le à son père.**

(*b*) An apostrophe should never occur at the end of a line. Divide

aujour-d'hui, not **aujourd'-hui;**
lors-qu'il viendra, not **lorsqu'-il viendra.**

§ **11.** The **Cédille** indicates that **c** has the sound [s] and not the sound [k] before **a, o, u.**

Une **leçon** de **français.** Je l'ai **reçu. Ç'a été** facile.

§ **12.** The **Tréma** indicates that a vowel must not be grouped in pronunciation with the vowel which precedes it.

Moïse, Saül, haïr, Caïn, ouï [ui] (compare **oui** [wi]), **ciguë.**

Thus adjectives ending in **-gu** have in the feminine a **tréma** on the **e,** to indicate that the **u** retains its full value.

aigu, aiguë [ɛgy].

§ **13.** The **Trait d'union,** or hyphen, is inserted without any attempt at consistency—

1. In many compound nouns, adjectives, and pronouns.

grand-père, chef-lieu, sourd-muet ;
moi-même, quelques-uns.

2. In many compound proper nouns.

les Pays-Bas, la Grande-Bretagne, les États-Unis.

Particularly in the ' départements ' of France.

Seine-et-Oise, Loire-Inférieure, Alpes-Maritimes.

And in all successions of Christian names.

Philippe-Auguste, Marie-Thérèse, Jean-Jacques Rousseau.

3. In numerals, between the tens and the units, when there is no conjunction **et.**

dix-sept, vingt-deux, le trente-troisième.

Also in **quatre-vingts,** etc. : **quatre-vingt-onze.**
But **vingt et un, trente et unième.**

4. In a few adverb phrases.

c'est-à-dire, peut-être, sur-le-champ.

But **tout de suite, à peu près,** etc.

5. To join **ci** and **là** to the word which they qualify.

ci-joint, là-bas, là-haut, là-dessus.

(But **là dedans.**)

celui-ci, cette maison-là.

6. Between verbs and a following subject or object pronoun.

Que vois-je ! Parle-t-il ? Que dirait-on ? Donnez-le-moi.

Note.—In texts printed before 1878, **très** was joined by a hyphen to the following adjective or adverb : **très-joli, très-bien.** This use of the hyphen is now obsolete.

§ **14. Capital Letters** are used less frequently than in English. The following examples will show the chief points of difference :

1. Il viendra **dimanche** ou **lundi.** Au mois de **février.**
2. Le **roi** Édouard VII ; le **docteur** Moreau ; le **duc** d'Aumale.
   Voici **monsieur, madame** et **mademoiselle** Dupuis.

(But Voici **M., Mme** et **Mlle** Dupuis.)

3. La **mer** Noire, l'**océan** Atlantique.
4. Le peuple **français,** l'armée **anglaise.**
   Il parle **russe** et **espagnol.** Il parle **le russe** et **l'espagnol.**

But usually

Les **Anglais** et les **Français.** Il est **Espagnol.**

Though many authors write and print

Les **anglais** et les **français.**

Note **saint** Jean, **saint** Étienne, etc. (the saints) ; but la **Saint-Jean** (the feast day), **Saint-Étienne** (the town), etc.

§ **15. Punctuation.** Single inverted commas are not used in quoting, and double inverted commas (**guillemets**) are used much more sparingly than in English. Thus :

" Entrez, dit-il, et asseyez-vous."

A FEW PRINCIPLES
GOVERNING WRITTEN AND SPOKEN FRENCH

§ **16.** The spelling of words in French is based largely on historical, instead of phonetic, considerations, and must be learnt chiefly through practice. There are, however, some governing principles which should be understood.

1. The proper use of the **Accents.** See § **8.**

2. Pronunciation and spelling of **g + vowel:**

(*a*) **ga** [ga] **ge** [ʒə] **gi** [ʒi] **go** [go] **gu** [gy] **gy** [ʒi]
(*b*) **gea** [ʒa] **geo** [ʒo] **geu** [ʒy]
(*c*) **gue** [gə] **gui** [gi]

(*a*) **garde, je mange, gilet, gorge, aigu, Égypte.**
(*b*) **Georges, je mangeais, gageure** [gaʒyːr].
(Compare Engl *changeable, manageable.*)
(*c*) **guerre, fatigue, Guillaume, long, longue.**

3. Pronunciation and spelling of **c + vowel**:

(*a*) **ca** [ka] **ce** [sə] **ci** [si] **co** [ko] **cu** [ky] **cy** [si]
(*b*) **ça** [sa] **ço** [so] **çu** [sy] (See § 11.)
(*c*) **que** [kə] **qui** [ki]

(*a*) **cahier, percer, cire, colère, curé, cygne.**
(*b*) **perçant, garçon, nous perçons, reçu.**
(Unlike Engl. *noticeable, serviceable.*)
(*c*) **public,** fem. **publique ; vaincre, nous vainquîmes.**

4. The group **euil** becomes **ueil** (reverting to an old spelling **ue** for **eu**, to avoid **ueu**) after **c** and **g**.

accueil, cueillir, orgueil.

5. The endings **au, eau, eu, œu** are followed by final **x** instead of **s**.

je vaux, les beaux chapeaux, je veux, les vœux, deux.
(Chief exceptions : **bleu,** pl. **bleus ; je meus.**)

6. The letter **v**, when final, changes to **f**.

vive, masc. **vif ; veuve,** masc. **veuf.**

7. Most consonant groups, *e.g.* **gn, rm, mm, nn, ss, tt,** are reduced and simplified when final, or when followed by the verbal endings **s, t**. Before the latter, **s, v,** and sometimes **t** are also dropped.

maligne, masc. **malin ; sonner, le son ; nommer, le nom.**

dorm+s>je **dors** ; **craign**+s>je **crains** ; **batt**+s>je **bats** ; **batt**+t>il **bat** ; **finiss**+s>je **finis** ; **finiss**+t>il **finit** ; **serv**+s>je **sers** ; **serv**+t>il **sert** ; **reçoiv**+s>je **reçois** ; **viv**+s>je **vis** ; **viv**+t>il **vit**.

Note.—To a stem ending in **d** no **t** is added, because final **d** = [t] : **Descend-il ?** = [desɑ̃t il]. Thus : **Il mord, il répond, il descend.**

8. Before another consonant, particularly before **x** (=s) and t, l usually becomes **u**.

cheval+s>**chevaux** ; **val**+s>je **vaux** ; **fall**+t>il **faut.**

Thus also **autel, faucon** ; cp. English *altar, falcon.*

9. The groups **nr, lr,** generate a **d.**

vien-rai > **viendrai** ; **val-rai** (> valdrai) > **vaudrai** ; **fall-ra** (>faldra)>**faudra** ; **absolv-re** (>absolre>absoldre)>**absoudre** ; **ceign-re**>**ceindre.**

Similarly **sr** generates a **t.**

connaiss-re (>connaistre)>**connaître.**

10. Between the groups **ai, oi, ui,** and a following vowel (not **e** mute) a [j] is always generated. From **roi+al** is formed, not [rwa-al], but [rwa-jal]=**roi-ial.** The resulting **ii** is spelt **y**: **royal.** Thus :

soie, soyeux ; **voir, voyant** ; **un essai, essayer** ; **fuir, fuyant.**

Note.—The present tense of **payer** is either **je paie** or **je paye,** because there are alternative pronunciations [ʒə pɛ] and [ʒə pɛːj]. So also with other verbs in **-ayer.**

11. In a French word, considered apart from its context, **the stress is on the last sounded syllable.** In all languages stress has a great influence on sound, and in many French words the stem syllable is pronounced differently according as it bears the stress or not.

The following are the most important correspondences :

	Unstressed	*Stressed*
(*a*)	[ə] **chandelier, appeler, modeler, semer, je ferai, nous prenons.**	[ɛ] **chandelle, j'appelle, modèle, je sème, faire, ils prennent.**
	[e] **Suédois, négresse, écolier, céder.**	[ɛ] **la Suède, nègre, écolière, je cède.**
(*b*)	[ə] **venir, maintenir, chenil.**	[jɛ, jɛ̃] **ils viennent, il vient, maintien, chien.**
	[e] **acquérir, matériel.**	[jɛ] **j'acquiers, ils acquièrent, matière.**
(*c*)	[ə] **me, recevez, buvant** (=bevant), **fenil.**	[wa, wɛ̃] **moi, reçois, boire, foin.**
(*d*)	[a] **clarté, nous savons, marin.**	[ɛ] **clair, je sais, mer.**
(*e*)	[u] **prouver, courage, vigoureux, mourir, vouloir.**	[œ] **preuve, cœur, vigueur, il meurt, ils veulent.**
	[u] **moulin, vouloir, pouvoir.**	[ø] **meule, je veux, il peut.**

THE PARTS OF SPEECH

§ **17.** 1. There are in French **eight** parts of speech, as in English.

It is convenient to treat apart those demonstrative adjectives of a special type and use generally known as **articles.**

2. There are **three genders,** as in English, but the **Neuter** gender is restricted to certain pronouns, and to certain uses of the adjectives.

3. There are **two numbers,** as in English.

4. There are **four cases: Nominative, Vocative, Accusative,** and **Dative.** The dative case is restricted to the personal pronoun.

French has **no Genitive case,** or rather, the only instances of a genitive are the personal pronoun **en** and the relative **dont.**

The nominative, vocative, and accusative of the noun and its adjuncts show no difference of form.

Certain **pronouns** have different forms in the nominative, accusative, and dative.

THE VERB

§ **18.** A French verb consists of **one** or **more stems** to which are added **endings** characteristic of person, tense, and **mood**: donn-**er**, finiss-**ons**, répond-**îmes.**

It may be divided, as in English, into **Indicative, Subjunctive,** and **Imperative** moods, **verb-nouns (Infinitive** and **Gerund),** and **verb-adjectives (Present** and **Past Participles).**

§ **19.** The tense system is more developed than in English, there being three tenses corresponding to the English simple past.

Compound tenses are formed with the auxiliaries **avoir** or **être**: il **a** donné, nous **sommes** venus. To every simple tense there is a corresponding compound tense formed with the past participle and the simple tense of the auxiliary, giving the following scheme:

Infinitive

Present	Perfect

Participle

	Past
Present	Perfect

Indicative

Present	Perfect [1]
Past Descriptive	Past Perfect
Past Historic	Second Past Perfect
Future	Future Perfect
Future in the Past	Future Perfect in the Past

Imperative [2]

Present	Perfect

Subjunctive [2]

Present	Perfect
Past	Past Perfect

§ **20.** There are **three voices : Active, Passive,** and **Pronominal.** In the active voice verbs may be **Transitive (directly** or **indirectly),** or **Intransitive,** or have both functions.

§ **21.** Verbs are named in the **present infinitive,** the characteristic endings of which are

-er	-ir	-re	-oir
donner	courir	répondre	avoir

and are divided into **two conjugations,** the **e** conjugation and the **s** conjugation, according to the ending of the first person singular of the present indicative.

e *conjugation*	**s** *conjugation*
je donne	je cours, je réponds, je vois

All verbs with infinitive in **-er,** except **aller,** belong to the e conjugation ; there are about 4000, and all new verbs, such as **téléphoner, stopper,** are formed according to this conjugation, which is still ' living.'

The s conjugation is ' dead,' *i.e.* it is incapable of forming new verbs. It consists of some 150 verbs which date back to the Latin spoken in Gaul, and of some 330 verbs in **-ir,** with present stem in **-iss,** which are for the most part of French formation, but to which none have been added during recent centuries.

---

[1] Used also as a conversational past.

[2] All the tenses of the imperative and subjunctive moods have also future value.

§ **22.** **Table of Endings of the French Verbs.**

1. *Infinitive*	e conjugation: **-er.**	s conjugation:	**-ir, -re, -oir.**
2. *Past Participle*	„ **-é**	„	**-i, -u (s, t)**

3.

Present Indicative e conj.	s conj.	*Present Subjunctive*	*Past Descriptive*	*Present Participle*
-e	-s (x)	**-e**	**-ais**	
-es	-s (x)	**-es**	**-ais**	
-e	**-t**	**-e**	**-ait**	
-ons		**-ions**	**-ions**	**-ant**
-ez		**-iez**	**-iez**	
-ent		**-ent**	**-aient**	

4.

Past Historic e conj.	s conj.	*Past Subjunctive*	5. *Future*
-ai	**-s**	**-sse**	**-ai**
-as	**-s**	**-sses**	**-as**
-a	**-t**	**^t**	**-a**
^mes		**-ssions**	**-ons**
^tes		**-ssiez**	**-ez**
-rent		**-ssent**	**-ont**

§ **23.** 1. The verb frequently shows different stems before the endings of groups 2, 3, 4. Thus:

1. **naître.**
2. **né.**
3. **je nais, nous naissons.**
4. **je naquis.**

2. The infinitive endings (group 1) are added to the same stem as the endings of group 3, but this stem is often affected and altered by the ending **-re.** *Cf.* § 16.9.

3. The past participle stem in a few verbs does not take the vowel endings of group 2. Thus:

écrire, past part. **écrit;**
mettre, past. part. **mis.**

4. The endings of group 3 are added to the 'present' stem of the verb. Thus: **plaire,** present stem **plais:**

je plais, nous plais-ons, je plais-e, je plais-ais, plais-ant.

5. The endings of group 4 are added to the 'past historic' stem of the verb, mostly with an intervening vowel. Thus:

vivre, past historic stem **véc**:

je véc-u-s, je véc-u-sse.

6. The future (group 5) has the infinitive, mostly in a shortened form, as a stem, and the present tense of **avoir** (though no longer felt as such) for its endings. A future in the past is formed with the stem of the future and the endings of the past descriptive.

recevoir, future stem **recev(oi)r**:

je recevrai, je recevrais.

7. The present imperative usually borrows its forms from the present indicative. The 2nd person singular does not take **s** after the vowels **e, a**; thus:

donne, va, ouvre, aie.

Except when followed by the pronouns **y** and **en**:

Donnes-en à ton frère. Vas-y. Aies-en bien soin.

§ **24.** There are three so-called 'regular' types of conjugation:

(1) The **e** conjugation;

(2) the **s** conjugation of verbs in **-ir** with 'present' stem in **-iss**;

(3) the **s** conjugation of a large group of verbs in **-re** in which the stem never alters. In the majority of these the stem ends in **d**, after which no **t** is added in the 3rd pers. sing. of the present (§ 16.7, note); but if the stem does not end in **d** the **t** reappears: **rompre, il rompt.** The only exception is **vaincre, il vainc.**

§ **25.** 1. In the so-called 'irregular' verbs the present tenses frequently show the stem in two forms, stressed and unstressed, as explained in § 16.11. Thus:

je mène	**je viens**	**je reçois**	**je meurs**
nous menons	**nous venons**	**nous recevons**	**nous mourons**

2. The stem may also drop one or more consonants before a consonantal ending, as explained in § 16.7, or show changes in accordance with § 16.8 and 10. Thus:

(§ 16.7)	**je fini(ss)s**	**je dor(m)s**	**je reçoi(v)s**
	il fini(ss)t	**il dor(m)t**	**il reçoi(v)t**
	nous finissons	**nous dormons**	**nous recevons**
(§ 16.10)	**j'envoie**	(§ 16.8)	**je vaux**
	nous envoyons		**nous valons.**

§ 26. 1. Three verbs have in the 2nd pers. plur. present indic. **-tes** instead of **-ez** :

être, êtes ; dire, dites ; faire, faites.

2. Four verbs have in the 3rd pers. plur. present indic. **-ont** instead of **-ent** :

avoir, ont ; être, sont ; faire, font ; aller, vont.

3. A few verbs in **-ir** form their present according to the **-e** conjugation (§ 37).

ouvrir, j'ouvre ;	**offrir**, j'offre ;	**cueillir**, je **cueille.**
couvrir, je **couvre** ;	**souffrir**, je **souffre** ;	**assaillir**, j'**assaille.**

4. In group 3 of § 22 the **present subjunctive** may as a rule be inferred from the **third person plural of the present indicative** :

ils **reçoivent**	je **reçoive**
ils **acquièrent**	j'**acquière**
ils **viennent**	je **vienne**
ils **prennent**	je **prenne**

But the following verbs show a stem peculiar to the subjunctive :

avoir	j'**aie**	**faire**	je **fasse**
être	je **sois**	**aller**	j'**aille**
savoir	je **sache**	**valoir**	je **vaille**
pouvoir	je **puisse**	**vouloir**	je **veuille**

Avoir, être, savoir, vouloir show the **subjunctive** stem in the **imperative** :

ayez, soyez, sachez, veuillez.

Avoir and **savoir** show it also in the **present participle** :

ayant, sachant.

§ 27. All transitive verbs in the **active voice,** and **most intransitive** verbs, form their compound tenses with the auxiliary **avoir,** as shown in § **31.**

A few intransitive verbs have the auxiliary **être** (§ 63). The compound tenses are then conjugated as follows :

Infinitive Perfect	**être arrivé(s)** *or* **arrivée(s)**	
Participle Perfect	**étant arrivé(s)** *or* **arrivée(s)**	
Indicative Perfect	**je suis arrivé(e)**	**nous sommes arrivé(e)s**
	tu es arrivé(e)	**vous êtes arrivé(e)**
		vous êtes arrivé(e)s
	il est arrivé	**ils sont arrivés**
	elle est arrivée	**elles sont arrivées**

(And thus throughout.)

The past participle agrees with the subject according to § **441.** When the subject is **vous** the past participle is in the singular or in the plural according as **vous** has **singular** or **plural** function (§ 215)

§ **28.** 1. In the **'inverted'** order, *e.g.* in interrogation, the subject pronoun immediately follows the verb or auxiliary. If the 3rd person singular of the verb ends in a vowel, it adds **-t-** before **il, elle, on.**

Que **vendez-vous** ?	Où **êtes-vous** allé ?
A-t-il un livre ?	Où **va-t-elle** ?
Que vous **donne-t-on** ?	

2. If the first person singular of the verb ends in a mute syllable, the latter takes the stress, **e** becoming **é,** before **je** (which never takes the stress; *cf.* § 313, note).

Vous **ennuyé-je** ? A qui **parlé-je** ? Vous **appelé-je** ?

But this construction is archaic, and hardly used to-day even in academic style, apart from the optative **Puissé-je** (le revoir, etc.).

The usual form of question in the first person singular is

Est-ce que je vous ennuie ? (§ 340.4.)
A qui **est-ce que** je parle ?

Note.—One does constantly say:

Où suis-je ? Que dois-je faire ?
Puis-je entrer ? Ai-je dit cela ?

But the inversion is avoided in the first person singular in the case of many other verbs ; thus one never says:

Où cours-je ? Mens-je ? Vends-je ?

§ **29.** In **negations, ne** precedes the verb or auxiliary, and any unstressed object pronouns ; **pas, plus, jamais,** etc., follow the verb or auxiliary, except in the infinitive.

Infinitive

ne pas donner	**ne pas avoir donné**
	or **n'avoir pas donné**

Participle

ne donnant pas	**n'ayant pas donné**

Indicative

je ne donne pas, etc.	**je n'ai pas donné,** etc.
je ne donnais pas	**je n'avais pas donné,** etc.

Imperative

ne donne pas, etc.	**n'aie pas donné,** etc.

Je ne vous en donnerai pas.
Nous ne le lui aurions jamais donné.
Ne leur en donnez plus.

Interrogative

Ne vous en donnera-t-il pas ?
Ne vous en a-t-on pas donné ?

§ 30. THE AUXILIARY VERBS *AVOIR* AND *ÊTRE*

Infinitivê

Present		*Perfect*
to have	*to be*	*to have had, been*
avoir	être	avoir eu, été

Participle

having	*being*	*having had, been*
avant	étant	ayant eu, été

Indicative Mood

Present		*Perfect and Conversational Past*
I have, am having, do have	*I am, am being*	*I have had, I had I have been, was*
j'ai	je suis	j'ai
tu as	tu es	tu as
il a	il est	il a } eu
nous avons	nous sommes	nous avons } été
vous avez	vous êtes	vous avez
ils ont	ils sont	ils ont

Past Descriptive		*Past Perfect*
I had, was having, used to have	*I was, was being, used to be*	*I had had, I had been*
j'avais	j'étais	j'avais
tu avais	tu étais	tu avais
il avait	il était	il avait } eu
nous avions	nous étions	nous avions } été
vous aviez	vous étiez	vous aviez
ils avaient	ils étaient	ils avaient

Past Historic		*Second Past Perfect*
I had	*I was*	*I had had, been*
j'eus	je fus	j'eus
tu eus	tu fus	tu eus
il eut	il fut	il eut } eu
nous eûmes	nous fûmes	nous eûmes } été
vous eûtes	vous fûtes	vous eûtes
ils eurent	ils furent	ils eurent

Future		*Future Perfect*	
I shall have	*I shall be*	*I shall have had, been*	
j'aurai	je serai	j'aurai	
tu auras	tu seras	tu auras	eu
il aura	il sera	il aura	
nous aurons	nous serons	nous aurons	été
vous aurez	vous serez	vous aurez	
ils auront	ils seront	ils auront	

Future in the Past		*Future Perfect in the Past*	
I should have	*I should be*	*I should have had, been*	
j'aurais	je serais	j'aurais	
tu aurais	tu serais	tu aurais	eu
il aurait	il serait	il aurait	
nous aurions	nous serions	nous aurions	été
vous auriez	vous seriez	vous auriez	
ils auraient	ils seraient	ils auraient	

Imperative Mood

Present (and Future)		*Future Perfect*	
have	*be*	*have had, been*	
aie	sois	aie	eu
ayons	soyons	ayons	
ayez	soyez	ayez	été

Subjunctive Mood

Present (and Future)		*Perfect*	
I have	*I be*	*I have had, been*	
j'aie	je sois	j'aie	
tu aies	tu sois	tu aies	eu
il ait	il soit	il ait	
nous ayons	nous soyons	nous ayons	été
vous ayez	vous soyez	vous ayez	
ils aient	ils soient	ils aient	

Past		*Past Perfect*	
I had	*I were*	*I had had, been*	
j'eusse	je fusse	j'eusse	
tu eusses	tu fusses	tu eusses	eu
il eût	il fût	il eût	
nous eussions	nous fussions	nous eussions	été
vous eussiez	vous fussiez	vous eussiez	
ils eussent	ils fussent	ils eussent	

§ 31. EXAMPLES OF 'REGULAR' VERBS

Infinitive

	Present		*Perfect*
to speak	*to finish*	*to sell*	*to have spoken, etc.*
parler	finir	vendre	avoir parlé, fini, vendu

Participle

	Present		*Perfect*
speaking	*finishing*	*selling*	*having spoken, etc.*
parlant	finissant	vendant	ayant parlé, etc.

Indicative Mood

	Present		*Perfect and Conversational Past*
I speak, am speaking, do speak	*I finish, etc.*	*I sell, etc.*	*I have spoken, etc. I spoke, etc.*
je parle	finis	vends	j'ai
tu parles	finis	vends	as
il parle	finit	vend	a } parlé, fini, vendu
nous parlons	finissons	vendons	avons
vous parlez	finissez	vendez	avez
ils parlent	finissent	vendent	ont

	Past Descriptive		*Past Perfect*
I spoke, was speaking, used to speak	*I finished, etc.*	*I sold, etc.*	*I had spoken, etc.*
je parlais	finissais	vendais	j'avais
tu parlais	finissais	vendais	avais
il parlait	finissait	vendait	avait } parlé, fini, vendu
nous parlions	finissions	vendions	avions
vous parliez	finissiez	vendiez	aviez
ils parlaient	finissaient	vendaient	avaient

	Past Historic		*Second Past Perfect*
I spoke	*I finished*	*I sold*	*I had spoken, etc.*
je parlai	finis	vendis	j'eus
tu parlas	finis	vendis	eus
il parla	finit	vendit	eut } parlé, fini, vendu
nous parlâmes	finîmes	vendîmes	eûmes
vous parlâtes	finîtes	vendîtes	eûtes
ils parlèrent	finirent	vendirent	eurent

	Future		*Future Perfect*	
I shall speak	*I shall finish*	*I shall sell*	*I shall have spoken, etc.*	
je parlerai	finirai	vendrai	j'aurai	parlé
tu parleras	finiras	vendras	auras	
il parlera	finira	vendra	aura	fini
nous parlerons	finirons	vendrons	aurons	
vous parlerez	finirez	vendrez	aurez	vendu
ils parleront	finiront	vendront	auront	

	Future in the Past		*Future Perfect in the Past*	
I should speak	*I should finish*	*I should sell*	*I should have spoken, etc.*	
je parlerais	finirais	vendrais	j'aurais	parlé
tu parlerais	finirais	vendrais	aurais	
il parlerait	finirait	vendrait	aurait	fini
nous parlerions	finirions	vendrions	aurions	
vous parleriez	finiriez	vendriez	auriez	vendu
ils parleraient	finiraient	vendraient	auraient	

Imperative Mood

	Present (and Future)		*Future Perfect*	
speak	*finish*	*sell*	*have spoken, etc.*	
parle	finis	vends	aie	parlé
parlons	finissons	vendons	ayons	fini
parlez	finissez	vendez	ayez	vendu

Subjunctive Mood

	Present (and Future)		*Perfect*	
I speak	*I finish*	*I sell*	*I have spoken, etc.*	
je parle	finisse	vende	j'aie	parlé
tu parles	finisses	vendes	aies	
il parle	finisse	vende	ait	fini
nous parlions	finissions	vendions	ayons	
vous parliez	finissiez	vendiez	ayez	vendu
ils parlent	finissent	vendent	aient	

	Past		*Past Perfect*	
I spoke	*I finished*	*I sold*	*I had spoken, etc.*	
je parlasse	finisse	vendisse	j'eusse	parlé
tu parlasses	finisses	vendisses	eusses	
il parlât	finît	vendît	eût	fini
nous parlassións	finissions	vendissions	eussions	
vous parlassiez	finissiez	vendissiez	eussiez	vendu
ils parlassent	finissent	vendissent	eussent	

§ 32. Peculiarities of Verbs in -er.

1. Verbs in **-cer** have **ç** before **a, o,** to retain the sound [s] (§ 11).

avancer, j'avance, nous **avançons,** **avançant,**
j'**avançais,** nous avancions,
j'**avançai,** nous **avançâmes.**

2. Verbs in **-ger** insert a mute **e** after **g** before **a, o,** to retain the sound [ʒ] (§ 16.2).

manger, je mange, nous **mangeons,** **mangeant,**
je **mangeais,** nous mangions,
je **mangeai,** nous **mangeâmes.**

3. Verbs with stem in **ai, oi, ui,** change these syllables to **ay, oy, uy,** before a sounded vowel, as explained in § 16.10.

essayer, j'essaierai, essayant, essayé,
j'essaie, nous **essayons,** vous **essayez,** ils **essaient.**
ployer, je **ploierai, ployant, ployé,**
je **ploie,** nous **ployons,** ils **ploient.**
essuyer, j'**essuierai, essuyant, essuyé,**
j'**essuie,** vous **essuyez,** ils **essuient.**

Note.—Verbs in -ayer may have ay throughout, as explained in § 16.10, note.

j'essaye, j'essayerai, etc.

4. Verbs with stem in [e] change [e] to [ɛ] when the stem takes the stress (§ 16.11.*a*).

céder	je cède	nous cédons	je céderai
	tu cèdes	vous cédez	
	il cède	ils cèdent	

régner	pénétrer	protéger
je règne	je pénètre	je protège

Note.—This does not apply to verbs in **-éer** : **créer,** je **crée.**

5. Verbs with stem in [ə] change [ə] to [ɛ] when the stem takes the stress (§ 16.11.*a*), and also before the following mute syllable in the future tenses.

semer	je sème	nous semons	je sèmerai
	tu sèmes	vous semez	
	il sème	ils sèment	

se lever	geler	acheter
je me lève	il gèle	j'achète

But a considerable number of verbs in **-eler** and **-eter** show the sound [ɛ] by doubling the **t** or the **l**, *i.e.* by showing a closed syllable in the stem (§ 7.2).

jeter	**je jette**	**je jetterai**
appeler	**j'appelle**	**j'appellerai**

Thus: **atteler, épeler, étinceler, renouveler, etc.**
épousseter, feuilleter, fureter, etc.

IRREGULAR VERBS

§ **33.** In the list below, the following parts are given:

1. The **Infinitive** (§ 22, group 1), from which the **Future** and the **Future in the Past** may be inferred. If the Future is not formed as shown in the 'regular' conjugations (§ 31), it is given also.

2. The **Past Participle** (group 2), which is given in the **Perfect** tense, in order to show the auxiliary used in the compound tenses.

3. The **First Persons Singular and Plural of the Present Indicative,** from which may in most cases be formed all the tenses shown in group 3. Thus:

Pres. Indic.	*Pres. Subjunct.*	*Imperat.*	*Descript. Past.*
je **meurs**	je meure		je mourais
tu meurs	tu meures	meurs	tu mourais
il meurt	il meure		il mourait
nous **mourons**	nous mourions	mourons	nous mourions
vous mourez	vous mouriez	mourez	vous mouriez
ils meurent	ils meurent		ils mouraient

Present Participle mourant

Note the regular alternation of stressed and unstressed stems, which will be referred to as '**strong**' and '**weak**,' and the similarity of Present Indicative and Present Subjunctive in the 3rd pers. plural.

All departures from the scheme shown above are given in full.

4. The **First Person Singular of the Past Historic,** from which the whole tense, and the **Past Subjunctive,** may always be inferred.

The parts of the verb are given in the following order:

(*a*) The 'principal' parts:

(1) **Infinitive.** (2) **Present Indicative.** (3) **Past Historic.** (4) **Perfect.**

(*b*) To which are added when necessary:

(5) **Future.** (6) **Present Subjunctive.** (7) **Present Participle.** (8) **Imperative.**

Note.—Compounds of prefix + verb usually have the conjugation of the simple verb. Thus the conjugation of **mettre** includes that of **remettre, transmettre, promettre, compromettre,** etc.

I. Verbs in -er

§ **34.** **Aller,** *to go.* Shows three stems, unrelated to each other.

(2) je **vais,** tu **vas,** il **va,** nous allons, vous allez, ils **vont.**

(3) j'allai. (4) je suis allé. (5) **j'irai.** (6) **j'aille,** tu **ailles,** il **aille,** nous allions, vous alliez, ils **aillent.** (7) allant. (8) **va,** allons, allez.

Note the conjugation of the pronominal form: **s'en aller,** *to go away.*

(2) je m'en vais. (3) je m'en allai. (4) je m'en suis allé (Conversationally: je me suis en allé). (5) je m'en irai. (6) je m'en aille. (7) s'en allant. (8) va-t'en, allons-nous-en, allez-vous-en. Negatively: ne t'en va pas, ne nous en allons pas, etc.

§ **35.** **Envoyer,** *to send.* (2) j'envoie (§ **16.**10). (3) j'envoyai. (4) j'ai envoyé. (5) **j'enverrai.**

II. Verbs in -ir

§ **36.** All verbs with present stem in **-iss** are regular, except

Haïr, *to hate.* (2) je **hais,** tu **hais,** il **hait,** nous haïssons, vous haïssez, ils haïssent. (8) **hais,** haïssons, haïssez. All other parts regular like **finir.**

§ **37.** Verbs with Present of the **e** conjugation.

Ouvrir, *to open.* (2) j'ouvre, tu **ouvres,** il **ouvre,** nous ouvrons. (3) j'ouvris. (4) j'ai ouvert. (8) **ouvre.**

Thus also: **couvrir,** *to cover*; **offrir,** *to offer*; **souffrir,** *to suffer.*

cueillir, *to pluck, gather.* (2) je **cueille,** nous cueillons. (3) je cueillis. (4) j'ai cueilli. (5) je **cueillerai.**

assaillir, *to assail.* (2) j'**assaille,** nous assaillons. (3) j'assaillis. (4) j'ai assailli. (5) j'assaillirai.

Thus also : **tressaillir,** *to start, shudder.*

§ 38. Verbs with strong and weak Present stems.

acquérir, *to acquire.* (2) j'**acquiers,** nous acquérons, ils **acquièrent.** (3) j'**acquis.** (4) j'ai **acquis.** (5) j'**acquerrai.** (6) j'acquière.

Thus also : **conquérir,** *to conquer,* etc.

tenir, *to hold.* (2) je **tiens,** nous tenons, ils **tiennent.** (3) je **tins,** nous **tînmes,** vous **tîntes,** ils **tinrent.** (4) j'ai **tenu.** (5) je **tiendrai.**

Thus also: **venir,** *to come.* (4) je suis **venu.**

mourir, *to die.* (2) je **meurs,** nous mourons, ils **meurent.** (3) il **mourut.** (4) il est **mort.** (5) je **mourrai.**

§ 39. Verbs with **shortened** Present stems (§ 16.7).

dormir, *to sleep.* (2) je **dors,** tu **dors,** il **dort,** nous dormons, vous dormez, ils dorment. (3) je dormis. (4) j'ai dormi.

Thus also :

mentir, *to lie (tell a falsehood).* (2) je **mens,** nous mentons. (4) j'ai menti.

partir, *to depart.* (2) je **pars,** nous partons. (4) je suis parti.

sentir, *to feel.* (2) je **sens,** nous sentons. (4) j'ai senti.

se repentir, *to repent.* (2) je me **repens,** nous nous repentons. (4) je me suis repenti.

sortir, *to go out.* (2) je **sors,** nous sortons. (4) je suis sorti.

servir, *to serve.* (2) je **sers,** nous servons. (4) j'ai servi.

bouillir, *to boil.* (2) je **bous,** nous bouillons. (4) j'ai bouilli.

§ 40. Stem in ui, uy (§ 16.10).

fuir, *to flee.* (2) je fuis, nous **fuyons,** ils fuient. (3) je fuis. (4) j'ai fui.

§ 41. **courir,** *to run.* (2) je cours, nous courons. (3) je **courus.** (4) j'ai couru. (5) je **courrai.**

vêtir, *to clothe.* (2) je vêts, nous vêtons. (3) je vêtis. (4) j'ai **vêtu.** (5) je vêtirai.

III. Verbs in -re

§ **42.** **vaincre**, *to be victorious, to overcome.* Conjugated like **vendre**, but with stems **vainc** and **vainqu** (§ **16**.3). (2) je vaincs, tu vaincs, il vainc (§ **24**), nous **vainquons**, vous vainquez, ils vainquent. (3) je **vainquis**. (4) j'ai vaincu. (7) **vainquant**.

Thus: **convaincre**, *to convince.*

§ **43.** Stems ending in a **vowel**.

rire, *to laugh.* (2) je ris, nous rions. (3) je **ris**. (4) j'ai **ri**.

Thus: **sourire**, *to smile.*

conclure, *to conclude.* (2) je conclus, nous **concluons**. (3) je **conclus**. (4) j'ai **conclu**.

Thus: **exclure**, *to exclude.*

§ **44.** Verbs with stem in **oi**, **oy**; **ai**, **ay** (§ **16**.10).

croire, *to believe.* (2) je crois, nous **croyons**, ils croient. (3) je **crus**. (4) j'ai **cru**. (6) je croie, nous **croyions**.

traire, *to milk.* (2) je trais, nous **trayons**, ils traient. (3) *None.* (4) j'ai **trait**. (6) je traie, nous **trayions**.

Thus: **extraire**, *to extract*; **soustraire**, *to subtract*, etc.

§ **45.** Verbs with stem in **tt** (§ **16**.7).

battre, *to beat.* (2) je **bats**, nous battons. (3) je **battis**. (4) j'ai battu.

Thus: **abattre**, *to knock down*; **combattre**, *to fight*, etc.

mettre, *to put.* (2) je **mets**, nous mettons. (3) je **mis**. (4) j'ai **mis**.

Thus: **admettre**, *to admit*; **commettre**, *to commit*, etc.

§ **46.** Verbs with stem in **s**.

coudre, *to sew.* (2) je **couds**, tu **couds**, il **coud**, nous cousons, vous cousez, ils cousent. (3) je cousis. (4) j'ai cousu.

plaire, *to please.* (2) je plais, il **plaît**, nous plaisons. (3) je **plus**. (4) j'ai **plu**.

taire, *to keep secret.* (2) je tais, il tait, nous taisons. (3) je **tus**. (4) j'ai tu.

Thus: **se taire**, *to be silent.*

faire, *to do, to make.* (2) je fais, nous faisons, vous **faites**, ils **font**. (3) je **fis**. (4) j'ai **fait**. (5) je **ferai**. (6) je **fasse**, nous **fassions**. (7) faisant. (8) fais, faisons, **faites**.

dire, *to say, to tell.* (2) je dis, nous disons, vous **dites**, ils disent. (3) je **dis**. (4) j'ai **dit**. (6) je dise. (8) dis, disons, dites.

Thus : **redire**, *to say again.*

Médire, *to slander*; **contredire**, *to contradict*; **interdire**, *to forbid*, have (2) and (8) (vous) médisez, contredisez, interdisez.

maudire, *to curse.* (2) je maudis, nous **maudissons**, vous maudissez. (3) je **maudis**. (4) j'ai **maudit**.

lire, *to read.* (2) je lis, nous lisons. (3) je **lus**. (4) j'ai **lu**.

Thus : **élire**, *to elect.*

suffire, *to suffice.* (2) je suffis, nous suffisons. (3) je **suffis**. (4) j'ai **suffi**.

confire, *to pickle, to preserve.* (2) je confis, nous confisons. (3) je **confis**. (4) j'ai **confit**.

§ 47. Verbs with stem in **aiss**, **oiss** (§ 16.9).

connaître, *to know.* (2) je **connais**, il **connaît**, nous connaissons. (3) je **connus**. (4) j'ai **connu**.

paraître, *to appear.* (2) je **parais**, il **paraît**, nous paraissons. (3) je **parus**. (4) j'ai **paru**.

Thus : **repaître**, *to feed.* But in the simple verb **paître**, *to graze*, (3) and (4) are wanting.

naître, *to be born.* (2) je **nais**, il **naît**, nous naissons. (3) je **naquis**. (4) je suis **né**.

croître, *to grow.* (2) je **croîs**, tu **croîs**, il **croît**, nous croissons. (3) je **crûs**. (4) j'ai **crû**. (6) je croisse. (8) **croîs**, croissons.

Takes a circumflex accent as a distinguishing mark where it might otherwise be confused for a part of **croire** (§ 8.3.*d*). But the compounds **accroître**, *to increase*, **décroître**, *to decrease*, have the accent only on the 3rd pers. sing. like **connaître**.

§ 48. Verbs with stem in **uis**.

conduire, *to conduct.* (2) je conduis, nous conduisons. (3) je conduisis. (4) j'ai **conduit**.

Thus nearly all verbs in **uire** :

introduire, *to introduce.* (2) **j'introduis**, **nous introduisons**.

produire, *to produce*. (2) je produis, nous produisons.

réduire, *to reduce*. (2) je réduis, nous réduisons.

traduire, *to translate*. (2) je traduis, nous traduisons.

construire, *to construct*. (2) je construis, nous construisons.

détruire, *to destroy*. (2) je détruis, nous détruisons.

cuire, *to cook*. (2) il cuit, ils cuisent.

nuire, *to harm*. (2) je nuis, nous nuisons. (3) je nuisis. (4) j'ai nui.

Thus : luire, *to shine*.

§ 49. Verbs with stem in v.

suivre, *to follow*. (2) je suis, tu suis, il suit, nous suivons. (3) je suivis. (4) j'ai suivi.

Thus : poursuivre, *to pursue*.

vivre, *to live*. (2) je vis, nous vivons. (3) je vécus. (4) j'ai vécu.

Thus : survivre, *to survive*.

écrire, *to write*. (2) j'écris, nous écrivons. (3) j'écrivis. (4) j'ai écrit.

Thus : décrire, *to describe* ; inscrire, *to inscribe*, etc.

§ 50. Verbs with stem in aign, eign, oign.

craindre, *to fear*. (2) je crains, nous craignons. (3) je craignis. (4) j'ai craint.

Thus : plaindre, *to pity*. (2) je plains.
contraindre, *to compel*. (2) je contrains.

peindre, *to paint*. (2) je peins, nous peignons. (3) je peignis. (4) j'ai peint.

Thus : atteindre, *to reach* ; ceindre, *to gird* ; éteindre, *to extinguish* ; feindre, *to feign* ; teindre, *to dye*, etc.

joindre, *to join*. (2) je joins, nous joignons. (3) je joignis. (4) j'ai joint.

Thus : oindre, *to anoint*.

§ 51. Verbs with stem modified by vocalisation of l (§ 16.8).

moudre, *to grind*. (2) je mouds, il moud, nous moulons. (3) je moulus. (4) j'ai moulu.

absoudre, *to absolve.* (2) **j'absous, il absout, nous absolvons, ils** absolvent. (3) *None.* (4) j'ai **absous.**

Thus: **dissoudre,** *to dissolve.*

The feminine of the past participles **absous, dissous,** is **absoute, dissoute.**

résoudre, *to resolve.* (2) je **résous, il résout, nous résolvons, ils** résolvent. (3) je **résolus.** (4) j'ai **résolu.**

There is also a past participle **résous,** *fem.* **résoute,** used in the scientific sense of the verb: La vapeur s'est **résoute** en eau.

§ 52. Verbs with strong and weak Present stems (§ 16.11).

boire, *to drink* (stem in **v**). (2) je **bois,** nous **buvons,** vous **buvez,** ils boivent. (3) je **bus.** (4) j'ai **bu.** (6) je boive, nous buvions.

prendre, *to take.* (2) je prends, il prend, nous **prenons,** ils **prennent.** (3) je **pris.** (4) j'ai **pris.** (6) je prenne, nous prenions.

Thus: **apprendre,** *to learn*; **comprendre,** *to understand*; **surprendre,** *to surprise,* etc.

§ 53. **être,** *to be.* (2) je **suis, tu es, il est,** nous **sommes,** vous **êtes,** ils **sont.** (3) je **fus.** (4) j'ai **été.** (5) je **serai.** (6) je **sois,** nous soyons, ils **soient.** (7) **étant.** (8) **sois,** soyons, soyez.

IV. Verbs in -oir

§ 54. Verbs with **strong** and **weak** Present stems.

recevoir, *to receive.* (2) je **reçois,** nous recevons, ils **reçoivent.** (3) je **reçus.** (4) j'ai **reçu.** (5) je **recevrai.**

Thus: **apercevoir,** *to catch sight of*; **concevoir,** *to conceive*; **décevoir,** *to deceive*; etc.

devoir, *to owe.* (2) je **dois,** nous devons, ils **doivent.** (3) je **dus.** (4) j'ai **dû.** (5) je **devrai.**

Past participle **dû** (§ 8.3.*d*), due, dus, dues.

pouvoir, *to be able, 'can.'* (2) je **peux** *or* je **puis, tu peux, il peut,** nous pouvons, ils **peuvent.** (3) je **pus.** (4) j'ai **pu.** (5) je **pourrai.** (6) je **puisse, nous** puissions, ils puissent. (7) pouvant. (8) *None.*

Interrog. 1st pers. sing. always **Puis-je?**
Negative either **Je ne peux pas** *or* **Je ne puis pas.**
The conversational form is **Je peux,** Est-ce que je peux?

mouvoir, *to move.* (2) je **meus,** nous mouvons, ils **meuvent.** (3) je **mus.** (4) j'ai **mû.** (5) je **mouvrai.**

Past participle **mû,** mue, mus, mues.

savoir, *to know.* (2) je **sais,** nous **savons,** ils **savent.** (3) je **sus.** (4) j'ai **su.** (5) je **saurai.** (6) je **sache,** nous **sachions.** (7) **sachant.** (8) **sachez,** sachons, sachez.

§ 55. **pleuvoir,** *to rain,* impersonal. (2) il **pleut.** (3) il **plut.** (4) il a **plu.** (5) il **pleuvra.** (6) il pleuve. (7) pleuvant.

Often used in the 3rd pers. plural with personal subject. Les flèches **pleuvent,** pleuvaient (§ 71.1, note).

§ 56. **vouloir,** *to will, wish.* (2) je **veux,** nous voulons, ils **veulent.** (3) je **voulus.** (4) j'ai **voulu.** (5) je **voudrai.** (6) je **veuille,** nous voulions, ils veuillent. (7) voulant. (8) **veuille** (bien), **veuillez** (bien) + Infinitive: Veuillez (bien) ouvrir la fenêtre.

But **veux,** voulons, voulez in the sense of 'exert your will.' **Voulez-le** et vous le pourrez.

§ 57. **asseoir,** *to seat.* (2) j'**assieds,** il assied, nous **asseyons,** ils asseyent. Or: j'**assois,** il assoit. (3) j'**assis.** (4) j'ai **assis.** (5) j'**assiérai,** *or* j'**asseyerai.** (6) j'asseye, nous asseyions. (7) asseyant. (8) **assieds** *or* **assois,** asseyez.

Thus also the much commoner form **s'asseoir,** *to sit down.*

§ 58. Verbs with stem modified by vocalisation of **l.**

valoir, *to be worth.* (2) je **vaux,** il **vaut,** nous valons, ils valent. (3) je **valus.** (4) j'ai **valu.** (5) je **vaudrai.** (6) je **vaille,** nous valions, ils **vaillent.** (7) valant. (8) vaux, valons.

Thus: **prévaloir,** *to prevail,* but with Pres. Subjunctive je **prévale.**

falloir, *to be necessary, 'must,'* impersonal. (2) il **faut.** (3) il **fallut.** (4) il a **fallu.** (5) il **faudra.** (6) il **faille.** (7) *None.*

§ 59. Verb with stem in **oi, oy** (§ 16.10).

voir, *to see.* (2) je vois, nous **voyons,** ils voient. (3) je **vis.** (4) j'ai **vu.** (5) je **verrai.**

prévoir, *to foresee,* has (5) je **prévoirai.**

pourvoir, *to provide,* has (3) je **pourvus.** (5) je **pourvoirai.**

§ **60.** **avoir,** *to have.* (2) **j'ai, tu as, il a, nous avons, vous avez, ils ont.** (3) **j'eus.** (4) **j'ai eu.** (5) **j'aurai.** (6) **j'aie, il ait, nous ayons, ils aient.** (7) **ayant.** (8) **aie, ayons, ayez.**

§ 61. DEFECTIVE VERBS

(Only the forms in commonest use are given)

écloper, *to lame, maim.* Past Participle **éclopé.** Il rentra de la guerre tout éclopé.

faillir, *to fail.* (2) **faut.** Le cœur me faut, *My heart fails me.* Used chiefly in the forms (3) **je faillis** + infinitive. (4) **j'ai failli** + infinitive. Je faillis me noyer, *I narrowly escaped drowning.* Elle a failli se trouver mal, *She nearly fainted.*

défaillir, *to faint.* (2) **nous défaillons, vous défaillez, ils défaillent.** Past Descriptive : **je défaillais,** etc. (4) **j'ai défailli.**

férir, *to strike.* The Infinitive is used in the phrase **sans coup férir,** *without striking a blow.*

gésir, *to lie.* (2) **il gît, nous gisons, vous gisez, ils gisent.** Past Descriptive **je gisais,** etc. (7) **gisant.** Used especially as a tombstone heading : **Ci-gît, Ci-gisent.** *Here lie(s).'*

honnir, *to put to shame.* Used only in the Infinitive and the Past Participle, as in the device of the Order of the Garter: Ho(n)ni soit qui mal y pense.

ouïr, *to hear.* The Past Historic and Past Participle, though archaic, are occasionally used : **J'ouïs** dire que . . . J'ai **ouï** dire que. In constant use is the phrase Savoir quelque chose **par ouï-dire,** *by hearsay.*

quérir, *to fetch.* Used only in such phrases as **aller quérir,** *to go for* ; **envoyer quérir,** *to send for.*

But the usual expressions are **aller chercher, envoyer chercher.**

transir, *to penetrate with cold, rain.* Past Participle **transi.** Nous étions transis, *we were soaked through* ; il était transi de froid, *he was chilled to the bone.*

accroire, used only in the phrase **en faire accroire à quelqu'un.** Il nous en fait accroire, *he is 'pulling our leg.'*

braire, *to bray.* (2) il brait, ils braient. (5) il braira.

bruire, *to rustle, ripple.* (2) il bruit, ils **bruissent.** Past Descriptive il bruissait. (7) bruissant.

clore, *to close.* (2) je clos, il clôt. (4) j'ai **clos.** (5) il clora. Juger une affaire **à huis clos,** *in camera.* The usual verb is **fermer.**

éclore, *to hatch, to bloom.* (2) il éclôt, ils éclosent. (4) il a (*or* est) **éclos.** (5) il éclora. (6) il éclose.

Thus: **enclore,** *to enclose.* (4) j'ai **enclos.**

s'ensuivre, *to follow, result.* Conjugated like **suivre,** but used only in the 3rd pers. singular and plural.

forfaire, *to forfeit.* Used chiefly in the compound tenses. (4) Il a **forfait à** l'honneur.

frire, *to fry.* (2) je fris, il frit. (4) j'ai **frit.** (5) je frirai.

Nearly always intransitive: **Le poisson frit.** The transitive form is usually **je fais frire.**

chaloir, *to matter.* Used only in the Infinitive and in (2) Peu m'en **chaut,** *It matters little to me.* The Present Participle is preserved in the adjective **nonchalant.**

choir, *to fall.* Used humorously in **se laisser choir.** In old fairy-tales are found Past Participle **chu** and Future **cherra.** The usual verb is **tomber.**

échoir, *to fall due, to occur.* (2) il échoit, ils échoient. Past Descriptive il échoyait. (3) il **échut.** (4) il est **échu.** (5) il **écherra.** (6) il échoie. (7) **échéant.**

Commonly used in the phrase **le cas échéant,** *if the need should arise.*

déchoir, *to fall, decline.* (2) je déchois, nous déchoyons. (3) je **déchus.** (4) j'ai **déchu.** (5) je **décherrai.**

Used chiefly in Past Participle: **un ange déchu,** *a fallen angel.*

ravoir, *to get back, recover,* Infinitive only. Je voudrais ravoir mon livre, *I should like to have my book back.*

seoir, *to be fitting, to suit.* (2) il sied, ils **seyent.** Past Descriptive il **seyait.** (5) il siéra. (7) seyant. Past Participle **sis,** *situated, located.*

§ 62. LIST OF IRREGULAR AND DEFECTIVE VERBS

abattre § 45
absoudre § 51
accroire § 61
accroître § 47
acquérir § 38
admettre § 45
aller § 34
apercevoir § 54
apprendre § 52
assaillir § 37
asseoir § 57
atteindre § 50
avoir § 60

battre § 45
boire § 52
bouillir § 39
braire § 61
bruire § 61

ceindre § 50
chaloir § 61
choir § 61
clore § 61
combattre § 45
commettre § 45
comprendre § 52
concevoir § 54
conclure § 43
conduire § 48
confire § 46
connaître § 47
conquérir § 38
construire § 48
contraindre § 50
contredire § 46
convaincre § 42
coudre § 46
courir § 41
couvrir § 37
craindre § 50
croire § 44
croître § 47
cueillir § 37
cuire § 48

décevoir § 54
déchoir § 61
décrire § 49
décroître § 47
défaillir § 61
détruire § 48
devoir § 54
dire § 46
dissoudre § 51
dormir § 39

échoir § 61
écloper § 61
éclore § 61
écrire § 49
élire § 46
enclore § 61
s'ensuivre § 61
envoyer § 35
éteindre § 50
être § 53
exclure § 43
extraire § 44

faire § 46
faillir § 61
falloir § 58
feindre § 50
férir § 61
forfaire § 61
frire § 61
fuir § 40

gésir § 61

haïr § 36
honnir § 61

inscrire § 49
interdire § 46
introduire § 48

joindre § 50

lire § 46
luire § 48

maudire § 46
médire § 46
mentir § 39
mettre § 45
moudre § 51
mourir § 38
mouvoir § 54

naître § 47
nuire § 48

offrir § 37
oindre § 50
ouïr § 61
ouvrir § 37

paître § 47
paraître § 47
partir § 39
peindre § 50
plaindre § 50
plaire § 46
pleuvoir § 55
poursuivre § 49
pourvoir § 59
pouvoir § 54
prendre § 52
prévaloir § 58
prévoir § 59
produire § 48

quérir § 61

ravoir § 61
recevoir § 54
réduire § 48
repaître § 47
se repentir § 39
résoudre § 51
rire § 43

savoir § 54
sentir § 39
seoir § 61
servir § 39
sortir § 39
souffrir § 37
sourire § 43
soustraire § 44
suffire § 46
suivre § 49
surprendre § 52
survivre § 49

taire § 46
teindre § 50
tenir § 38
traduire § 48
traire § 44
transir § 61
tressaillir § 37

vaincre § 42
valoir § 58
venir § 38
vêtir § 41
vivre § 49
voir § 59
vouloir § 56

THE ACTIVE VOICE

§ **63.** It has already been stated (§ **27**) that in the active voice all transitive verbs form their compound tenses with the auxiliary **avoir,** according to the paradigms shown in § **31.**

Most intransitive verbs also have the auxiliary **avoir,** but a few denoting **change of place or state,** and also **rester,** have the auxiliary **être,** and are conjugated as shown in § **27.**

1 This is always the case with the verbs

aller	**arriver**	**entrer**	**naître**	**devenir**
venir	**partir**	**sortir**	**mourir**	**rester**

Je **suis allé** le voir. Elle **est venue** me trouver.

Nous **étions arrivés** la veille. Je **suis né** le quinze mars.

Je ne sais pas ce qu'elle **est devenue,** mais je ne pense pas qu'elle **soit restée** à Londres.

2. The verbs **monter, descendre, accourir, tomber,** usually have the auxiliary **être,** but **avoir** is also found.

Je suis (J'ai) monté me coucher à **onze heures.**
Louis était monté sur le trône en 1643.
Je suis monté dans **le train.**
Nous avons monté à l'**assaut.**
Je suis descendu à sept heures **ce matin.**
Déjà le soleil **était descendu** derrière les **cimes des arbres.**
La lune a descendu dans les brumes **de l'horizon.**
Elle **est accourue** immédiatement. Les agents **ont accouru.**
Je suis **tombé** et me suis fait mal (always **être** in this sense).

But : La pluie **a tombé** (*or* **est tombée**) à torrents.

And impersonally nearly always **avoir.**
Il a tombé de la pluie.

Note.—The verbs **monter, descendre,** of course take **avoir** when they have a cognate accusative (§ 126).

Nous **avons monté les degrés de** l'escalier.
Nous **avions redescendu la rue** de La Harpe.

And **monter, descendre, entrer, sortir,** have also the value of **transitive** verbs = to take up, down, in, out.

A-t-on **descendu** les malles ?
On **avait rentré** les tables **avant** la **nuit.**

3. On the other hand, verbs which denote not merely change of place, but also a certain form of **physical activity,** always take **avoir.** Thus :

marcher, courir, galoper, sauter, nager, voler.
J'ai couru le retrouver. **J'ai sauté** à terre.

§ 64. Verbs of the type of

changer, geler, grandir, vieillir, rajeunir, embellir,

denoting change of condition, are sometimes said to take both auxiliaries, **avoir** to denote the action, and **être** to denote the state.

It is more accurate to say that they are conjugated with the auxiliary **avoir :**

Il **a gelé** fort cette nuit,
Comme cette enfant **a embelli !**
Vous **avez vieilli** pendant vos voyages,
J'avais beaucoup **grandi** entre les âges de sept et dix **ans,**

but that their past participle is also used as a predicative adjective :

Comme cette enfant **est embellie !**
Comme vous **êtes changé** (**grandi, vieilli**) !
L'eau **était gelée** dans ma cuvette,

in which examples we have merely the present and the past descriptive of **être,** rather than tenses of **grandir, geler,** etc.

Note.—The same remark applies to such verbs as **sortir, rentrer, descendre, mourir, partir,** studied in § 63. Thus :

Madame **est sortie** = *Mrs* (*Smith*) *is out.*
Est-ce que monsieur **est rentré** ? = *Is your master home yet ?*
Son père **est mort** = *His father is dead.*

These sentences are really in the present tense, so that the construction

Je suis descendu depuis sept heures,
Les hirondelles sont parties depuis un mois,
La fête de Pâques est passée depuis plus de quinze jours,

shows no departure from the rule given in § 73.1.

In the following, on the other hand, we have the conversational past :

Il **est rentré** fort tard. *Came home.*
Madame **est sortie** à deux heures. *Went out.*
Son père **est mort** il y a deux ans. *Died.*

The same distinction must be made between the past tense of the pronominal verbs in

Je me suis assis. *I sat down,*
Je me suis levé. *I got up,*
Je me suis couché. *I went to bed,*

and the present tense in

Je suis assis. *I am seated,*
Je suis levé. *I am up,*
Je suis couché. *I am in bed,*

in which the past participle is used as a predicative adjective, just as in

La porte est **fermée** (**§ 66.2**).

THE PASSIVE VOICE

§ **65.** The **Passive Voice** is formed by adding to the verb **être,** in all its tenses, the **Past Participle** of a directly transitive verb. The past participle agrees with the subject.

INFINITIVE

Present.	être respecté(e)(s)	*Perfect.*	avoir été respecté(e)(s)

PARTICIPLE

Present.	étant respecté(e)(s)	*Perfect.*	ayant été respecté(e)(s)

INDICATIVE

Present.	je suis respecté(e)	*Perfect.*	j'ai été respecté(e)
	tu es respecté(e)		tu as été respecté(e)
	il est respecté		il a été respecté
	elle est respectée		elle a été respectée
	nous sommes respecté(e)s		nous avons été respecté(e)s
	etc.		etc.
Past Descript.	j'étais respecté(e)	*Past Perf.*	j'avais été respecté(e)
	etc.		etc.

and so on throughout the conjugation of **être** as given in § 30.

§ 66. Use of the Passive Voice.

1. The object of a directly transitive verb becomes subject, and is shown as 'suffering' the action, the agent being then governed by the prepositions **par** or **de** (§ 67).

{ Jean **a frappé** la petite Louise.
{ La petite Louise **a été frappée par** Jean.

{ Tout le monde **respecte Pierre.**
{ **Pierre est respecté de** tout le monde.

2. If the agent is not mentioned, it becomes important to distinguish between **être, auxiliary of the passive,** and **être followed by an adjective complement,** there being no **action** in progress. Thus:

Pierre est respecté=On respecte Pierre,
La Suisse est bien gouvernée=On gouverne bien la Suisse,

and we have here the passive **voice** of **respecter, gouverner,** in the present tense.

But **La porte est fermée,** *The door is shut,* is not equivalent to **On ferme la porte**; no action is being 'suffered' by the door, we have merely an indication of its state or position, and **fermée** is **adjectival and predicative.**

Pierre est respecté is felt as being in the passive because the verb **respecter** denotes an **enduring** action.

La porte est fermée is not felt as a passive, if no agent is mentioned, because **fermer** denotes a **momentary** action, which is felt as having now been completed.

3. English easily distinguishes between 'The door is shut' (completed action, or state), and 'The door is being shut,' by the use of the continuous present, but as French lacks this construction, the **present and past descriptive passive of verbs denoting momentary action are not often used unless the agent is mentioned.** They are replaced by

(*a*) The active voice with **on** as subject.
  On ouvre la porte. *The door is (being) opened.*

(*b*) The pronominal voice.
  La porte **s'ouvre.** *The door opens.* (§ 70.3.*c*.)

4. This restriction does not apply to the past tenses, as the past historic and conversational past denote action as opposed to state (descriptive past).

La porte **fut** (**a été**) **ouverte.** *The door was opened* (passive).
La porte **était ouverte.** *The door was open* (not passive).
Le pauvre oiselet **fut tué, plumé** et **mis** à cuire dans une petite casserole, car il devait **être servi** à part au fils du roi.

5. It is permissible in English to make a dative or a prepositional object the subject of the passive.

John gave me an apple. I *was given* an apple by John.
People laughed at me. I *was laughed at.*

This construction is impossible in French. Note especially that indirectly transitive verbs have no passive voice.

Such sentences as

On répondit à sa question. Son fils lui succédera. On ne peut résister à cette tentation,

cannot be recast in the passive, except occasionally as in § 71.4.

Note.—To the verbs **obéir à** qqn, **désobéir à** qqn, **pardonner à** qqn, correspond the passive constructions

Il **est obéi** de tous. Elle **fut** souvent **désobéie.** Vous serez **pardonné.**

But these exceptions are only apparent. The passive of these verbs dates from a time when they were directly transitive

One also says:

C'est une chose **convenue.** *That's agreed upon,*

although the active construction is **convenir de** qq**ch.**

§ **67.** 1. The relation of the **agent** to the action suffered by the subject is expressed either by **de** or by **par.**

De expresses a vague, indeterminate, habitual relation.
Par expresses a definite, special, or unusual relation.

Il est respecté **de** tout le monde, et même **par** son domestique.

Monsieur Durand s'en allait faire une petite promenade en auto, accompagné **de** sa famille ; ayant dépassé la limite de vitesse, il dut se rendre au poste de police, accompagné **par** deux agents.

2. While in the older language the agent was usually introduced by **de,** it is to-day with the majority of verbs introduced by **par.**

Louise a été battue, frappée, **par** son frère.
La fenêtre fut ouverte **par** un des élèves.
Ce château a été construit **par** un architecte du dix-huitième siècle.
Cette œuvre fut commencée **par** Guillaume de Lorris et achevée **par** Jean de Meung.

Note.—When there is no conscious volition on the part of the agent, **de** is the more usual preposition.

Perché au sommet d'une colline, le village est battu **de** tous les vents du ciel.
Je fus frappé **de** cette réponse.

3. The preposition **de** is the more usual

(*a*) With verbs denoting an **action of the mind,** such as
être aimé, respecté, estimé, haï, détesté, honoré, craint;

(*b*) With verbs denoting what is mostly a habitual action, such as
être suivi, accompagné, escorté, précédé.

But the general rule given under 1 must always be borne in mind.

(*a*) Il est estimé **de** tout le grand public, et même **par** ses adversaires.
Elle est aimée **de** tous ceux qui la connaissent.
Dans sa jeunesse, elle fut aimée **par** son cousin.

(*b*) Le prince s'avançait, précédé **de** ses gardes.
La décadence militaire fut précédée **par** la décadence politique, comme l'effet l'est toujours **par** la cause.
Un bon bourgeois passa, suivi **de** son chien.
L'armée se retira, suivie de près **par** les troupes ennemies.

4. Thus also with **être vu, entendu, lu, obéi, favorisé, etc.**

Le soleil est vu **de** tout le monde, mais il y a des corps célestes qui n'ont été vus que **par** quelques astronomes.
Ce maître est toujours obéi **de** ses élèves.

§ 68. The instrument, as opposed to the agent, is usually introduced by **de**, rarely by **par**, and only to denote a special and unusual occurrence, in which the instrument is referred to as an agent.

Il fut blessé **par** une balle perdue (*a spent bullet*).

But :

Il fut blessé **d'**une flèche, **d'**un coup de fusil.
Il était éclairé **des** lumières de la foi.
Nous étions menacés **d'**une tempête.
Tout le peuple fut frappé **de** la peste.

Note that in these sentences the adverbial complements would stand equally if the verb were in the active voice.

Un sauvage le blessa **d'**une flèche.
Dieu l'éclairait **des** lumières de la foi.

See also § 287.

THE PRONOMINAL VOICE

§ 69. The verbal endings are those of the active voice ; the auxiliary is **être**, the object pronouns **me, te, se, nous, vous,** cling to the verb or auxiliary. For the concords of the past participle, see **§§ 448, 449.**

INFINITIVE

Present.	se hâter	*Perfect.*	s'être hâté(e)(s)

PARTICIPLE

Present.	se hâtant	*Perfect.*	s'étant hâté(e)(s)

INDICATIVE

Present.	je me hâte	*Perfect.*	je me suis hâté(e)
	tu te hâtes		tu t'es hâté(e)
	il se hâte		il s'est hâté
	elle se hâte		elle s'est hâtée
	nous nous hâtons		nous nous sommes hâté(e)s
	vous vous hâtez		vous vous êtes hâté(e)(s)
	ils se hâtent		ils se sont hâtés
	elles se hâtent		elles se sont hâtées
Past Descr.	je me hâtais	*Past Perf.*	je m'étais hâté(e)
	etc.		etc.

IMPERATIVE

Present.	hâte-toi	ne te hâte pas	*Perfect. None.*
	hâtons-nous	ne nous hâtons pas	
	hâtez-vous	ne vous hâtez pas	

Note.—In the Infinitive and Participle, the pronominal object is that which suits the sense.

Je dois **me** hâter. Il nous a dit de **nous** hâter.
J'évitai l'orage, **m'**étant hâté de rentrer.

§ **70.** The pronominal verbs form three distinct groups.

1. An ordinary transitive verb has the subject as either (*a*) direct object, or (*b*) indirect object. The verb becomes **reflexive.**

(*a*) Marie **s'est coupée.** Elle **s'est coupée** au doigt.
Pourquoi **vous louez**-vous au lieu d'attendre qu'on vous loue ?

(*b*) Marie **s'est coupé** le doigt.
Vous **vous nuisez** par votre inexactitude. (Nuire **à** quelqu'un, *to injure some one.*)

Note.—The transitive verb **s'arroger**, which has a pronominal object in the dative, also belongs here, although it is always reflexive.

Ils **se sont arrogé** des droits que nous ne pouvons leur concéder.

2. The pronominal object indicates reciprocal action on the part of two or more agents. The verb is **reciprocal,** with object (*a*) direct or (*b*) indirect.

L'un l'autre, l'un à l'autre, etc. (§ 251.7) is a frequent adjunct which removes any ambiguity.

(*a*) Ces enfants **s'aiment** comme frères et sœurs.
Aimez-vous les uns les autres.

(*b*) Les deux chiens **se montraient** les dents.
Ces deux magasins sont trop rapprochés, ils **se nuisent l'un à l'autre.**

Notes.—(*a*) The verb may be singular with **on, tout,** etc., as subject.

Il y a toujours quelque chose de solennel dans un départ, même quand **on se quitte** pour peu de temps.
Entre voisins **on se rend** de petits services.
Dans une âme vraie **tout se tient :** ce qu'elle aime dans les paroles, elle l'aime aussi dans la vie.

(*b*) A few verbs show reciprocity of action by prefixing **entre.**
Dans le panier les bouteilles **s'entre-choquaient.**

3. In many verbs the action has never been felt, or has long ceased to be felt, as reflexive or reciprocal ; the object pronoun merely indicates the interest which the subject has in the action. These verbs are not as a rule reflexive or reciprocal in English. They include

(*a*) **Verbs always pronominal.** Some of these are indirectly transitive (generally with **de**), *e.g.* **s'emparer, se moquer, se repentir, se souvenir, se fier ;** others are intransitive, *e.g.* **s'envoler, s'évanouir, s'enfuir.**

Il **se moque de** vous. Je **me repens de** ma faute. Il **s'est emparé de** mon argent. Je ne **me fie** pas **à** lui.
L'oiseau **s'envola.** Elle **s'était évanouie.**

(*b*) **Active verbs** which assume **a new meaning,** transitive or intransitive, in the pronominal form. Compare:

Ne battez pas vos camarades.	Il s'est battu avec **courage.**
J'aperçois quelqu'un.	Je m'aperçois de mon erreur.
Il attendait une lettre.	Il s'attendait à un accident.
Ne me plaignez pas.	Ne **vous plaignez** pas **de ma** conduite.
Il va à l'école.	Il s'en va.
Il tait la vérité.	Il se tait.

(*c*) **Active verbs** which take the pronominal form with **passive meaning** (§ 66.3.*b*). They are numerous. The subject is usually **a 'thing,'** seldom a person.

La clef **s'est retrouvée.** *The key has been found.*
Une maison ne se bâtit pas en un jour. . . . *is not built.*
Cet article **se vend** partout. . . . *is sold everywhere.*
Cet article **se vend** bien. . . . *sells well.*
L'Académie des Sciences jouissait d'une faveur **qui s'explique** aisément.

Notes.—(*a*) Many verbs in English have both transitive and intransitive function without change of form. In most cases the verb becomes pronominal in French when it is intransitive in English.

J'arrête la pendule. *I stop the clock.*
Je m'arrête. *I stop.*

Je ne peux pas hâter les événements. *I cannot hasten events.*
Je ne peux pas **me hâter.** *I cannot hasten.*

(*b*) The verbs described in group 3 above are so numerous, as a page taken at random from any French book will show, that the collection and study of examples is of the utmost importance.

IMPERSONAL VERBS

§ **71.** The grammatical subject is always neuter **il,** followed by a singular verb. A logical subject may or may not follow.

1. The verb is a complete predicate. To this class belong verbs describing the weather.

Il pleut, il neige, il vente, il grêle, il tonne.

Note.—By extension of meaning the impersonal verb may take an object (which, however, may also be parsed as a logical subject):

Il pleut des balles;

or it may be used with a personal subject:

Les balles pleuvent. Les canons tonnent.

2. The verb is not a complete predicate. Such verbs are:

(*a*) **Faire + adjective or noun**, describing the weather.

Il fait beau (temps), vilain, froid, un temps glacial.
Il fait du vent, du brouillard, du soleil.

(*b*) **Il faut, il y a,** with an object noun, pronoun, infinitive, or clause.

Il y a de la craie dans le pupitre. **Il y en a** aussi dans la boîte. **Qu'est-ce qu'il** y a ? *What is the matter?* Il y a **que je suis très inquiet.**
Il faut travailler. Il faut **que nous travaillions.**

And with a dative of the person interested.

Il **lui** a fallu beaucoup travailler.
Il **nous** faudra deux heures pour faire ce travail.

(*c*) **Il est** + an expression of time.

Il est tard. Il est midi. Il est trois heures.

3. **Il** is used as a provisional subject, the real subject being the following clause, which, if in the infinitive, is introduced by **de.**

Il convient **d'être poli** avec tout le monde.
Il importe **de faire** vite.
Il paraît **que vous partez** en voyage.

Thus also with the construction **il est + adjective.**

Il n'est pas **facile de** se passer de pain.
Il est vrai qu'on m'a aidé.

There may be a dative of the person interested.

Il ne **me** convient pas de suivre ce conseil.
Il ne **nous** est pas facile de nous passer de pain.

Notes.—(1) The adjective may be replaced by an equivalent.

Dieu nous a donné le souvenir, et **il n'est au pouvoir** de **personne** de nous le retirer. (Au pouvoir de = possible à.)

(2) The construction **il est + adjective** belongs to literature and **to** 'careful' speech. In familiar speech **ce** is generally used.

Ce n'est pas facile de se passer de pain. C'est vrai qu'on m'a aidé.

4. **Il** is used as a provisional subject in order to bring the real subject (a noun) into stressed position.

Il est venu **beaucoup de monde. Il** va arriver **un accident.** **Il** est **un Dieu.**

This construction extends to the pronominal verbs with passive meaning (§ 70.3.*c*).

Il se trouva enfin **un homme** qui sut diriger les **événements.**
Il se vend à Paris **beaucoup d'articles anglais.**

And occasionally to verbs in the passive voice:

Au cours de mon voyage il me fut raconté **des choses très curieuses.**

USE OF THE TENSES OF THE INDICATIVE MOOD

§ 72. The Present Tense.

As in English and other languages, the **present** has in French a **threefold** value.

1. It indicates the **entire carrying out of an action**, from inception to completion, **now.**

Je **ferme** la porte.

On a line of time, such an action may be plotted as occupying a very short interval of time, or, for the sake of simplicity, a point in time.

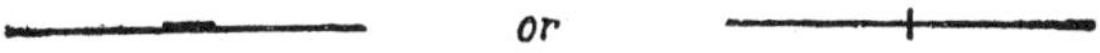

Thus:

Je **saisis** (1) le bouton de la porte, je **tourne** (2) le bouton, j'**ouvre** (3) la porte, j'**entre** (4) et je **referme** (5) la porte,

may be plotted.

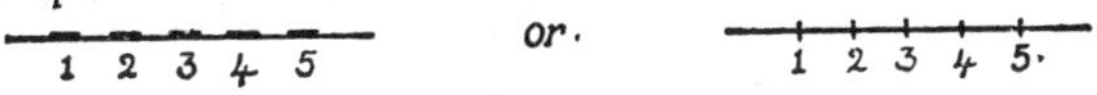

Such enumerations of actions, frequent in the past and future tenses, are rare in the present, but do occur; thus a lecturer will say:

Je **prends** ce flacon, j'y **verse** de l'eau, j'**ajoute** quelques gouttes d'acide sulfurique, j'y **laisse tomber** des fragments de zinc . . .

performing each action while he makes the relative statement.

2. It indicates that an action or state is **in progress, now.** The **beginning and the end of the action or state are not considered,** nor the extent of its duration.

Il **pleut.** Il **fait froid.**

Such statements cannot be plotted at or within definite points on a line of time; they may, however, be represented as follows:

the parallel to the line of time expressing that **now** (at A, where the line is thickest) the action is in progress, while its inception and completion belong vaguely to the past and the future.

Thus the statement,

Je **ferme** (1) la fenêtre parce qu'il pleut (2),

would be plotted

3. The present is also used when we refer to an action or state, not necessarily as taking place now, but as being (*a*) **always true,** or (*b*) **habitual.**

(*a*) L'eau pure est inodore et sans saveur.
Pierre qui roule n'amasse pas mousse.
(*b*) Je déjeune toujours à huit heures.
Quand il pleut je prends un parapluie.

Here, again, the actions or states referred to cannot be plotted at any definite point on a line of time ; but if always true, they may be represented graphically in the form

as above ; and if habitual, they would be represented by an indefinite number of points on such a parallel.

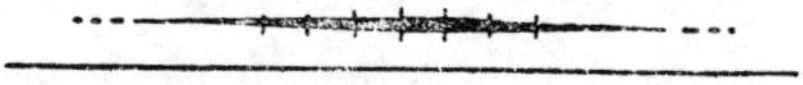

If these various uses of the present tense are clearly grasped and differentiated, there will be little difficulty in understanding the uses of the past tenses.

§ **73.** The present tense has a number of further uses.

1. As in most European languages *except English,* it shows that an action or state **begun at some past time** is still in progress. English has the present perfect.

Je suis à Londres **depuis deux ans.** *I have been in London for two years.*
Il y a déjà **deux** ans que je suis ici.
Voilà une demi-heure que je vous attends.

2. As in English, it is used familiarly as an immediate future.
J'arrive dans un instant. *I'm coming in a minute.*

3. It is used for the **future** after **si,** in adverbial clauses.
Si je **réussis** je vous écrirai.

4. It is used as an **immediate** past, especially of the verbs **arriver, revenir, sortir, rentrer.**

Il arrive de Paris. *He has just come from Paris.*
Il sort à l'instant. Elle sort du couvent.
Il rentre du régiment, du service militaire.

5. It is used, much more frequently than in English, of **past events,** especially when a **climax** in the narrative is being reached, to make the scene more vivid by substituting description for narrative (affective use, chiefly literary). This is often called the **present historic.**

> Il ouvrit, il posa la lampe, puis il **entre** pieds **nus.**
> C'est à ce moment que j'entrai . . . Un vrai coup de théâtre ! La petite **pousse** un cri, le gros livre **tombe,** les canaris, les mouches **se réveillent,** la pendule **sonne.**

Notes.—(*a*) The English continuous present may be rendered by the phrase **être en train de + infinitive.**

> Je suis **en train de préparer** mon discours. *I am preparing . . .*

(*b*) The 'emphatic' use of 'do' may be rendered by **bien** (cp. § 162).

> J'espère **bien** qu'ils reviendront ! *I do hope they will come back !*

§ 74. Past Historic.

Any action which in the present would be plotted as occupying a **point,** or a **definite interval,** in time, when it has become a past action, is expressed in literary style in the **past historic.** Thus, let the action of closing the door, which occurred at the time A,

be considered from a point in time B, it will be expressed,

> Je **fermai** la porte.

Thus also, narrated when we have reached a point in time B,

> Le conférencier **prit** (1) un flacon, y **versa** (2) de l'eau, **ajouta** (3) quelques gouttes d'acide sulfurique, puis y **laissa** (4) tomber des fragments de zinc . . .

When viewed in the past, it is immaterial whether the time occupied by the action or state was of short or long duration, provided that it is **viewed as a whole.**

> Louis XIV **régna** soixante-douze ans.

> Tel **fut** l'équipement de l'armée pendant trois siècles.

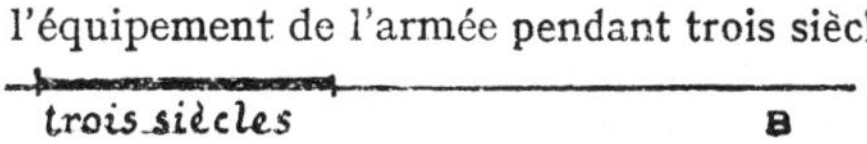

§ 75. Past Descriptive.

Any action which in the present is plotted under the forms

is expressed, when considered from a point in time B, in the **past descriptive.** Thus

Il pleut. Il fait froid,

become

Il **pleuvait.** *It was raining.* Il faisait froid.

Thus

Je déjeune toujours à huit heures

becomes

Je **déjeunais** toujours à huit heures. *I used to breakfast . . .*

§ 76. In accordance with the principle explained above, the past descriptive has the following uses :

1. It **describes** people, things, as they **appeared in the past.**
   Notre maison **était** petite, mais confortable.
   Mon hôte **portait** une perruque poudrée.

2. It is the tense of **habitual action.**
   Quand il **pleuvait** nous **prenions** un parapluie. *Whenever it rained, we used to take . . .*

3. It describes what **was in progress** at the time when some other event occurred or was occurring.
   Nous nous **préparions** à sortir quand sa lettre arriva.
   Il **écrivait** une lettre pendant que les obus **éclataient.**

Note.—Here also **être en train de** may be used.
   Nous **étions en train de déjeuner** quand sa lettre arriva.

4. It is used to **report statements and questions** originally expressed in the present tense, when they are dependent on a main verb in the past.
   Il nous a écrit qu'il **était** malade.
   Il demanda si tout **était** prêt.

§ **77.** The past descriptive has a number of further uses, most of which correspond to uses of the present tense explained above.

1. It describes an action or state, begun at a remoter period in the past, **as still in progress at a given past time.** English has the past perfect (cp. § 73.1).

> **Nous étions** à Londres **depuis un an** lorsque la guerre éclata. *We had been . . .*
>
> **Il y avait huit jours** que nous **l'attendions.**
> **Nous connaissions de longue date** l'homme auquel nous **avions** affaire.

2. It is used for the **future in the past** after **si,** in adverbial clauses (cp. § 73.3).

> Il nous promit qu'il nous écrirait **s'il réussissait.**
> **S'il** vous **voyait** ici, il serait bien étonné.
> **Si** la situation **changeait** pendant mon absence, vous me feriez prévenir.

3. It is used as an immediate past, anterior to a given moment in the past, especially of the verbs **arriver, sortir,** etc. (cp. § 73.4).

> Je rencontrai un journaliste qui **arrivait** de Paris. *Who had just come . . .*
> Elle **sortait** à peine du couvent lorsqu'il la demanda en mariage.
> Il **rentrait** du régiment lorsque je fis sa connaissance.

4. It is used occasionally for the **future perfect in the past,** to express vividly, as actually occurring, what might have happened under certain conditions (affective use).

> Un pas de plus et je **tombais** dans l'abîme (=et je serais tombé).
> Si l'on ne m'eût prévenu à temps, je **commettais** une faute irréparable (=j'aurais commis).

5. Modern writers frequently use the past descriptive instead of the past historic to make the narrative more vivid (affective use). This may be explained as a setting back into the past of the present historic (cp. § 73.5).

> Joe, immédiatement relevé après sa chute, à l'instant où l'un des cavaliers se précipitait sur lui, **bondissait** comme une panthère, **l'évitait** par un écart, se **jetait** en croupe, **saisissait** l'Arabe à la gorge . . . **l'étranglait,** le **renversait** sur le sable, et **continuait** sa course effrayante.
>
> Ce jour-là, elle **partait** de bonne heure avec sa bonne qui lui donnait le bras et portait un pliant. Près du cimetière, elle **entrait** chez une marchande de couronnes qui la connaissait depuis de longues années. . . . Là, elle se **reposait** quelques instants, puis, chargeant Germinie de couronnes d'immortelles, elle **passait** la porte du cimetière, **prenait** l'allée à gauche du cèdre.

§ **78.** The fact that the English simple past is represented in French sometimes by the past historic and sometimes by the past descriptive, constitutes one of the chief difficulties of French grammar. A little practice in plotting the tenses will, however, soon lead to a clear under standing of how to differentiate between them.

Consider the following French passage :

> La semaine suivante, toutes celles qui avaient (1) huit ans descendirent (2) au grand dortoir. J'eus (3) un lit placé près d'une fenêtre. Marie Renaud et Ismérie restèrent (4) mes voisines. Souvent, quand nous étions (5) couchées, sœur Marie-Aimée venait (6) s'asseoir près de ma fenêtre. Elle me prenait (7) une main qu'elle caressait (8), tout en regardant dehors. Une nuit, il y eut (9) un grand feu dans le voisinage. Tout le dortoir était (10) éclairé. Sœur Marie-Aimée ouvrit (11) la fenêtre toute grande, puis elle me secoua (12), en disant : " Réveille-toi, viens voir le feu ! "

It will be plotted as follows :

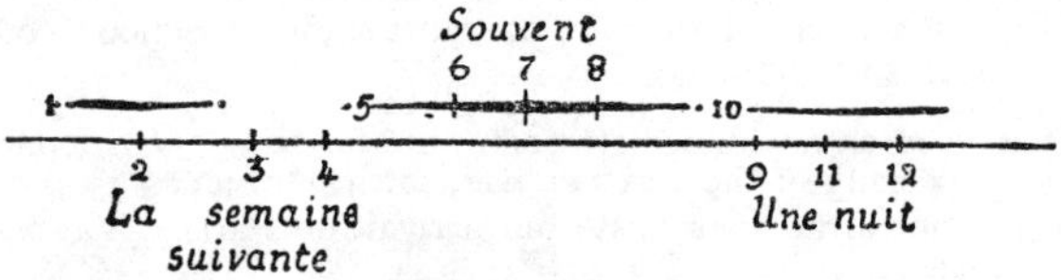

Note that verbs 5, 6, 7, 8, introduced by souvent, denote habitual action, and are located apart from, and not on, line A B.

In a like manner, in the following English passage, we should plot on the line A B every verb that carries the narrative a step forward.

> I *was* (1) in a hurry to get back to town, and *took* (2) a cross-road which *was pointed out* (3) to me. Unfortunately, the mist *grew* (4) thicker and thicker, no stars *shone* (5) in the sky ; at last the darkness *became* (6) so complete that I *went astray* (7). *I tried* (8) to retrace my steps, and *found* (9) myself completely lost.

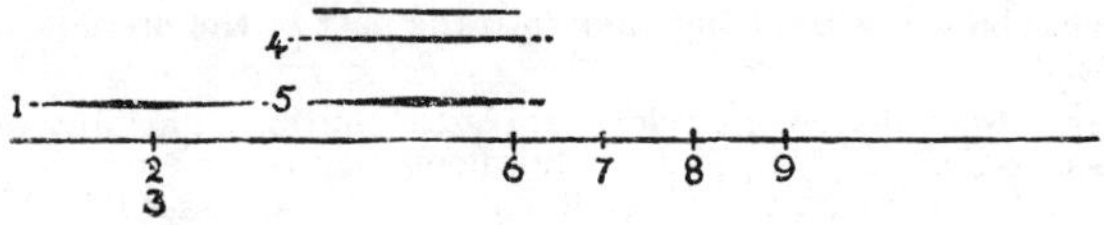

The tenses in French will then appear as follows :

> J'avais (1) hâte de regagner la ville, et pris (2) un chemin de traverse que l'on m'indiqua (3). Par malheur, la brume s'épaississait (4) de plus en plus, aucune étoile ne brillait (5) au ciel ; enfin l'obscurité devint (6) si profonde que je perdis (7) mon chemin. Je voulus (8) retourner sur mes pas, et me trouvai (9) complètement égaré.

The passage below should be treated in the same manner, and then compared with the French.

"While she *sang*, darkness *was falling* from the great trees, and the moonlight *shone* on her alone. She *stopped*, and no one *dared* to break the silence. The lawn *was covered* with mist, which *rolled* over the blades of grass. We *thought* ourselves in Paradise. At last I *rose*, and *ran* to the flower-beds of the castle, where some laurel bushes *stood*. I *brought* back two branches, which *were woven* into a wreath and tied with a ribbon. I *set* on Adrienne's head this ornament, the lustrous leaves of which *shone* above her fair hair. She *resembled* the Beatrice of Dante. . . . Adrienne *rose*, and *ran back* into the castle. She *was*, we *were told*, the grand-daughter of a descendant of a family connected with the ancient kings of France; the blood of the Valois *flowed* in her veins. . . . When I *came* back to Sylvia, I noticed that she *was weeping*. The wreath offered to the lovely singer *was* the cause of her tears. I *offered* to go and gather another one, but she *said* she *did* not in the least *desire* it."

A mesure qu'elle **chantait**, l'ombre **descendait** des grands arbres, et le clair de lune **tombait** sur elle seule. Elle se **tut**, et personne **n'osa** rompre le silence. La pelouse **était couverte** de vapeurs, qui **roulaient** sur les pointes des herbes. Nous **pensions** être en paradis. Je me **levai** enfin, et **courus** au parterre du château, où se **trouvaient** des lauriers. Je **rapportai** deux branches qui **furent tressées** en couronne et nouées d'un ruban. Je **posai** sur la tête d'Adrienne cet ornement, dont les feuilles lustrées **éclataient** sur ses cheveux blonds. Elle **ressemblait** à la Béatrice de Dante. . . . Adrienne se **leva**, et **rentra** en courant dans le château. C'**était**, nous dit-on, la petite-fille de l'un des descendants d'une famille alliée aux anciens rois de France; le sang des Valois **coulait** dans ses veines. . . . Quand je **revins** près de Sylvie, je m'aperçus qu'elle **pleurait**. La couronne donnée à la belle chanteuse **était** le sujet de ses larmes. Je lui **offris** d'en aller cueillir une autre, mais elle **dit** qu'elle n'y **tenait** nullement.

Compare also, and plot, the following groups of sentences:

Il **était** bien triste quand il reçut ma lettre. *He was feeling very sad at the time when he received my letter.*
Il **fut** bien triste quand il reçut ma lettre. *The contents of my letter made him very sad.*

Nous attaquâmes l'ennemi, qui se **retirait**. *We attacked the enemy, who were retiring.*
Nous attaquâmes l'ennemi, qui se **retira**. *We attacked the enemy, who then retired.*

Je **savais** à trois heures ce qui était arrivé. *At three o'clock, I already knew what had happened.*
Je **sus** à trois heures ce qui était arrivé. *I learnt at three o'clock what had happened.*

Il **connaissait** la misère. *He was acquainted with want.*
Il **connut** la misère. *He made acquaintance with want.*

§ 79. The Perfect.

1. Shows an action as **now completed** (present perfect).

J'ai fini mon devoir. **J'ai appris** ma leçon.

And is not used if the action is still in progress. See § 73.1 above.

2. Shows an action as having taken place at a **past time not specified.**

J'ai lu cela quelque part.
C'est des Arabes que nous **avons appris** l'algèbre.
J'ai été faible, n'étant qu'un homme.

3. Is used familiarly as a future perfect (cp. § 73.2).

Ne vous en allez pas, **j'ai fini** dans un instant.

4. And also after si in adverbial clauses (cp. § 73.3).

Si demain il **n'a** pas encore **répondu**, nous n'attendrons plus.

5. Is used as a **past tense, instead of the past historic,** in conversation, letter-writing, etc., especially when recent events are referred to. When thus used it is best called the **Conversational Past.**

J'ai vu votre frère ce matin. Le roi **est mort** hier dans la soirée. Nous **avons attaqué** l'ennemi, qui **s'est retiré. J'ai su** à trois heures ce qui était arrivé.

La semaine dernière, toutes celles qui avaient huit ans **sont descendues** au grand dortoir. **J'ai eu** un lit placé près d'une fenêtre.

Hier soir il y **a eu** un grand feu dans le voisinage. Tout le dortoir était éclairé. Sœur Marie-Aimée **a ouvert** la fenêtre toute grande, puis elle **m'a secouée,** en disant: " Réveille-toi, viens voir le feu."

Poil de Carotte, tu n'as pas **travaillé** l'année dernière comme j'espérais.

Note.—In modern French **the past historic is never used in conversation,** except in some of the remoter provinces, such as Brittany, and in the South.

§ 80. The Past Perfect.

1. As in English, the past perfect is used of an action anterior to the period in the past which is engaging our attention.

Louis XIII mourut en 1643; Richelieu **était mort** cinq mois auparavant.
Il arriva en retard ; il **avait manqué** son train.

On avait fini de déjeuner quand nous sommes **arrivés.**
Quand nous **avions** bien **travaillé** on nous accordait un demi-congé.
Avant d'être "des vieux," ils **avaient été** "un ménage d'ouvriers rangés." Ils **avaient possédé** un mobilier complet.

2. Statements and questions spoken in the past **historic** or in the **conversational** past are **reported in the past perfect,** when dependent on a main verb in the past.

Il nous a écrit qu'il **avait été** malade.
Il demanda quand nous **étions arrivés.**

This rule is strictly observed, and the looseness frequent in English is not permissible. "I was ill when you called" is often reported in English in the form "He explained to us that he was ill *when we called.*" But in French, "J'étais malade quand vous **êtes venus** pour me voir" must be reported

Il nous expliqua qu'il était malade quand nous **étions venus** pour le voir.

(Note that the descriptive past, "J'étais malade," is not set back into the past perfect.)

Several examples are to be found in Baudelaire's translation of *The Gold Bug.*

Driving a peg into the ground at the precise spot where the beetle fell, *my friend now produced from his pocket a tape-measure.* Mon ami enfonça dans la terre une cheville, à l'endroit précis où le scarabée **était tombé**, et tira de sa poche un ruban à mesurer.

§ 81. The Second Past Perfect is used

1. In simple sentences as a **past historic indicating the completion of an action.** It is then always accompanied by an adverb or adverb phrase indicating the time taken to accomplish the action, or its rapid accomplishment.

En huit jours le géant **eut terminé** son château.
En trois heures j'**eus visité** la ville et ses environs.
En moins d'un quart d'heure il **eut achevé** un portrait de mon lézard.
Il **eut bientôt fait** de s'habiller.
En vingt bonds il m'**eut dépassé.**
Je voulus nous garantir au moyen de la couverture, le vent l'**eut bien vite roulée.**

Thus also:

Avant qu'on eût pu saisir le voleur, il **eut sauté** par la fenêtre.

2. To indicate that the completion of an action was **immediately anterior** to another action in the **past historic**; *i.e.* it is used **in tense sequence with the past historic** (§ 395.2):

(*a*) In principal clauses introduced by **à peine, ne pas plus tôt**;

(*b*) In dependent clauses introduced by **quand, lorsque, dès que, aussitôt que, après que,** etc.

(*c*) In adjective clauses.

(*a*) **A peine fut-il arrivé** qu'il **fut** obligé de repartir.
La femme **ne fut pas plus tôt rentrée** chez elle que le diable **arriva.**

(*b*) **Quand** il **eut fini** de parler, il **vint** à moi.
Dès que la femme **fut rentrée** chez elle, le diable **arriva.**

(*c*) Ceux qui **eurent fini** les premiers **attendirent** les autres dans la cour.

And as in 1 above:

La trappe soulevée laissa paraître Télémaque . . . Il riait entre deux bouteilles de bière, qu'il **eut immédiatement débouchées** pour les servir aux militaires attablés.

Note.—The tense sequence must of course connect two successive actions, and does not obtain when events and description are intermingled.

Je veillai toute la nuit. Lorsque j'**eus fait** les dernières retouches à mon travail, le soleil se **levait** à l'horizon (*was rising*). *Cf.* § 395.2, note 1.

§ 82. 'Temps Surcomposés.' (*Cf.* § 395.2.)

The second past perfect belongs to 'historic' narrative; the corresponding conversational tense is termed in French 'surcomposé,' *i.e.* the auxiliary is itself in a compound tense. It occurs only with the auxiliary **avoir.**

En trois heures j'**ai eu visité** la ville et ses environs.
J'**ai eu** bientôt **fait** de m'habiller.
Quand j'**ai eu fini** mon devoir, je suis allé jouer.

This tense may be thrown back into a remoter past.

Les cinquante hommes **avaient eu** vite épuisé les maigres provisions du cabaret.
Quand j'**avais eu fini** mon devoir, j'étais allé jouer.

Or forward into the future.

Quand il **aura eu fini** son devoir, il sera allé jouer (§ 83.3).

And it may occur in the subjunctive.

Avant que l'omnibus **ait eu chargé** les bagages et pris les voyageurs, la nuit est venue.

§ 83. The Future and Future Perfect

1. Are used as in English, of **future time.**

Il arrivera demain. J'**aurai fini** avant vous.

2. Are used, chiefly in **dependent time clauses** and **adjective clauses,** in tense sequence with a future or imperative (which has future value) in the main clause (§ 395.2). Here English usually has the present or the perfect.

Appelez-moi quand vous **serez** prêt. ... *when you are ready.*
Appelez-moi quand vous **aurez fini.** ... *when you have finished.*
Je ferai ce qui me **plaira.**
Je viendrai aussitôt que je le **pourrai** ; dès que j'**aurai déjeuné.**
Faites comme vous **voudrez.**

3. Are used to express **supposition** or **probability.** The future simple is comparatively rare ; the future perfect constantly used.

On sonne. Ce **sera** le médecin. *It must be ...*
Il **aura** encore **fait** quelque bêtise.
Ma lettre lui **sera parvenue** trop tard.

4. The future is frequently used as an **imperative.**

Vous **ferez** ce que je vous dis. *You must do ...*
Les lecteurs **sauront** que M. Jeannot père avait acquis des biens immenses.

§ 84. The Future and Future Perfect in the Past.

1. These tenses are used when the future and future perfect, in uses 1 and 2 above, become dependent on a main verb in a past tense, or even in independent clauses, when the whole narrative is in the past.

Il se vanta qu'il **aurait fini** avant moi.
Il m'écrivait qu'il se trouvait retenu à Paris. Il **arriverait** le lendemain.
Il m'a dit de l'appeler quand je **serais** prêt. *When I was ready.*
Il refusa de me conseiller. Je **ferais** comme je voudrais.

2. (*a*) The **future simple in the past** is used as a somewhat diffident, and therefore polite, form, instead of the present **tense,** in statements, requests, and questions.

Je n'**affirmerais** pas que ce soit de sa faute.
Je ne **saurais** (= Je ne puis) me ranger à cette opinion (§ 94.1.).

Je **voudrais** bien vous demander quelque chose.
Voudriez-vous bien me passer le sucre, s'il vous plaît ?
Pardon, monsieur, **pourriez-vous** m'indiquer un bureau de tabac ?
Où donc est Henri aujourd'hui ? **Serait-il** malade ? *Can he be . . .*

(*b*) Both tenses are so used especially when one is not willing to vouch for the truth of a statement.

Vous avez entendu l'explosion ? D'après les journaux du soir, il y **aurait** deux cents morts.
Ce **seraient** les Chinois qui **auraient inventé** la poudre à canon.

(*c*) Both tenses are used in adjective clauses to express a fact which is only imaginary or hypothetical.

Il est honteux comme un renard qu'une poule **aurait pris.**
On a proposé de percer un tunnel qui **relierait** directement les deux vallées.
Un étranger qui **arriverait** au pays pourrait croire qu'il est dans cette île dont parle l'Arioste.

§ **85.** A 'then' clause with a dependent adverb clause of condition, or 'if' clause, is usually in one of the four future tenses. (Note that the 'if' clause is never in the future.)

(*a*) If the event is admitted as real or probable, the future and future perfect are used.

S'il vient, je lui **parlerai.**
Si l'on m'attaque, je me **défendrai.**
S'il est parti lundi, il **sera arrivé** hier à sa destination.

(*b*) If the event is presented as hypothetical, contrary to reality, the future and future perfect in the past are used.

S'il **venait**, je lui **parlerais.**
Si l'on m'attaquait, je me **défendrais.**
Si l'on m'**avait** attaqué, je me **serais défendu.**
S'il **était parti** lundi il **serait arrivé** hier à sa destination.

Notes.—1. In literary style the past perfect subjunctive is often used in both the 'if' and the 'then' clauses.

Si on **l'eût attaqué**, il se **fût défendu.**

2. The 'if' clause may be lacking, as in English.

Je **n'aurais** jamais pensé à cela !

§ 86. Auxiliary Uses of aller, venir, devoir.

1. The **present** and the **past descriptive** of **aller** are used with the infinitive to form an 'immediate' future and a corresponding future in the past. This construction is much more frequent than in English, which often uses the simple future although the action will follow immediately.

> Je **vais** lui **écrire.** *I am going to write to him.*
> Maintenant nous **allons réciter** la leçon. *Now we shall say the lesson.*
> **J'allais** lui **écrire** quand il est arrivé.

2. The present and the past descriptive of **venir** are used with de and the infinitive to form an 'immediate' past and a corresponding past perfect.

> Je **viens de** lui **écrire.** *I have just written to him.*
> Je **venais de sortir.** *I had just gone out.*

3. The verb **devoir** is used to form the future of the subjunctive mood, when it is necessary to distinguish the future from the present.

> Est-il vrai qu'il **doive** vous **écrire** de Londres ?

(*That he will write* . . ., a shade of meaning which would not be clearly expressed by " qu'il vous écrive.")

Also to form a future in the past.

> Richelieu mourut en 1642. Louis XIII **devait mourir** cinq mois plus tard.

THE IMPERATIVE MOOD

§ 87. The **Imperative** has only two tenses, called **present** and **perfect**, but which are usually future and future perfect in meaning ; thus we have seen that the imperative is equivalent to a future in § **83.2**.

A third person singular and plural is borrowed from the subjunctive present and perfect (§ 365).

> **Venez tout** de suite. **Ayez fini** avant mon retour.
> **Qu'il vienne** tout de suite. **Qu'ils aient fini** avant midi.

Note.—Much more common in French than in English is an 'ethic' or affective use of the first person of the imperative in giving orders to others.

> Vite le couvert, mes petites ! La table au milieu de la chambre, la nappe du dimanche. . . . Et ne **rions** pas tant, s'il vous plaît ! Et **dépêchons-nous** !

THE SUBJUNCTIVE MOOD

§ 88. The correspondence between the four tenses of the subjunctive and the tenses of the indicative is dealt with in § **395**.5.

For the uses of the subjunctive mood, see §§ **371–392**.

THE INFINITIVE

§ **89.** The infinitive, partaking of the nature of the verb, may form an **infinitive clause**, with a subject expressed or understood.

Que **répondre** à cela ?
Ainsi dit le renard, et **flatteurs d'applaudir.** (Historical Infinitive, § 109.)
Je déclare **avoir dit** la vérité (Je is subject to both verbs).
Je ne savais que **lui répondre** (§ 203.3).
Nous entendons les oiseaux **chanter** dans les arbres.
(**Les oiseaux**, object of **entendons**, is subject to **chanter.**)

§ **90.** The infinitive, partaking of the nature of the noun, is used as a **noun equivalent.** It may be governed by a preposition. Its chief functions are :

(*a*) **Subject,** grammatical or logical :
Trop parler nuit.
Marcher était difficile autant que pénible.
Mieux valait **partir** tout de suite.
Il vaut mieux **ne rien dire.**

(*b*) **Predicative noun equivalent :**
Mon destin est **de finir** sur les champs de bataille.
Voir, c'est **croire.**
Ne pas dire la vérité, cela s'appelle **mentir.**
Il me semble **avoir raison.** *He appears to me to be right.*
(May also be impersonal, coming under (*a*) above: *It seems to me that I am right.*)

(*c*) **Object** (with or without a governing preposition) :
Je déclare **avoir dit la vérité.** Je veux **sortir.**
J'aime **à me promener.**

(*d*) **Adjective equivalent** (with a governing preposition) :
J'ai plusieurs lettres **à écrire.**

(*e*) **Adverb equivalent** (with or without a governing preposition):
Il faut manger **pour vivre.**
Il est sorti **se promener.**

§ **91.** The dependent infinitive, *i.e.* the infinitive in uses *c, d, e* above, requires much study, and the constant collection of examples from the texts read. It is convenient to consider separately its use: *A,* without a governing preposition ; *B,* with the preposition **à** ; *C,* with certain other prepositions ; *D,* with the particle **de.**

A. The Dependent Infinitive without a Preposition

§ 92. The Factitive Verb.

1. The verb **faire** forms with a dependent infinitive a combination which may be considered as the **factitive** aspect of the verb Compare :

{ Les pommes **rôtissaient** devant le feu.
{ Nous **faisions rôtir** les pommes.

{ Les flèches **pleuvaient** sur les chevaliers français.
{ Les archers **firent pleuvoir** leurs flèches sur les chevaliers.

2. In this construction, extremely common in French, the dependent infinitive is always in the **active voice**. (For the word-order, see also § **332**.)

J'ai **fait venir** un médecin. *I called in a doctor.*
Faites entrer ces messieurs. *Show the gentlemen in.*
Faites-les **entrer**. Je les **ai fait entrer**.
Tout le monde est là. Vous pouvez **faire servir**. *You may order dinner to be served.*
Elle **fit apporter** les gâteaux que l'on rangea sur une table.
Je **me fais faire** un pardessus au Bon Marché. *I am having an overcoat made (for myself) at the B.M. stores.*
Il s'est fait punir. *He got punished.*
Elle se disposait à nous servir en se **faisant aider** par Madeleine.

3. As the double accusative is unknown in French, the personal object of the factitive verb has the **indirect construction** whenever there is another object. Compare :

Je fais travailler **mes élèves**. Je **les** fais travailler.
Je fais travailler l'algèbre **à mes élèves**.
Je **leur** fais travailler l'algèbre.
Faites boire **ce pauvre blessé**. Faites-**lui** boire un peu de vin.

The accusative object may be a clause, or neuter **le** standing for a clause.

Faites savoir à vos amis **que j'arriverai demain.**
Faites-le-leur savoir. Je **le** leur ferai savoir.

Note.—To avoid ambiguity, the personal object may be governed by **par**.

J'ai fait porter ma lettre **par** un des garçons de l'hôtel.
I got a waiter to take my letter.

Par *must* be used in such a sentence as

Il se faisait lire le journal **par** son fils,

since a double dative is as impossible as a double accusative.

4. If the dependent infinitive is a pronominal verb, the reflexive pronoun is dropped.

Faites taire ces enfants.
Je vous **ferai repentir** de ces paroles.
C'était une joie pour elle de me **faire reposer** un instant.

Unless the verb is truly reflexive or reciprocal (§ 70.1, 2), in which case the reflexive pronoun may be retained to avoid ambiguity or misunderstanding.

C'est moi qui les ai fait **se connaître.**
Je l'ai fait **se sécher** devant le feu du salon.

(C'est moi qui les ai fait connaître = *It was I who brought them into prominence* (*made them known*). Je l'ai fait sécher = *I dried him.*)

Note.—English 'to make' + predicative adjective is expressed in French by the verb **rendre** + predicative adjective.

Sa cuisine nous a tous **rendus malades.** *Made us all ill.*
Cette nouvelle le **rendra joyeux.** *This news will make him glad.*

§ **93.** Closely allied in construction to the verb **faire** are the verbs **voir, entendre,** sentir, and **laisser.** The dependent verb is in the active voice, and the personal object takes the indirect construction, or is governed by **par,** as in § **92.**3 above; but the combination is a looser one, and the two verbs are frequently felt and treated as separate entities, each verb having an accusative, provided two accusatives do not come together.

Je vous **vois pâlir.** Je **l'entends appeler.**
En montant au lac, je **vois grandir** l'horizon, *or* je **vois** l'horizon **grandir.**
Je sentais mes cheveux **se hérisser.**
Le (*or* **Lui**) **laisserez-vous faire** cela ?
Il ne se laissera pas **tromper.**
Je **lui ai** (*or* **l'ai**) **entendu dire** qu'il viendrait.
Je **le lui ai entendu dire** (*Not* Je le l'ai . . . ! But one may say : Je l'ai entendu le dire.)
J'étais **désolée** de **leur** (*or* **les**) **voir quitter** la maison.

The construction is frequently ambiguous. Thus **Je l'entends appeler** = either *I hear him calling* or *I hear him being called.*

J'ai entendu dire **à mon** père que la maison passait pour être hantée = either *I have heard my father say* . . . or *I have heard my father told* . . .

If the sense is not quite clear, other constructions are available.

Je l'entends **qui appelle.** *I hear him calling.*
J'ai entendu dire **par** mon père que . . .

Notes.—(*a*) **Voir,** like **entendre,** often has a dependent relative clause instead of the infinitive.

Je le vois **qui vient.** Le voyez-vous **qui arrive** en courant ?

(*b*) **Se voir** is often followed by a predicative past participle passive.
Il se vit **forcé** d'obéir.

§ **94.** 1. The verbs **pouvoir, savoir, vouloir, devoir,** which correspond in part to the English modal auxiliaries **can, may, will, must, shall,** take an infinitive as direct object.

Pouvez-vous **répondre** à ma question ? *Can you . . . ?*
Puis-je **ouvrir** la fenêtre ? *May I ? Shall I ?*
Il **a pu se tromper.** *He may have made a mistake.*

(Note that here in French the infinitive remains in the present tense.)

Savez-vous **jouer** aux échecs ? *Can you* (*Do you know how to*) *?*
Je ne **saurais me ranger** à votre avis (§ 84.2.*a*).
Il ne **veut** pas **travailler.** *He will not . . .*
Il **veut bien** nous **accompagner.** *He is willing to . . .*
Il **voudrait bien** nous **accompagner.** *He would like to . . .*
Veuillez (bien) vous **asseoir.** *Kindly sit down.*

2. The verb **devoir** has a number of uses, some of which are peculiar to certain tenses.

Je **dois** honorer mes parents. *I should* (general precept).
Je **dois** partir demain. *I am to start to-morrow.*
Je **dois** me plier à tous ses caprices. *I have to fall in with all his fancies.*
Vous **devez** avoir faim. *You must be hungry.*

Je **devais** partir hier. *I was to have started yesterday.*
Je **devais** me plier à tous ses caprices. *I had to . . .*
Il **devait** avoir faim. *He must have been hungry.*

Je **dus** (J'**ai dû**) partir sur-le-champ. *I had to start at once.*
Il **dut** (Il **a dû**) se tromper de chemin. *He must have mistaken the way.*

J'**avais dû** partir sur-le-champ. *I had had to start at once.*
Il **avait dû** se tromper de chemin. *Must have mistaken.*

Il **devra** partir sur-le-champ. *He will have to* (*must*) *start.*

Il **devrait** aller le voir. *He ought to* (*should*) *go and see him.*
Il **aurait dû** aller le voir. *He ought to have gone . . .*

Je suis heureux qu'il **doive** nous rejoindre. *I am glad he will join us again.* (**Devoir** used as auxiliary of the future in the subjunctive, § 86.3.)

Note the differences between

(*a*) The French and the English construction in such sentences as **Il a pu se tromper. Il a dû se tromper. Il aurait dû aller.**
(*b*) The uses of **pouvoir** and **savoir** = 'can.'
(*c*) **Je dois** and **je devrais** = 'I should.'
(*d*) 'Shall,' 'should,' 'will,' 'would,' used with full meaning in the examples above, and the same verbs used as tense auxiliaries.

§ **95.** To **vouloir** may be assimilated other verbs of will or desire, such as **désirer, préférer, aimer autant, aimer mieux, prétendre, entendre, oser.**

Je **désire** vous parler. Je **préfère** attendre. J'**aimerais autant** rester ici. J'**aime mieux** ne rien dire. Je **prétends** (J'**entends**) faire ce qui me plaît. Je n'**ose** pas l'aborder.

§ **96.** The infinitive stands as object (*a*) to 'declarative' verbs such as **affirmer, avouer, déclarer, dire, reconnaître, nier** ; (*b*) to verbs of 'believing' and 'hoping' such as **croire, penser, se figurer, espérer, compter.** This construction is little used in familiar speech (§ 403).

(*a*) Il **affirme** (**dit, jure, déclare**) nous avoir aperçus.
Il **avoue** (**reconnaît, nie**) y être allé.

(*b*) Je ne **croyais** pas si bien dire. Je ne **comptais** pas vous voir ici. Je **pense** (J'**espère**) partir demain. Je **me figurais** le revoir tel que je l'avais connu.

§ **97. Intransitive verbs of motion,** and the verbs **mener, envoyer,** have an adverbial infinitive of purpose.

Je **suis allé** le **voir**. **Venez** me **trouver** demain.
Il **courut** le **prévenir**. Julie **est sortie acheter** du beurre.
Il **est descendu déjeuner**. J'**ai envoyé chercher** le sergent de ville.
Il **retourna** à l'église **attendre** son curé.

Note.—The preposition **pour** is used to insist on the idea of purpose (§ 106.1), especially when the purpose remained unfulfilled.

Il est descendu **pour** mieux entendre notre conversation.
Je suis allé **pour** le voir, mais il n'y était pas (. . . *was not at home*).

§ **98.** An infinitive without preposition, which has come to be looked upon as the logical subject, follows the impersonal verbs **il semble, il me semble, il faut, il fait + adjective.**

Il **semble** pleuvoir. Il **me semble** entendre quelque chose. Il **faut** faire de notre mieux. Il **fait mauvais** voyager par ces routes en hiver. Il **fait cher** vivre en temps de guerre.

Note.—Somewhat similar is the personal construction **avoir beau + infinitive.**

J'**ai beau** crier, on ne m'écoute pas. *I shout in vain, no one listens.*

B. The Dependent Infinitive governed by à denotes Tendency, Aim, Direction

§ **99.** Dependent on a verb.

1. It stands as **adverb equivalent** instead of a noun.

Je l'engage à la persévérance.	Je l'engage **à persévérer.**
Je consens à votre départ.	Je consens **à vous laisser partir.**
Il se met au travail.	Il se met **à travailler.**
On l'oblige au repos.	On l'oblige **à se reposer.**
Je me plais à la lecture.	Je me plais **à lire.**
Il passe son temps à des riens.	Il passe son temps **à ne rien faire.**
Il est à son travail.	Il est **à travailler.**

2. It may replace a **direct object** after **aimer, chercher, demander, offrir, apprendre,** commencer, etc.

Il aime les distractions.	Il aime **à se distraire.**
Il cherche le succès.	Il cherche **à réussir.**
Il demande du vin.	Il demande **à boire.**
Il m'offrit un verre de vin.	Il m'offrit **à boire.**

And is thus used also as object of **avoir** :

J'ai **à vous parler.** J'ai **à faire une visite.**

3. It is used with certain verbs which do not take a dependent noun, *e.g.* **tarder, hésiter, s'étudier.**

Il tarde **à rentrer.** Il hésite **à accepter.** Il s'étudie **à nous faire plaisir.**

4. It stands in adverbial relation to a verb with a noun-object which is not particularized.

J'ai une visite **à faire.**
J'ai eu de la peine, de la difficulté, **à le retrouver.**
J'aurai beaucoup de plaisir **à vous revoir.**
Quel plaisir trouvez-vous **à le taquiner** ?
Pourquoi prenez-vous plaisir **à le taquiner** ?
Ces voix joyeuses font plaisir **à entendre.**

Note.—If the noun is particularized, the infinitive is usually adjectival to the noun, and governed by **de.**

Aurai-je bientôt le plaisir **de vous revoir** ?
Donnez-vous la peine **de vous asseoir.**

§ **100. Dependent on a noun.**

1. Certain abstract nouns corresponding to verbs or **adjectives** followed by **à** have the same construction as the verb or adjective.

Quel acharnement à les dénigrer ! *How he persists in running them down!*

Son **adresse à** se tirer d'affaire était proverbiale.

Compare : Il s'acharne à les dénigrer. Il est **adroit à** se tirer d'affaire.

2. The Infinitive with **à** is an adjective equivalent in many compound nouns (§ 147.1.*b*).

Une chambre **à** coucher ; une salle **à manger** ; du **bois** à brûler.

§ **101. Dependent on an adjective.**

1. Many adjectives take an adverbial infinitive governed by **à**. Such are **prêt**, **prompt**, **lent**, **facile**, **difficile**, **bon**, **mauvais**, **léger**, **lourd**, and their synonyms.

Je suis **prêt à** vous écouter.
Il était **lent à** prendre une décision.
Ce passage est **facile** (**difficile**) **à** traduire.
Ce fruit n'est pas **bon à** manger.

2. Thus also **unique**, **seul**, **dernier**, and the ord'nal **numbers**.

Il fut **le seul à** nous encourager.
Il est toujours **le premier à** réclamer.
Le troisième à mourir fut un des mousses.

§ **102.** The infinitive governed by **à** has a number of important idiomatic uses.

1. Adjectival.

(*a*) Ce devoir est **à refaire**. Maison **à louer**. Voici un problème **à résoudre**. Il est bien **à plaindre**.

Note that the dependent infinitive is always in the active voice in this construction.

(*b*) Il est homme **à réussir** dans toutes ses entreprises. *He is the kind of man who will succeed . . .*

2. Adverbial.

(*a*) **A vous croire** tout serait perdu.
A dire vrai, j'étais trop loin pour bien entendre.
A le voir, on ne le croirait pas si vigoureux.

(*b*) Il riait **à se tordre**. Il courait **à perdre haleine**.
Il gèle **à pierre fendre**. Vous dansez **à ravir**, mademoiselle !

(*c*) Je me gâte la vue **à lire votre écriture**.
Mais je me tue **à vous répéter** que vous **avez raison** !

C. The Dependent Infinitive governed by après, par, sans, pour

These constructions are all adverbial

§ **103. Après + perfect infinitive** = 'after' + gerund.

Après avoir fini mes devoirs, je suis sorti jouer.
After finishing my work, I went out to play.

§ **104. Par + infinitive** = 'by' + gerund, after the verbs **commencer, débuter, finir, achever.**

Nous commençons par faire nos devoirs, ensuite nous apprenons nos leçons.
Ils avaient fini par croire que la race des meuniers **était** éteinte.

§ **105. Sans + infinitive** = 'without' + gerund.

Entrez sans frapper. Ne partez pas sans m'avoir **donné** une réponse.

§ **106. Pour + infinitive :**

1. = '(in order) to' (cp. § 97, note).

Il faut manger **pour vivre** et non pas vivre **pour manger.**

2. = 'to' (expressing a result, as in 1) after **trop, assez + adjective, suffire, suffisant, insuffisant.**

Vous êtes **assez grand pour** savoir cela.
Tu es **trop petit pour** venir avec nous.

(But, of course : Vous êtes trop bon **de** m'aider ainsi, *It is too good of you to help me thus*).

Ce manteau **suffira pour** me protéger contre le froid.
Je n'ai pas des connaissances **suffisantes pour** étudier cette question.

3. = 'to' (= 'considering that').

Vous ne savez pas beaucoup de français **pour l'avoir étudié** si longtemps.

4. = 'for' (= 'because of') + gerund. The infinitive is always in the perfect.

Il est en retenue **pour avoir ri** en classe.
He is in detention for laughing during the class.

Note.—The infinitive is also governed by **entre, jusqu'à.**

Entre lui **donner** et lui prêter il n'y avait guère de différence.
Il est allé **jusqu'à** m'adresser des injures.

D. The Dependent Infinitive governed by de

§ **107.** **Non-prepositional de** (§ 281) is the most usual link between verb, noun, or adjective and a dependent infinitive. The cases are too numerous to be committed to memory ; given a thorough knowledge of the construction of the dependent infinitive without a preposition, and with the prepositions **à, par, pour,** etc. (§§ 92–106), it may be assumed that in cases which have not come under observation the link is **de.**

Thus, **de** may link up the infinitive with

(*a*) Verbs.

Je vous **dis de** vous taire.
Nous avons **résolu de** repartir demain.
Je vous **prie de** rester encore quelques jours.
Je vous **conseille de** faire ce devoir sans dictionnaire
Ne **craignez** pas **de** nous déranger.
Vous m'aviez **promis de** venir.

(*b*) Verb phrases.

J'ai **besoin de** marcher, **de** courir.
J'ai **honte d**'arriver si tard.
Il **fait semblant de** dormir.
Vous **courez risque de** vous tuer.

(*c*) Nouns.

Aurons-nous le **plaisir de** vous voir ? (§ 99.4, note.)
Je n'ai pas les **moyens de** vivre sans rien faire.
Il est **temps de** songer à notre train.

(*d*) Adjectives.

Je suis **certain de** réussir.
Nous sommes **heureux d'**apprendre cette nouvelle.
Êtes-vous **capable de** résister aux fatigues du voyage ?
Vous êtes bien **bon de** m'inviter. *It is very kind of you to invite me.*

Note.—With the last example compare **Ce fruit n'est pas bon à manger,** . . . *is not fit to eat* (§ 101.1). Distinguish between the infinitive dependent on **bon** (='good,' 'fit'), as in **Un fruit bon à manger,** and the infinitive linked up by **de,** not to **bon,** but to the statement **Vous êtes bien bon.**

§ **108. De** is still felt as prepositional in

Je **viens de** lui écrire (§ 86.2).

§ **109.** The infinitive is linked to the subject by **de** in the construction known as the **historical infinitive** (always affective). The subject is always stressed.

On emmena le soldat et le paysan. Et **eux de s'indigner !**
Un médecin consultait ses fiches (*dockets*) et disait : " Tu as une plaie au bras droit ? " Et **l'homme de répondre** avec modestie : " Oh ! c'est pas une plaie, c'est seulement un trou."

§ **110.** The infinitive is also linked up by **de** when it is a logical subject following the predicate (§ 71.3) ; compare :

{**Perdre la vue** est un grand malheur.
{C'est un grand malheur (que) **de perdre la vue.**

{**Faire mieux** serait impossible.
{Il serait impossible **de faire mieux.**

{**Gambader** dans la bruyère, quel plaisir !
{Quel plaisir **de gambader** dans la bruyère !

Traduire ce passage, c'est difficile.
Il est difficile (facile) **de traduire** ce passage.

And when it forms the second term in a comparison (see § 156, note 1).

Note.—Compare also

Ce passage est **facile (difficile) à traduire.**

Distinguish between an infinitive dependent on **facile, difficile,** and governed by **à** (§ 101.1), and the infinitive which is a logical subject, and linked up to the predicate by **de.**

§ **111.** The infinitive is also governed by a number of prepositional phrases ending with **de,** such as **au lieu de, avant de, faute de, près de, de peur de.** *Cf.* § 405.

§ **112.** 1. Many verbs take different constructions according to the meaning. Compare the following groups :

{J'aime **à** me promener dans les bois.
{J'aime mieux me taire.

{Nous avons décidé **de** rester ici.
{Ce fut à grand'peine qu'on le décida **à** entrer.

{Je demande **à** parler.
{Nous demandons au professeur **de** nous raconter une histoire.

{Il dit le savoir d'une source sûre.
{Je lui ai dit **de** venir tout de suite.

{Finissez **de** faire tant de bruit !
{Il a fini **par** tout avouer.

{Laissez-moi entrer.
{Je vous laisse **à** penser comment il fut reçu.
{Il ne laissa pas **de** revendiquer ses droits. *He stoutly asserted his rights* (Literally : *He did not omit to . . .*).

Note particularly the pronominal construction of certain verbs:

Je l'ai entendu dire. *I have heard it said.*
Il s'entend à marchander. *He is a good hand at bargaining.*

Nous décidâmes **de** rester où nous étions. *Decided to ...*
Nous nous décidâmes **à** rester où nous étions. *Decided, reluctantly, to ...*

J'essaye **d'**apprendre le russe.
Je m'essaye **à** écrire dans les journaux. *I am trying my hand at ...*

Vous risquez **de** vous tuer.
Je ne me risquai pas **à** répondre. *Did not venture to ...*

Sometimes with little or no difference in meaning, other than the 'ethic' value which goes with the use of the reflexive pronoun.

J'ai offert **de** l'accompagner.
Je me suis offert **à** l'accompagner.

Je refuse **de** croire cela.
Je me refuse **à** croire cela.

Note also the construction of certain impersonal verbs.

Quelques mots aimables suffirent **à** (or **pour**) lui rendre sa bonne humeur.
Il suffira **d'**emporter des provisions pour trois jours.

Ils tardent **à** rentrer.
Il me tarde **de** le revoir.

In these examples the dependent infinitive after the impersonal verb is the logical subject (§ 71.3).

2. If a verb has two objects, one being an infinitive clause and the other a person, (*a*) the latter is most frequently in the dative.

permettre, conseiller,
demander, défendre,
dire, crier,
écrire, télégraphier, } à qqn de faire qqch.

(*b*) But a few verbs have the accusative of the person.

prier, conjurer,
avertir, menacer,
empêcher, } qqn de faire qqch.

(*a*) Je demanderai à mon **frère** de m'aider.
Je conseillai à ma **famille** de rester à Paris.
Pourquoi ne **lui** avez-vous pas dit de venir!
J'ai écrit à ma **famille** de m'envoyer de l'argent.

(*b*) Priez-**le** de venir.
Empêchez-**le** de sortir.
Il avertit **ses amis** de se dépêcher.
Je conjurai **le capitaine** de quitter le navire.

PARTICIPLES AND GERUND

§ 113. The verbal form in **-ant** has three main functions.

1. It indicates a **passing** or **temporary** activity or state, and is then a true **present participle**, with verbal functions; *i.e.* it may have an object, may be constructed with a negation, may be qualified by adverbs (which must follow it) and by adverb phrases of time and place.

It is related to the noun or pronoun to which it stands in closest proximity, but **remains invariable** (§ 438).

Ma serviette était surmontée d'une carte **portant** mon nom.
Ne **sachant** que faire, nous sommes entrés dans un café.
Bien que **pouvant** à peine mettre une jambe devant l'autre, c'était moi maintenant qui traînais Vitalis.
Ne **s'étant** pas encore **fait** d'amis, il vivait solitaire.
De rares promeneurs **osant** braver l'humidité parcourent les allées **où** les gouttes **tombant** des arbres semblent continuer l'averse.
On les trouva **vivant** encore. ... *still living.*

2. It indicates an **enduring, habitual** quality or characteristic of a noun, has a purely **adjectival** function, and is treated in every respect as an adjective; *i.e.* it agrees with its head noun, which it may either precede or follow; it is preceded by its adverb. It may then be called a **verbal adjective.**

Le café a des vertus **excitantes** et **stimulantes.**
Ce sont de **charmants** voisins.
Nous arrivâmes **à** la nuit **tombante.**
On les trouva encore **vivants.** ... *still alive.*

Notes.—(*a*) The forms in **-ant** are also used as nouns: **un négociant, un commerçant, un étudiant, un mendiant, un passant, un penchant;**

And a few have become prepositions (§ 300): **durant, pendant,** with derived conjunctions: **pendant que** (§ 263).

(*b*) The verbal adjective and verbal noun have in a number of cases retained an older form or an older spelling of the participle. Thus:

	Participle	*Verbal Adjective*
savoir	sachant	**savant**
pouvoir	pouvant	**puissant**
valoir	valant	**vaillant**
convaincre	convainquant	**convaincant**
fatiguer	fatiguant	**fatigant**
vaquer	vaquant	**vacant**
		Verbal Noun
aimer	aimant	**amant**
fabriquer	fabriquant	**fabricant**

On the other hand, such words as **différent**, **excellent**, **négligent**, **précédent**, are not participial forms of the French verbs **différer**, **exceller**, etc., but are borrowed directly from Latin.

(c) Verbal adjectives, like the true present participle, have as a rule an active meaning, *e.g.* des voisins **obligeants** = des voisins **qui nous obligent volontiers**; but there are a few phrases in which the adjective has passive force. Thus:

de l'argent **comptant** (*ready cash*) = de l'argent **qui est compté** sur-le-champ.

Thus also:

une couleur **voyante**, *a loud colour*; une soirée **dansante**;
une place **payante**; faire quelque chose séance **tenante**.

3. Governed by **en**, the form in -ant is called **gerund**, and forms invariable adverb phrases or clauses of time, manner, means, etc., qualifying a verb (§ 410).

Il répondit **en riant**.
Elle marchait lentement **en regardant** tout le monde.
Tout le monde sortit de la maison **en courant**. . . . *ran out.*
Vous vous ferez respecter **en vous faisant obéir**. *You will win respect by compelling obedience.*

Notes.—(1) The gerund is not used to express the *reason* for an action; this is a function of the present participle, as in the sentence in 1 above:

Ne **sachant** que faire, nous sommes entrés dans un café.

(2) The adverb **tout** may qualify the gerund, either (*a*) to insist on the **simultaneity** of two actions, or (*b*) to express concession.

(*a*) Elle me prenait une main qu'elle caressait, **tout en regardant** au dehors.
Tout en la **suivant**, je l'examinais curieusement.
Bouilleron riait sans lever les yeux, **tout en polissant** son ceinturon.

(*b*) **Tout en désirant** la paix, l'Angleterre dut déclarer la guerre. *Although desirous of peace, England was compelled to declare war.*
Tout en reconnaissant votre bonne volonté, je ne puis m'empêcher de vous faire certaines observations.

§ **114.** The gerund should refer to the subject of the sentence, while the present participle is related to subject, object, or complement, whichever stands nearest to it.

Je la rencontrai **en revenant** du marché. *I met her as I came back . . .*
Je **la** rencontrai **revenant** du marché. *I met her coming back* (i.e. *as she came back*) . . .

See, however, § 411.

§ **115. Synopsis of English forms in -ing.**

1. **Adjective.**

An obliging little girl.	Une petite fille **obligeante.**
Smiling faces.	Des visages **souriants.**
A raging storm.	Une tempête **furieuse.**
The leaning tower of Pisa.	La tour penchée de Pise (§ **116,** note *c*).

2. **Present Participle.**

(*a*) Forming continuous tenses.

I am working. **Je travaille.** Je suis **en train de travailler.**

(*b*) Forming adjectival clauses. Various constructions.

I found him reading the paper. Je le trouvai **lisant** le journal. Je le trouvai **en train de lire** le journal.

I spent an hour waiting for him. Je passai une heure **à l'attendre.**

And with verbs of 'seeing and hearing.'

I could see him running toward them. Je le voyais **courir** vers eux. Je le voyais **qui courait** vers eux.

Je le voyais **courant** vers eux (comparatively rare construction).

I hear them laughing. Je les entends **rire.**

(*c*) Forming adverbial clauses.

Not knowing what to do, I decided to wait. Ne **sachant** que faire, je résolus d'attendre.

And in absolute constructions.

The hotel being far from the beach, the visitors were few. L'hôtel **se trouvant** éloigné de la plage, les visiteurs étaient peu nombreux.

The troops entered the town with drums beating. Les troupes entrèrent dans la ville tambour **battant.**

3. **Gerund.** To the many uses of the gerund in English correspond a variety of constructions in French. The following examples are typical, but by no means exhaustive:

(*a*) As subject or predicative complement, it is usually rendered by the **infinitive.**

Seeing is believing. **Voir,** c'est **croire.**

(*b*) As object to a verb, it is rendered by the **infinitive** :

Do you like skating, cycling? Aimez-vous **à patiner, à faire de la bicyclette?**

The whole house needs cleaning. La maison entière a besoin **d'être nettoyée.**

or by a noun :

He is fond of hunting, fishing, skating. Il aime **la chasse, la pêche, le patinage.**

Cease firing. **Cessez le feu.**

(*c*) Forming an adverbial clause, it is frequently rendered by the gerund.

On learning the news I hurried home. En apprenant cette nouvelle je me hâtai de rentrer.

While listening to him, I thought of his father. En l'écoutant je pensais à son père.

By learning to swim you will add to your personal worth. En apprenant à nager vous ajouterez à votre valeur personnelle.

You will oblige me by all leaving the room. Vous m'obligerez en sortant tous.

(*d*) But after prepositions other than en = 'while,' 'in,' 'by,' 'on,' the infinitive will be used.

Thanks for reminding me. Je vous remercie de m'y avoir fait songer.

I was spared the trouble of writing. On m'épargna la peine d'écrire.

He is making progress without knowing it. Il fait des progrès sans le savoir.

After hesitating a long time he consented. Après avoir longtemps hésité, il y consentit.

He was punished for telling the truth. Il fut puni pour avoir dit la vérité.

I reproached him for deceiving me. Je lui reprochai de m'avoir trompé.

We always end by liking those who are sincere. Nous finissons toujours par aimer ceux qui sont sincères.

Women should pride themselves on being good housekeepers. Les femmes doivent se piquer d'être de bonnes ménagères.

Have you done discussing the question? Avez-vous fini de discuter cette question ?

He burst out laughing. Il éclata de rire.

(*e*) If the head verb and the gerund have different subjects, the gerund is usually rendered by a clause in a finite mood.

His indisposition is due to his eating too much. Son malaise vient de ce qu'il mange trop.

He had no idea of his end being so near. Il ne soupçonnait pas que sa fin fût si proche.

He comes home without anyone knowing it. Il rentre sans qu'on le sache.

I have my doubts as to this being true. Je doute que cela soit vrai.

(*f*) Adjectival gerund in compound nouns.

A sewing-machine.	Une machine à coudre.
A dining-room.	Une salle à manger.
A dancing-room.	Une salle de danse.
A riding lesson.	Une leçon d'équitation.

§ **116. The Past Participle** is used

1. With the auxiliaries **avoir** and **être** to form the compound tenses of the verb.

(*a*) With active force.

Il m'a donné un livre. Il **s'est coupé.** Il est **venu** hier.

(*b*) With passive force.

Il **est respecté** de tous.

2. As a simple adjective, attributive or predicative.

On lut le testament devant la famille **assemblée.**
La porte est **fermée.** Vous semblez **fatigué.**

Notes.—(*a*) Adjectival past participles are usually passive in meaning, but a few have active force, *e.g.* **appliqué, décidé, dissimulé, entendu, osé, serré.**

Voilà un garçon **appliqué** (=qui s'applique à son travail).
Un homme **dissimulé** (=qui dissimule sa pensée).
Un caractère **osé** (=qui ose, audacieux).
Une femme **serrée** (=**qui serre** son argent, avare).

(*b*) Past participles are also used as nouns, *e.g.* **un reçu, une vue**; and as prepositions: **attendu, excepté, vu, y compris, passé, supposé** (§ 440); with derived conjunctions: **attendu que, vu que, supposé que** (§ 311.2).

Vous lui ferez signer **un reçu** pour le montant de la somme.
Je ne vous punis pas pour cette fois, **attendu** votre bonne conduite habituelle.
Vous serez puni, **attendu que** c'est la troisième fois que vous me désobéissez.
Excepté la Prusse, aucun pays n'a jamais prétendu que la force prime le droit.

(*c*) A number of French verbs, chiefly pronominal verbs expressing attitudes of the body, are used in French in the past participle denoting the state, where English has the present participle denoting the action.

Thus: **s'agenouiller, s'appuyer, s'asseoir, se coucher, se pencher.**

Nous restâmes un moment **agenouillés.** *Kneeling.*
Appuyé contre un mur, il se chauffait au soleil. *Leaning.*
Je l'ai trouvé **assis** à table. *Seated* or *sitting.*
Couché sur un canapé, il lisait le journal. *Lying, reclining.*
Penché hors de la fenêtre, il me regardait. *Leaning.*

Thus also: **se composer de, poser, (sus)pendre.**

Un dîner **composé** de trois plats. *Consisting in.*
Il vit deux nids **posés** côte à côte. *Lying.*
Un jambon **suspendu** au plafond. *Hanging from.*

GOVERNMENT OF VERBS

§ **117.** The guiding principles are the same as in English. Verbs are on the one hand **predicative** (directly or indirectly) or **non-predicative**, on the other **transitive** (directly or indirectly) or **intransitive.**

§ **118.** Are **predicative.**

1. Such intransitive verbs as (*a*) **être, sembler, devenir, rester, mourir, passer** ; (*b*) **passer pour, mourir (se battre,** etc.) **en.**

(*a*) Il est mon ami. Il mourut pauvre. Vous semblez fatigué. Il devient ridicule.
Il est passé sergent. *He has been promoted to be a sergeant.*
(*b*) Il passe pour riche. *He is said to be wealthy.*
Il mourut en soldat. Il se battit en héros.

To which may be assimilated certain verb phrases and pronominal verbs such as **avoir l'air** (=sembler), **se faire** (=devenir):

Il a l'air malade. Nous nous faisons vieux.

And impersonally :

Il se fait tard. *It is getting late.*

2. Transitive verbs such as (*a*) **appeler, nommer, élire, déclarer, rendre, faire, croire** ; (*b*) **prendre pour, choisir pour, regarder comme, traiter de.**

(*a*) On m'appelle l'homme à tout faire. . . . *Jack of all trades.*
On l'a nommé (élu, fait) président.
Les médecins le déclarèrent apte au service. . . .*fit for military service.*
Cette nouvelle le rendit malheureux (cp. § 92.4, note).
On me croit savant . . . j'ai une réputation, . . . mais grâce à qui ?
(*b*) Ils prirent (choisirent) ce chef pour roi.
Il m'a traité de lâche. *He called me a coward.*
On le regardait comme fou. *We looked on him as (took him for) a madman.*

With the verbs of group (*a*) the predicative accusative becomes a nominative in the passive voice.

Il a été élu (fait) président.

Note.—The predicative complement, when indicating one out of a group, is often omitted before the partitive noun.

Soyez de mes amis (=un des mes amis. Cp. § 177).
Les gens d'Auray le tenaient en haute estime; il était du conseil municipal.

§ 119. Transitive verbs are

(*a*) Directly transitive, with or without a remoter object of the person (a dative pronoun or a dative equivalent with the preposition **à**):

J'aime **Pierre.** J'appelle **Paul.** Je **l'**appelle.
Je donne un livre **à Pierre.** Je **lui** donne un livre.

(*b*) Indirectly transitive, the object being governed by the prepositions **à** or **de.**

J'obéis **à mes parents.** Je **leur** obéis. Je pense **à vous** (§ 237.4).
Je me repens **de ma faute.** Il se moque **de nous.**

§ 120. In French as in English many verbs are used with both transitive and intransitive function.

La cloche sonne.	Je sonne la cloche.
L'heure sonne.	Je sonne du cor.
J'attends.	J'attends un ami.
Vous rêvez.	J'ai rêvé de naufrage.

But it has been seen (§ 70.3, note *a*) that in numerous cases the verb becomes pronominal in French when it is used intransitively in English. Further examples:

La terre **se meut.** *The earth moves.*
La porte **s'ouvre.** *The door opens.*
Le feu **s'allume.** *The fire kindles.*
La nouvelle **se répand.** *The news is spreading.*

§ 121. Many verbs directly transitive in English are indirectly transitive in French, and *vice-versa.* Thus:

(*a*)	**médire de,** *to slander.*	**obéir à,** *to obey.*
	jouir de, *to enjoy.*	**résister à,** *to resist.*
	convenir de, *to admit.*	**répondre à,** *to answer.*
	manquer de, *to lack.*	**ressembler à,** *to resemble.*
	changer de, *to change.*	**succéder à,** *to succeed.*
(*b*)	**attendre,** *to wait for.*	**chercher,** *to look for.*
	regarder, *to look at.*	**écouter,** *to listen to.*

(*a*) Elle médit **de** ses voisins. Nous jouissons **de** notre liberté.
Je conviens **de** ma faute. Nous manquions **de** tout.
Il changea **de** visage. *His face changed.*
(But: Il a changé ses habitudes. *He has changed his habits.*)

Obéissez **à** vos maîtres. Il faut résister **à** la tentation.
Répondez **à** sa question, **à** sa lettre; répondez-**lui.**
Vous ressemblez **à** votre frère. Il succéda **à** son père.

(*b*) J'attends une lettre. Regardez le tableau. Je cherche mes lunettes. Écoutez ce que je vous dis.

§ **122.** Again, verbs such as the following, which according to the general rule take a direct object, and a remoter object of the person (§ 220), show a variety of constructions in English.

Présenter qqch. à qqn	Une jeune fille lui présenta un bouquet. *A maiden presented her with a bouquet.*
Inspirer qqch. à qqn	Il inspire de la crainte à tous. *He inspires all with awe.*
Demander qqch. à qqn	Il me demanda du tabac. *He asked me for some tobacco.*
Pardonner qqch. à qqn	Je lui pardonne sa grossièreté. *I forgive his rudeness.*
Payer qqch. à qqn	Je lui paye son travail. *I pay him for his work.*
Reprocher qqch. à qqn	Je lui reprochai sa paresse. *I reproached him for his laziness.*
Enseigner qqch. à qqn	J'enseigne le français à mes enfants. *I teach my children French.*

§ **123.** Note also the following:

1. **Prendre, voler, arracher,** acheter, *To take, steal, tear, buy,* **Emprunter,** extorquer, cacher, *To borrow, extort, hide,* } qqch. à qqn. *something from some one.*

Prenez-lui ce canif, il va se blesser. *Take that knife from him.*
On lui a volé son porte-monnaie. *His purse has been stolen from him.*
On ne put arracher à l'accusé aucun aveu. *They were unable to extract any confession from the prisoner.*
J'emprunterai un parapluie à un ami. *I shall borrow an umbrella from a friend.*
J'achetai à la petite toute sa marchandise. *I bought from the child all her wares.*
On lui extorqua une forte rançon. *They extorted a heavy ransom from him.*
On cacha la vérité aux parents. *The truth was concealed from the parents.*

2. **Se nourrir, vivre, déjeuner, dîner, souper de** qqch. *To feed, live, lunch, dine, sup on something.*

Nous nous nourrissons de fruits et de légumes. *We feed on fruit and vegetables.*
De quoi vivez-vous ? *What do you live on ?*
Ce sont des artichauts dont vous déjeunez là ?
On pêcha du poisson, dont on dîna. *We caught some fish, which we dined on,* or *off which we dined.*
En cercle autour du feu, nous soupions d'un morceau de pain arrosé de bouillon.

3. **Dépendre de**, **rire de**, approcher **de**, penser **à**.
To depend on, to laugh at, to draw near to, to think of.

Cela dépend **de** vous, **des** circonstances.
On rit **de** sa réponse. Pensez **à** moi.
Nous approchons de Paris. Approchez votre chaise **du feu**.

4. With certain verbs, French asks the question *where ?* when English asks the question *where from ?*

Où avez-vous pris cela ? *Where did you get that from ?*
Une cotisation de quelques sous par semaine, le produit d'une loterie annuelle, . . . composent un fonds modeste **où** l'on prend tous les jours sans jamais l'épuiser.

And in the answer French uses the prepositions **dans**, **à**, **sur**, **entre**, when English uses the prepositions *from, out of.*

Thus with the verbs **prendre**, **choisir**, **puiser**, **boire**, **manger**.

Prenez un verre dans l'armoire. *Out of the cupboard.*
Je pris un livre sur la table. *From the table.*
Je prends un seul fait **entre** mille. *Out of a thousand.*
Ces exemples ont été choisis **dans** un journal français.
A trois sous les oranges, mesdames ! Choisissez **dans** le tas ! *Choose out of the lot !*
A quelle source avez-vous puisé ces renseignements ?
Il boit **dans** mon verre !
Les pigeons viennent nous manger dans la main (§ 178.3).
Ils mangeaient tous les trois **au** même plat, et buvaient **à** la même bouteille.

But with verbs which in themselves denote *taking from, extraction,* the adverbial extension is introduced by **de**. Thus with **tirer**, **arracher**.

Je tire mon mouchoir **de** ma poche.
Je lui arrachai le revolver **des** mains.

§ **124.** Pronominal verbs of § 70.3 are indirectly transitive, since the pronoun object stands grammatically as an accusative. Thus :

Se charger d'une tâche.	*To undertake a task.*
Se repentir de sa dureté.	*To repent one's harshness.*
S'acquitter d'une dette.	*To discharge a debt.*
S'apercevoir de son erreur.	*To notice one's mistake.*
S'attendre à un événement.	*To expect an event.*
S'approcher d'un endroit.	*To approach a place.*
Se démettre de ses fonctions.	*To resign one's office.*
Se servir de quelque chose.	*To use something.*
Se tromper de chemin.	*To mistake the way.*
Se fier à quelqu'un.	*To trust some one.*
Se défier de quelqu'un.	*To distrust some one.*
Se souvenir de quelqu'un.	*To remember some one.*
But : se rappeler quelqu'un.	With this verb **se** is a dative.

§ 125. Many verbs have different constructions according to the meaning.

Thus :

User. J'use mes souliers à trotter par la ville.
J'userai de la permission. *I shall avail myself of the permission.*
Vous en usez mal avec moi. *You are dealing badly with me.*

Servir. Il sert bien son maître.
Son valet **lui** sert **de** secrétaire.
Je **me** sers **de** ce livre.
A quoi sert tout cela ?

Jouer. Il nous a joués. *He has tricked us.*
Il joue Hamlet. *He acts the part of Hamlet.*
Il joue **du** piano, **du** violon, **du** tambour, etc.
Il joue **aux** cartes, **au** billard, **au** football, etc.

Penser. Je pense **à** mes amis, **à** mes affaires.
Que pensez-vous **de** cette affaire ?

Rêver. Il rêve **à** son avenir.
Il a rêvé **de** naufrage.

Manquer. Il a manqué son train, son ami. *He missed his train, his friend.*
Il manque **de** pain. *He lacks bread.*
Il a manqué **à** son devoir. *He has failed in his duty.*
Vous lui avez manqué **de** respect. *You were discourteous to him.*
Ses amis **lui** manquent. *He misses (is unhappy without) his friends.*
Il **lui** manque cinq francs. *He is five shillings short.*

Note.—The verbs of which examples are given in the last few paragraphs are numerous ; the student should note and classify further instances in the course of his reading.

§ 126. Intransitive verbs, as in English, occasionally take as a 'cognate accusative' some word closely associated in its meaning with that of the verb. Thus are formed a number of phrases belonging to everyday speech, such as :

monter l'escalier, descendre un fleuve, courir les rues, la campagne, jouer gros jeu (*high stakes*), **parler une langue, grelotter la fièvre** ;

while other groupings belong entirely to literary style :

dormir son dernier sommeil, combattre le bon combat ;

and poets have obtained striking effects from this construction ; thus Lamartine :

N'ai-je pas, comme toi, sué mon agonie ?

Note.—The cognate accusative must not be confused with the construction

marcher deux heures, marcher dix kilomètres, vivre cent ans, vivre de nombreuses années, peser deux kilos, etc.,

in which the verb is followed by an adverbial extension (§ 446).

NOUNS AND QUALIFYING ADJECTIVES

Gender of Nouns

§ **127.** The gender of nouns in French must be acquired by careful observation, for names of 'things' are distributed between the masculine and the feminine genders, and it cannot even be stated as an absolute rule that names of males are masculine and names of females feminine.

The gender of many nouns may, however, be inferred from consideration of (1) their meaning; (2) their derivation; (3) their ending.

§ 128. Gender according to Meaning.

1. Are **masculine :** (*a*) Names of males. (*b*) Names of trees; metals; seasons, months and days of the week; points of the compass; decimal weights and measures. (*c*) Names of countries and rivers not ending in mute **e.**

(*a*) **Le père, le chat.**
(*b*) **Le chêne ; le fer ; le printemps ; le nord ; le gramme.**
(*c*) **Le Japon, le Portugal, le Rhin.**

Exceptions.—Some names usually applied to males, and others which apply equally to both sexes, are always feminine.

La sentinelle, la recrue, la vigie, la personne, la dupe, la victime.
La sentinelle tira sur mon père, qui se trouva ainsi **la victime d'une** erreur déplorable.
L'esprit est toujours **la dupe** du cœur.

Note in particular the names of a number of animals :

Une baleine, une autruche, une girafe.
Une baleine **mâle**, une baleine **femelle.**

2. Are **feminine :** (*a*) Names of females. (*b*) Most abstract nouns. (*c*) Names of countries and rivers ending in mute **e.**

(*a*) **La mère, la chatte.** (*b*) **La douleur, la foi, la parenté.**
(*c*) **La France, la Seine, la Loire.**

Exceptions.—To (*a*) Some names applicable to both sexes are always masculine, thus : **témoin, ange.**

Elle a été **le seul témoin** de l'accident. Sa femme est **un ange.**

Thus also some nouns which more usually refer to males : **écrivain, auteur, médecin.**

Cette femme est **un** de nos meilleurs **écrivains.**

Thus also the names of a certain number of animals.

Un éléphant, un hippopotame, un vautour.
Un éléphant **mâle**, un éléphant **femelle.**

To (*b*) A few abstract nouns such as **le vice, l'état,** and those in which the gender is determined by the suffix, *e.g.* **le courage, l'accablement.**

To (*c*) **Le Mexique, le Hanovre,** etc.; **le Rhône, le Danube, le Tibre,** etc.

§ 129. Gender by Derivation.

1. Latin **masculine** and **neuter** > French **masculine**.
Lat. murum > **le mur** ; Lat. corpus > **le corps.**

Latin feminine > French **feminine.**
Lat. luna > **la lune** ; Lat. caritatem > **la cherté.**

Exceptions, however, are numerous, so that Latin etymology is an unsafe guide. Thus :

(*a*) Trees, feminine in Latin, are masculine in French: **un arbre, un aune.**
(*b*) Abstract nouns in -orem, masculine in Latin, > feminine in French, with ending **-eur**; colorem > **la couleur.**
(*c*) In many Latin nouns a neuter plural was mistaken for a feminine singular: folia > **la feuille**; vela > **la voile**, *sail.*
(But velum > **le voile**, *veil.*)
(*d*) Miscellaneous (fairly numerous):

dentem > **la dent**;	mare > **la mer**;
artem > **un art**;	aestatem > **un été**;
rem > **un rien**;	frontem > **le front.**

2. Words and expressions not originally nouns, when used as such, are masculine.

un oui, un non ; le déjeuner, le devoir ; le savoir-faire, le pourboire, le tête-à-tête.

3. Verbal roots are for the most part feminine if ending in mute **e**, otherwise masculine.

la marche, la chasse, la visite.
le refus, le soutien, un emploi, le choix, un espoir.

4. Adjectives and participles used as nouns retain the gender shown by their ending.

le plat, le traité, le penchant.
la nouvelle, une allée, la sortie.

Compare **le droit** (*legal right*), **la droite** (*right hand*);
le fait, la défaite ; le couvert, la découverte.

5. Compounds of two nouns one of which is an adjective equivalent have the gender of the head-noun.

le chou-fleur, le chef-d'œuvre.

Compounds in which the first element is verbal are masculine.
le tire-bottes, le parapluie (= pare à pluie).

§ 130. Gender by Endings.

	Masculine		*Feminine*	
1.	**-eur** (*agent*)	le flatteur, un acteur	-euse	la flatteuse
			-trice	une actrice
2.			-eur (*abstract*)	la couleur
3.	**-er, -ier**	le plancher, le papier, le fer	-ère, -ière	une artère, la lumière
4.	**-eau**	le chapeau	-elle	la chapelle
5.	**-t**	le chocolat, le sujet, le mot, le but, le monument	-te, -tte	la date, la compote, la patte, une allumette, la botte, la butte
			-de	la peuplade, une habitude
6.	**-c**	le lac, un accroc	-che	la tache, la niche, la cloche
7.	**-age** (*suffix*)	le village, le courage	-age (*not suffix*)	la rage, une image
8.	**-ail**	le poitrail, le détail	-aille	la trouvaille
9.	**-oir**	le miroir, le mouchoir	-oire	la gloire, une histoire
10.	**-é**	le dé, le péché	-ée	la journée, une épée
			-té (*abstract*)	la bonté, la calamité
			-tié	la moitié, une amitié
11.	**-on**	le clairon, le bâton	-onne	la couronne, la tonne
			-aison	la raison, la déclinaison
			-ison	la guérison, la prison
			-ion	la nation, la ration
12.	**-acle**	le miracle, un obstacle		
13.	**-ège**	le piège, le collège		
14.	**-ème**	le poème, le thème		
15.	**-o**	le zéro, le numéro		
16.	**-ou**	le clou, le genou		
17.			-esse	la paresse, l'ivresse
18.			-ie	la colonie, une infamie
19.			-ine	la colline, la mine
20.			-une	la rancune, la fortune
21.			-ure	la nature, une armure
22.			-ance, -anse	la vengeance, la danse
			-ence, -ense	la prudence, la défense

Exceptions.—2. Un honneur, le labeur.

3. La mer, la cuiller; nouns in -ère borrowed from the Greek, such as le mystère, le caractère.

4. Une eau, la peau, in neither of which is -eau a suffix.

5. La dot, la forêt, la dent, la jument, etc.

6. Le manche (*handle*), le reproche, le caniche.

9. Many learned and technical words in -oire, such as le laboratoire, un observatoire, and a few more: un bel ivoire.

10. Words in -ée borrowed from the Greek are masculine: un musée, un lycée, un apogée. Note also le comté, originally feminine.

11. La boisson, la rançon, etc.; le poison; le pion, etc. (in which -ion is not a suffix).

14. La crème.

18. Un incendie, le génie.

21. Le murmure, le mercure.

22. Le silence.

Plural of Nouns and Adjectives.

§ **131.** 1. General rule : add **s** to the singular.

le petit enfant, les petits enfants.

2. The endings **s, x, z,** remain unchanged.

le vieux bois, le gros nez, la voix ; les vieux bois, les gros nez, les voix.

3. The endings **au, eau, eu,** add **x** (§ 16.5).

mon nouveau neveu, mes nouveaux neveux.

Except **bleu,** *plur.* **bleus.**

4. The ending **ou** adds **s,** as a rule.

Cet Indou est fou, ces Indous sont fous,

but six nouns in very common use add **x** :

bijou(x), caillou(x), chou(x), genou(x), hibou(x), joujou(x).

5. The ending **al** changes to **aux** (§ 16.8).

un rival loyal, des rivaux loyaux ; le cheval, les chevaux.

But a few nouns take **s,** *e.g.* **le bal, les bals** ; and the masculine plural of many adjectives is uncertain, and usually avoided.

6. The ending **ail** takes **s,** as a rule.

le détail, les détails ; le poitrail, les poitrails ;

but a few nouns change **ail** to **aux** :

le travail, les travaux.

7. Notice also : **le ciel, les cieux ; l'œil, les yeux ; l'aïeul, les aïeuls** (*grand-parents*), **les aïeux** (*ancestors*).

Note.—The plural ending **-x** is 'dead,' *i.e.* it is not attached to any new formations in the language :

un landau, des landaus ; un pneu (*pneumatic tyre*), des pneus ; un Zoulou, des Zoulous.

§ **132. Compound nouns** written in one word add **s.**

le pourboire, les pourboires ; le gendarme, les gendarmes ; la grand'mère, les grand'mères.

But the following should be noted

monsieur, madame, mademoiselle ; messieurs, mesdames, mesdemoiselles.

(Abbreviated M., Mme, Mlle ; MM., Mmes, Mlles.)

le bonhomme, le gentilhomme ; les bonshommes, les gentilshommes.

§ **133.** The plural of compound nouns written in two or more words is complicated, often illogical, and uncertain. The guiding principle is that those elements vary which took the sign of the plural before the group came to be looked upon as a compound. Thus :

1. **Noun and adjective,** or noun and **appositive noun :** both vary.

le beau-père	les beaux-pères
le grand-père	les grands-pères
le chou-fleur	les choux-fleurs

2. **Noun and adjective equivalent :** the noun alone varies.

un ver à soie	des vers à soie
un aide-de-camp	des aides-de-camp
un arc-en-ciel	des arcs-en-ciel
un timbre-poste	des timbres-poste (=timbres de poste)
un avant-poste	des avant-postes ('avant' is an adverb with adjectival function)

3. **Noun governed by a preposition :** the compound should be invariable.

un après-midi	des après-midi
un hors-d'œuvre	des hors-d'œuvre

But : un sous-sol, des sous-sols ; and also des après-midis.

4. **Verb** and **noun-object :** the compound is usually invariable.

un coupe-gorge	des coupe-gorge

But most dictionaries give

un essuie-main	des essuie-mains
un tire-botte	des tire-bottes

instead of the more logical

un essuie-mains	des essuie-mains

Une quantité innombrable d'objets ont été convertis en porte-réclames : les sous-main, les coupe-papier, les canifs, les porte-allumettes.

5. **No noun :** the compound is invariable.

un passe-partout	des passe-partout

Note.—For the plural and feminine of compound adjectives, see § 417.

§ 134. Plural of Proper Nouns.

1. Family names are invariable.
   J'ai dîné chez les **Dupont.**

2. With Christian names usage varies.
   les deux **Henri** *or* les deux **Henris.**

3. With dynastic names usage varies.
   les **Stuarts,** les **Bourbons.** les **Hohenzollern,** les **Romanoff.**

§ 135. 1. Some nouns are used in the plural only, (1) because they come from Latin plurals, or (2) on account of their collective meaning.

archives, f. *archives*	**pincettes**, f. *tongs*
armoiries, f. *coat of arms*	**ténèbres**, f. *darkness*
environs, m. *surroundings*	**vivres**, m. *provisions*
dépens, m. *costs*	**entrailles**, f. *entrails*
frais, m. *expenses*	**fiançailles**, f. *betrothal*
mœurs, f. *manners*	**funérailles**, f. *funeral*
obsèques, f. *obsequies*	**tenailles**, f. *pincers*

2. A number of nouns have a special meaning attached to the plural.

le ciseau, *chisel*	**les ciseaux**, *chisels, scissors*
la lunette, *field-glass*	**les lunettes**, *field-glasses, spectacles*
la défense, *defence*	**les défenses**, *defences, tusks*
la vacance, *vacancy*	**les vacances**, *vacancies, holidays*
le gage, *pledge*	**les gages**, *pledges, wages*
l'affaire, *affair*	**les affaires**, *affairs, business*

§ 136. Only nouns, adjectives, and pronouns, and words which have taken on a *permanent* noun or adjective function, can have the sign of the plural. Thus, no **s** in

Il faut peser les **pour** et les **contre** avant de prendre une décision.

J'aime ce parler un peu rude, avec ses **u** gutturaux.

Feminine of Nouns.

§ 137. Most nouns denoting males have corresponding feminine forms. The feminine may be

1. Formed by the addition of mute **e**: **un ami, une amie.**
2. Formed with a special suffix: **un acteur, une actrice.**
3. Expressed by an entirely different word: **le coq, la poule.**
4. Expressed by the same word as the masculine: **un(e) élève.** The number of such nouns is small.
5. Expressed by the words **femelle** (of animals only), **femme** (§ 128).

§ 138. The addition of mute **e** frequently involves a further alteration of the masculine. The following are typical instances:

1. **Berger, bergère; ouvrier, ouvrière** (§ 16.11.*a*).
2. Final **t** and **n** are doubled: **chat, chatte; chien, chienne; lion, lionne; Jean, Jeanne; paysan, paysanne.**
3. Final **p** and **f**>**v**, **x**>**s**: **loup, louve; veuf, veuve; époux, épouse.**
4. The ending **-eur**>**-euse**, and **-eau**>**-elle**: **baigneur, baigneuse; chameau, chamelle.**

§ **139.** The commonest feminine suffixes are

-esse: **nègre, négresse; chasseur, Diane chasseresse; abbé, abbesse; duc, duchesse; dieu, déesse.**

-trice: **lecteur, lectrice; directeur, directrice; tuteur, tutrice; bienfaiteur, bienfaitrice.**

Note.—Nouns in **-eur** have the feminine in **-euse** if they are formed from the present stem of a French verb; thus **liseur, liseuse** is formed from **lire, nous lisons,** while **lecteur, lectrice** is a borrowing from Latin.

But nevertheless: **inspecteur, inspectrice; persécuteur, persécutrice.**

Note also: **empereur, impératrice; ambassadeur, ambassadrice.**

§ **140.** A few words alter or lose the suffix in the feminine.

serviteur, servante; canard, cane; compagnon, compagne.

Gouverneur, gouvernante, are generally coupled, but are to-day so different in meaning that the one can hardly be considered as the feminine of the other. (**Gouverneur**: *governor* [of a province, etc.]; **gouvernante**: *housekeeper*.)

Feminine of Adjectives.

§ **141.** Adjectives ending in **-e** in the masculine have the same form in the feminine.

un jeune homme **aimable** — une jeune fille **aimable**

§ **142.** All other adjectives add **-e** in the feminine.

un petit garçon **appliqué** — une petite fille **appliquée**

Note **long, longue** (§ 16.2); also **aigu, aiguë,** and thus all adjectives ending in **-gu** (§ 12).

§ **143.** The addition of **-e** frequently involves a further alteration of the masculine form.

1. The ending **-er** > **-ère** (§ 16.11.*a*).

léger, légère — **premier, première** — **cher, chère**

Thus also **-et** > **-ète** in learned borrowings from the Latin.

(in)**complet, complète** — (in)**discret, discrète**
secret, secrète — **inquiet, inquiète**

2. The consonant is doubled in the endings **-as, -eil, -el, -en, -et, -on.**

bas, basse — **pareil, pareille** — **mortel, mortelle**
ancien, ancienne — **muet, muette** — **bon, bonne**

Also in the following:

nul, nulle	**sot, sotte**
épais, épaisse	**gros, grosse**

3. Final **-f** > **-ve** (§ 16.6).

bref, brève	**actif, active**	**neuf, neuve**

4. The endings **-eur** and **-eux** > **-euse.**

menteur, menteuse	**courageux, courageuse**

But **un** poteau **indicateur,** une plaque **indicatrice** (cp. § 139, note).

Adjectives in **-eur** derived from a Latin **comparative** have feminine in **-eure.**

meilleur, meilleure	**intérieur, intérieure**

5. Final **-c** > either **-que** (§ 16.3) or **-che.**

public, publique	**turc, turque**	**grec, grecque**
blanc, blanche	**franc, franche**	**sec, sèche**

6. The following show 'irregularities' which are explained by their etymology; the feminine shows the true stem.

doux, douce	**frais, fraîche**	**malin, maligne**
jaloux, jalouse	**faux, fausse**	**bénin, bénigne**
roux, rousse	**favori, favorite**	**gentil, gentille**

§ **144.** The adjectives

bel, belle	**nouvel, nouvelle**	**vieil, vieille**
mol, molle	**fol, folle**	

which form their feminine as explained in § 143.2, have altered their masculine forms to

beau	**nouveau**	**vieux**	**mou**	**fou**

according to § 16.8.

The latter masculine forms are now used in all positions except when the adjective precedes a noun beginning with a vowel sound, and occasionally when two adjectives are joined by **et.**

un **beau** jardin	de **beaux** jardins
un **bel** arbre	de **beaux** arbres
une **belle** allée	de **belles** allées
un **nouvel** élève	de **nouveaux élèves**
un **vieil** ami	de **vieux** amis
un **vieil** habit	de **vieux** habits
Que cet arbre est **beau**!	Je me fais **vieux**

Tout cela est **bel et bon,** mais cela ne vous excuse pas. *That's all very fine, but* . . .

Nous venons d'admirer un **nouvel et éclatant** exemple de son **talent.**

§ **145**. Adjectives which in Latin had one form only for the masculine and the feminine, presented only one form in early French. Thus are explained the compounds **grand'mère, grand'messe**, etc. (§ **10**) ; such names as **Rochefort** (from **la roche**) ; adverbs of the type of **prudemment** (§ 150.5) ; and the expression **se faire fort de**, in which **fort** does not take the feminine **-e**.

Elle se fait fort de réussir. *She is confident of success.*

§ **146**. A very few adjectives never take the feminine form, *e.g.* grognon, chic.

Une petite fille **grognon**. Ta robe est très **chic** ! Une **chic** cérémonie.

§ **147**. 1. **Adjective equivalents** (other than adjective clauses) generally consist in French of (*a*) a noun governed by the prepositions de, à, en (§§ 279.2, 282.3, 284) ; or (*b*) an infinitive governed by **à** (§ **100.2**).

(*a*) Un homme **de talent**. *A talented man.*
Un homme **à barbe grise**. *A grey-bearded man.*
Une salle **d'attente**. *A waiting-room.*
Un garçon **de café**. *A café attendant.*
Une tasse **à café**. *A coffee cup.*
Un moulin **à vent**. *A windmill.*
Une montre **en or**. *A gold watch.*
Un cheval **de** (*or* **en**) **bois**. *A wooden horse.*

(*b*) Une salle **à manger**. *A dining-room.* (§ 100.2.)
Voici une lettre **à expédier**. . . . *to be dispatched.*
Une histoire **à mourir de rire**. *A side-splitting story.*

Note.—From **un garçon de café** distinguish the construction **une tasse de café**, in which **café** is the main noun.

2. The adjective equivalent may also be a noun joined to its headword without any preposition.

La loi **Bérenger**. Le code **Napoléon**.
La rue **Racine**. Le boulevard **Haussmann**.

§ **148**. Adverbs occasionally have adjectival function.

Un jeune homme **très bien**. *A very proper young man.*

§ **149**. The adjective is used with nominal function

1. In the masculine and feminine, much more frequently than in English.

Taisez-vous, **malheureuse** ! *Wretched woman !* Va-t'en, **ingrat** !
L'imprudent réfléchit à ce qu'il a dit ; **le sage** à ce qu'il va dire.

2. In the sense of a neuter.

L'expérience est **le passé** qui parle **au présent**.
Il a **poussé l'étrange** jusqu'à **l'horrible**.

ADVERBS OF MANNER

§ **150.** Closely related to qualifying adjectives are the adverbs of manner of cognate meaning.

Like all adverbs in French they are invariable.

1. A few adverbs come directly from Latin:

bien **mieux** **mal** **pis** **peu** **moins**

They correspond to the adjectives:

bon **meilleur** **mauvais** **pire** **petit** **moindre**

2. Most adverbs are derived from the feminine of the adjective by the adjunction of the suffix **-ment** (originally a feminine noun).

grandement, heureusement, fièrement.

Note, however: **bref, brièvement; grave, gravement** and **grièvement (blessé).**

3. In a few cases the **e** of the feminine becomes **é,**

profondément, obscurément,

by analogy with other adverbs such as

aveuglément, opiniâtrément,

derived from forms in **é** (the past participles **aveuglé, opiniâtré).**

Note also **impunément,** formed under the influence of Latin 'impune.'

4. If the masculine adjective ends in a vowel, feminine **e** is dropped.

hardiment, aisément, résolument.

But **gaiement** or **gaîment.** The contraction is also shown in

assidûment, indûment, goulûment, etc.

Note also **gentil** [ʒɑ̃ti], **gentiment.**

5. Adjectives in **-ant** and **-ent** had only one form in early French (§ 145), so that feminine **e** does not appear in the derived adverbs.

savant + ment > savamment; prudent + ment > prudemment.

Thus also **constamment, violemment, négligemment,** etc.

But **lent, lentement; présent, présentement.**

§ **151.** Certain adverbs in **-ment** have to-day no corresponding adjectives. Thus:

incessamment, *at once*	**notamment**, *particularly*
journellement, *daily*	**sciemment**, *knowingly*
profusément, *profusely*	**nuitamment**, *by night*

§ **152.** 1. From certain adjectives no adverbs may be formed. Such are

(*a*) Adjectives of colour : **blanc, rouge, vert,** etc.

Except in a figurative sense, *e.g.* **tancer vertement,** *to give a good scolding.*

(*b*) **Possible, content, crédule, hautain.**

2. In place of all these, adverb phrases are used.

(*a*) Une porte peinte **en vert.**
Une jeune fille vétue **de blanc.**
Ell' voit venir son page
Tout **de noir** habillé.

(*b*) Il répondit **d'un air content** (*or* **avec satisfaction).**
Il m'écoute **avec crédulité.**
Il me regardait **d'un air hautain** (*or* **avec hauteur).**

Or another construction is resorted to.

Il **m'est impossible** de venir. *I can't possibly come.*

Note.—Adverb phrases are widely used in place of existing adverbs, some of which are long and heavy.

Il s'est battu **avec courage** (courageusement).
Il agit **avec prudence** (prudemment).
Je l'ai cherché **en vain** (vainement).
Je l'aime **à la folie** (follement).
Ne répondez pas **à la légère** (légèrement).
Je l'aime **d'instinct** (instinctivement).
Il s'apaisa **peu à peu** (graduellement).
Il se leva **tout à coup** (subitement).

And also to express shades of meaning for which no adverb exists.

Il me regarda **à la dérobée.**
Il vient nous voir **de temps à autre.**
Je lui écrirai **de nouveau.**

§ **153.** Many adjectives may be used adverbially, but only in expressions which must be acquired by practice. Thus :

parler **haut,** *to speak loud,*	*but*	avouer hautement.
parler **bas,** *to speak low,*	,,	agir bassement.
chanter **juste,** *to sing in tune,*	,,	être puni justement.
coûter **cher,** *to cost dear,*	,,	aimer chèrement.
travailler ferme, *to work hard,*	,,	croire fermement.
refuser **net,** *to decline point blank,*	,,	s'expliquer nettement.

Thus also :

sentir bon, mauvais. s'arrêter **court.**

Note.—**Vite,** originally an adjective, is now used only as an adverb.
Courez **vite !**

The derived adverb **vitement** is now obsolete.

COMPARISON

Comparative. Two or more terms may be compared in respect of their quality or their **quantity.**

§ **154. Qualitative Comparison.** The comparative of adjectives and adverbs is formed with the adverbs **plus,** *more*; **aussi,** *as, so*; **si,** *so*; **moins,** *less.*

The second term of comparison is always introduced by the conjunction **que.**

Henri { est **plus** grand, court **plus** vite, / est **aussi** grand, court **aussi** vite, / n'est pas **si** grand, ne court pas **si** vite, / n'est pas **aussi** grand, ne court pas **aussi** vite, / est **moins** grand, court **moins** vite, } que Paul.

Henri est **plus grand** et **plus fort que** Paul.
Henri est **plus grand que** Paul ou **que** Jules.

§ **155. Quantitative Comparison.** The comparative is formed with the adverbs **plus (de), autant (de), tant (de), moins (de).**

Henri { travaille **plus** / a **plus de** patience / travaille **autant** / a **autant de** patience / ne travaille pas (au)**tant** / n'a pas (au)**tant de** patience / travaille **moins** / a **moins de** patience } **que Paul.**

§ **156.** 1. The comparison is usually between two terms which are opposed to each other; these may be (*a*) nouns (and pronouns); (*b*) adjectives, adverbs, or adverb phrases; (*c*) verbs.

(*a*) Henri est plus grand que **Paul.**
Henri est plus grand que **moi.**
Henri court plus vite que **vous.**

(*b*) Il est plus **intelligent** que **travailleur.**
Le ciel n'est pas aussi pur **en hiver** qu'**en été.**
Il s'est conduit avec plus **de courage** que **de prudence.**

(*c*) Vous **écrivez** plus correctement que vous (ne) **parlez** (§ 277.6).
Il vaut mieux **se taire** que de **mentir.**

2. Occasionally there is no opposition between two terms, the so-called second term of comparison being a clause adverbial to an adjective or adverb.

Il est **plus** intelligent **que vous** (ne) **pensez.**
(=Il est intelligent—plus que vous ne pensez.

This adverbial clause may be elliptical.

Je vais aussi bien que **possible** (=qu'il est possible d'aller).

Notes.—1. If the two terms of comparison are in the infinitive, the second is usually introduced by **que de,** unless the infinitives are already governed by another preposition.

Il est plus honteux de mentir que **d'être puni.**
J'aime mieux être puni que **de mentir.**
J'aime autant être puni que de mentir.

But : Il s'applique plus **à** jouer qu'**à travailler.**
Nous pensions moins **à** suivre ses conseils qu'**à nous moquer** de ses petites manies.

2. The second term of comparison may be entirely omitted.

Plus vers la gauche, s'élevait une véritable ville formée de **tentes** écrues.

3. Comparison may also be expressed by the adverb **davantage,** which, however, should always be in end (*i.e.* stressed) position.

Henri est travailleur, mais Paul l'est **davantage.**
(=Paul est plus travailleur que Henri.)
Henri a beaucoup d'amis, mais j'en ai **davantage.**
(=J'ai plus d'amis que Henri.)

§ 157. The following have retained the Latin comparative :

Adjectives.	**bon,** *good*	**meilleur,** *better*
	mauvais, *bad*	**pire** or **plus mauvais,** *worse*
	petit, *small, little*	**moindre,** *less* ; **plus petit,** *smaller*
Adverbs.	**bien,** *well*	**mieux,** *better*
	mal, *badly*	**pis** or **plus mal,** *worse*
	peu, *little*	**moins,** *less*

The student must be careful to distinguish between **adjective and adverb.**

Son devoir est **meilleur** que le vôtre, *His exercise is better than yours.*
Il travaille **mieux** que vous, *He works better than you.*
Ses souffrances sont **moindres** que les vôtres. *His sufferings are less than yours.*
Il a **moins** souffert que vous. *He suffered less than you.*

§ **158.** The following constructions should be noted:

1. Comparison is often expressed by **auprès de**, by **comme**, by **autre**, **autrement.**

Que sont les peines du corps **auprès des** tourments de l'âme ?
Son travail est **autre** (**autrement** consciencieux) **que** le vôtre.

Note.—Intensifying similes are always introduced by **comme.**

Il était pâle **comme la mort.** *As pale as death.*
Il est gai **comme un pinson.** *As merry as a cricket.*
Il est sourd **comme un pot.** *As deaf as a door-post.*
Il était blanc **comme un linge.** *As white as a sheet.*
Il s'est montré doux **comme un agneau.** *As gentle as a lamb.*

2. **Plus . . . plus ; moins . . . moins.** *The more . . . the more ; the less . . . the less.* **Autant . . . autant.**

Plus on avançait, **plus** on s'égarait.
Plus on le punit, **moins** il travaille.
Plus vous aimerez Dieu, **meilleur** vous serez.
Autant l'un des frères a d'intelligence native, **autant** l'autre a d'application soutenue.

3. **De plus en plus, de moins en moins.** *More and more, less and less.*

Il se fatigue **de plus en plus.**

4. **D'autant plus (moins) . . . que.** *All the more (less) . . . as.*

Il travaille **d'autant plus** fiévreusement **que** les examens approchent.
On l'appréciait d'**autant** moins que sa timidité l'empêchait de se faire valoir.

5. Il a trois ans **de plus** que moi.
Il est plus âgé que moi **de trois ans.** } *He is three years older than I.*

§ **159.** The **Superlative** is formed by prefixing **le, la, les,** or the **possessive adjective,** to the comparative.

Le plus grand n'est pas **le plus puissant,** c'est **le plus juste.**
Le chien est **le meilleur** ami de l'homme. Mon chien est **mon meilleur** ami. Jean est **le plus âgé** de la famille. Marie est **la moins âgée.** L'éléphant est **la plus grosse** des bêtes.

Notes.—(*a*) After the superlative, de is prepositional, and the article is not omitted, as the superlative singles out one or more from a whole group or class, *i.e.* the dependent noun is always particularized or generalized.

(*b*) In English the superlative is often followed by 'in'; French always has **de** (§ 280, note).

Le meilleur élève **de** la classe. *The best boy in the class.*

(*c*) The distinction made in English between 'the younger' and 'the youngest' can have no counterpart in French.

I! **est le plus âgé** des **deux, des trois.**

§ **160.** If the adjective follows the noun, it is preceded by the article.

Voilà l'élève **le** plus intelligent de la classe.
Un de mes amis **les** plus dévoués.

§ **161.** The article **le** is invariable before **an** adverb.

C'est elle qui travaille **le mieux.**

Also in adverbial phrases

C'est lui qui a agi avec **le plus** de prudence.

Grammarians also teach that the article remains invariable (*i.e.* is in the neuter) when an individual is compared, not with another, but with himself.

C'est parmi ses compagnes d'enfance qu'elle est **le plus heureuse.**
C'est au mois de mai que nos campagnes sont **le plus fleuries.**

But the rule is frequently ignored, even in literary French, and was at no date in the language strictly observed.

Note the partitive construction:

Je fais **de** mon mieux. *I do (am doing) my best.*

And this other partitive construction, in which the superlative remains undetermined:

Je vous donne ce que j'ai **de** meilleur.

§ **162.** A so-called **absolute superlative** is formed by prefixing to the adjective such adverbs as **très, fort, extrêmement, bien.**

Ce vin est **très bon, fort bon.**
J'en ai été **extrêmement surpris.**

Bien is always affective (§ 171.5, note).

Il est **bien malheureux !**
Qui fut **bien étonné ?** Ce fut Pierrot !

and is never used if no emotion is implied ; it would be quite out of place in such a sentence as :

Cet acide a une odeur **très** forte et **très** caractéristique.

§ **163.** Various other affective constructions are used instead of normal **très.** Thus :

Sa famille est { **des plus respectables.** / **tout ce qu'il y a de plus respectable.** }

C'est un brave **entre les braves !**

Il est { **on ne peut plus laborieux.** / **laborieux au possible.** }

Il est { **richissime.** / **archi-riche.** / **riche, riche !** } Humorous or familiar uses.

THE ARTICLES

§ 164. Definite Article.

The	**le** père	**la** mère	**l'**enfant	**les** parents
Of the	**du** père	**de la** mère	**de l'**enfant	**des** parents
To the	**au** père	**à la** mère	**à l'**enfant	**aux** parents

Before '**h muette**': **l'**homme, **de l'**homme, etc.
Before '**h aspirée**': **le** héros, **du** héros, etc., **la** hauteur, etc.

Du, au, des, aux are contractions of **de** and **à** with the definite article, and are commonly called in French *articles contractés.*

Notes.—1. There is no possessive case in French. 'The pupil's book' is **Le livre de l'élève.**

2. In old French, **en les** was contracted to **es**, now spelt **ès**, and still retained in **bachelier ès sciences, licencié ès lettres**, etc. But **licencié en droit, docteur en médecine.**

§ 165. Indefinite Article.

a(n)	**un** livre	**une** plume	**un** encrier	The plural is
of a(n)	**d'un** livre	**d'une** plume	**d'un** encrier	the partitive
to a(n)	**à un** livre	**à une** plume	**à un** encrier	**des, de.**

§ 166. Partitive Article (derived from the definite article).

some, any	**du** pain	**de la** viande	**de l'**eau	**des** enfants
of some, any	**de** pain	**de** viande	**d'**eau	**d'**enfants
to some, any	**à du** pain	**à de la** viande	**à de l'**eau	**à des** enfants

§ 167. The Definite Article has two main functions.

1. Its original function, dating from old French, and similar to its function in English, is to **particularize** a noun.

Ouvrez **la** fenêtre. *Open the window*, i.e. *that window.*
Les élèves **du** collège furent invités **à la** fête.

2. Its new function, highly developed in modern French, is to **generalize** a noun. In English this use is restricted to class names.

Le chien est le meilleur ami de l'homme. *The dog is man's best friend.* J'aime **les** chiens. *I like dogs.*
Je préfère **le** café au thé. **L'**avarice est un vice.
L'ignorance est toujours suivie de l'obstination.
Le fer est le plus utile **des** métaux.

§ **168.** The definite article is used in French, though not in English:

1. Before names of continents, countries, provinces, mountains, many islands, etc.

l'Asie, la France, la Normandie, le mont Blanc, la Corse.
Thus also: **La Seine,** *the river Seine*; **le Rhône,** *the river Rhone*; **les Vosges** [vo:ʒ], *the Vosges mountains*, etc.

Note.—The article is omitted:

(*a*) After **en**: **en France, en Normandie** (§ 284.1.*a*).

(*b*) In adjective phrases: **les vins de France** (*French wines*), **l'histoire de France, de l'eau de Seine, un chapeau de paille d'Italie, le roi** (**la couronne, le trône**) **d'Espagne. Les côtes de Bretagne** *or* **de la Bretagne.**

(*c*) Usually, after **arriver de, revenir de**: **Il arrive d'Espagne.**

But the article is usually retained before masculine names of countries (§ 284, note 1): **Il revient du Portugal, du Danemark.**

(*d*) Before names of towns: **Je connais bien Paris et Londres.**

Unless the article is an inherent part of the name (taking a capital), as in **Le Havre** (*lit.* 'The Haven'), **La Rochelle** ('The Rock'), **La Fère, La Ferté, La Mecque, Le Caire.**

Je reviens du Havre. Je me rends au Caire.

2. Before titles preceding proper nouns, and before proper nouns qualified by an adjective.

Le roi Georges, le capitaine Moreau, le petit Jules, le grand Corneille, la Rome antique.

Note the construction with **monsieur, madame, mademoiselle.**

Bonjour, docteur, or **Bonjour, monsieur le docteur.**
Je me plaindrai à madame la directrice.
Je me soumets à votre décision, monsieur le président (*Mr Chairman*).
Entrez, messieurs les voyageurs.

Thus also with the possessive adjective.

Comment se porte madame votre mère ?

3. Before the names of most feast-days.

La Saint-Jean, la Toussaint, la Fête-Dieu.

But **Pâques, Noël.**

Nous avons congé à Pâques, à la Fête-Dieu, à la Toussaint, et à Noël.

In familiar style, **Noël** often has the article.

Deux jours avant la Noël, maître Sylvain se prépara à tuer le porc.

Note that in every case the article is feminine, **fête** being understood when not expressed: **la fête de saint Jean, la fête de Noël.**

4. Sometimes, in colloquial French, before a noun in the vocative.

Eh, **l'homme**, que faites-vous donc là ?
Combien vos fromages, **la petite mère** ?

5. With nouns used distributively, after adverbial extensions of price.

Le sucre coûte onze sous **la livre**.

In expressions of time, **par** is more usual in the distributive sense.

Il gagne cinquante francs **par semaine**.
Il vient nous voir trois fois **par an**.

But also : Il vient nous voir trois fois **l'an**.

And always : Il vient nous voir **le lundi** (*on Mondays = each Monday*), with which compare

Il viendra (est venu) nous voir **lundi**. *He will come on Monday (came last Monday).*

6. In many phrases which must be acquired by practice.

La semaine dernière ; vers le soir ; avez-vous le temps ? apprendre le français ; partir le premier, etc.

7. With parts and attributes of the body, etc. See §§ 178, 179.

§ 169. The **Indefinite Article** is used, on the whole, as in English, except that it has no distributive function (see § 168.5 above).

Prêtez-moi **un** livre. Adressez-vous à **un** ami.

Note, however :

I have a *sore throat.*	J'ai mal à **la** gorge (§ 178.1).
He has a *large mouth.*	Il a la bouche grande (§ 179).
What a *house!*	Quelle maison ! (§ 182).

§ 170. Omission of the definite and indefinite articles.

In old French the noun originally had no article when it was not particularized. Many instances of the older construction have survived. Thus, the articles are omitted

1. In proverbs handed down from a remote past.

Pauvreté n'est pas **vice** (= **La** pauvreté n'est pas **un** vice).
Humilité est sagesse.

2. In headings, titles, inscriptions, postal addresses, etc.

Dictée Thème Version

Traité d'Algèbre Livre I, chapitre 4

BOULEVARD HAUSSMANN	MAISON FÉLIX POTIN

Il demeure rue Saint-Honoré, numéro 137.

3. In enumerations (literary construction).

Grands et **petits**, **nobles**, **bourgeois** et **paysans**, étaient animés du même espoir.

And frequently when nouns are grouped in pairs.

Il y avait des routes mitoyennes (*common to both sectors*) où **Français** et **Anglais** voisinaient.

Elle prépara **crayons** et **couleurs** . . . et fit le portrait d'un paysan basané.

4. In appositions to a noun or a clause.

Le maire est un monsieur Durand, **ancien épicier**.
Il fut nommé colonel, **honneur** qu'il méritait bien.
Vous habitez la province, **mauvaise condition** pour faire du théâtre (*to write plays*).

But the article is used before the noun in apposition

(*a*) To **particularize** it, as is done in English.

Vous trouverez ça chez M. Durand, **l'épicier** du coin.

(*b*) With an **affective** value.

C'est une mélodie de Gounod, **le grand compositeur français.**
. . . *the great French composer, you know.*

The article is used here to show that the apposition is not intended to convey information, but to remind us of a fact assumed as known.

Note.—Appositive nouns, in French as in English, are sometimes introduced by the particle **de**, without any article.

La ville **de** Paris. L'ancienne province **de** Normandie.
Adieu, charmant pays **de** France !
Il a pris le grade **de** docteur.

Compare the use of **de** in predication, § 118.2.*b*.

5. Before predicative nouns, especially when, having no epithet, they may themselves be considered as adjectival.

Son père est **avocat**. Êtes-vous **père**, monsieur ?
On l'a élu **président**. Il a été élu **président**.

But the article is used if the predicative noun is particularized, or qualified.

Son père est **l'avocat** qui m'a défendu.
Son père est **un avocat** distingué, **un excellent homme**.

But again:

Il s'est montré **honnête homme**,

the group **honnête homme** being practically a compound noun.

There is really no absolute rule ; taste often decides.

Les dieux sont **gardiens** des coutumes traditionnelles.

6. Before nouns forming adjectival phrases (§ 147).

Un sac **d'école.** Un homme **de talent.** Une cuiller **à thé.**
On voyait à l'horizon un clocher **d'église.**

Unless the dependent noun is particularized, or qualified.

On voyait à l'horizon **le clocher de l'église.**
C'est un homme **d'un talent rare.**

In fact, both head noun and dependent noun take the articles as the sense may require. Thus:

Quand on lit dans un livre **le récit d'une** bataille, on se figure volontiers que sur **un** champ **de** bataille, chacun sait ce qu'il fait.

7. In adverb phrases.

Travaillez **avec courage** (=courageusement).

But: **Avec du courage,** vous réussirez,

in which sentence we could not substitute 'courageusement.'

Thus: **avec patience, avec prudence,** etc. (§ 152, note).

Thus also: **en prison, en cachette** (*secretly*), **à terre, par terre, par exemple, de but en blanc** (*point-blank*), etc.

8. In many expressions belonging to business or official style.

On paye les vignerons chaque jour **après réception de** dépêches fixant le cours aux Halles (The 'Covent-Garden' of Paris).

9. In many so-called verb-phrases, such as

perdre courage, perdre connaissance (*to faint*), **avoir besoin** de qqch., **tenir tête** à qqn, **rendre service** à qqn, **livrer bataille, prendre garde,** etc.

avoir faim, soif, froid, chaud, raison, tort, sommeil, etc.

Note, however, that many verb-phrases have the article, *e.g.* **demander l'aumône, faire la guerre, garder le silence,** etc.

10. Before nouns introduced by sans, and by **ni . . . ni.**

Il est arrivé **sans argent.**
Il n'avait **ni dignité ni aisance** dans ses manières.
Je ne le ferai **ni** pour or **ni** pour **argent.**

Unless the nouns are particularized.

Il est revenu **sans l'argent.** *He came back without the money.*
Il n'avait **ni la dignité ni l'aisance** de son père.
Comme il n'y a pas de religion **sans temple,** il n'y a pas de famille **sans l'intimité du foyer.**
Je m'élançai seul sur cet orageux océan du monde, dont je ne connaissais **ni les ports ni les écueils.**

11. Frequently before an unparticularized subject or object when the verb is negatived by **jamais.** The partitive article is also omitted in the plural.

Jamais musique ne m'a paru aussi funèbre.
Je n'ai depuis **jamais** vu **folie** triste et douce comme la sienne.
Jamais éclats de rire ne furent si brusquement arrêtés.

§ **171. Partitive de.** 1. The particle **de** combines with the articles and with adjectives to form determinatives indicating **a part of a whole** (English 'some,' 'some of,' 'any'). The noun thus introduced is treated **not as an accusative governed by prepositional de,** but as a **nominative subject, accusative object,** etc. (§ 281.2).

Nous avons bu **du** vin. Nous avons bu **d'un** vin exquis.
Donnez-moi **de ce** vin. Il nous a fait boire **de son** vin.
Donnez-nous **de vos** nouvelles.
Des personnes malveillantes vous diront le contraire.
Il empruntera **de l'**argent à **des** amis.
On nous servit du bœuf rôti avec **de la** gelée de groseilles.
Nous avons bu **d'excellent** vin. Donnez-lui **de bons** conseils.

Notes.—(*a*) In familiar French, the article is very commonly used before those qualifying adjectives which usually precede the noun (§ 347).

Nous avons bu **du** bon vin. Voilà **de la** vraie poésie !
En voilà **des** beaux enfants !

It is always so used before the numerous adjective + noun groups which are felt as compound nouns, such as :

des grands-pères ; **des** chauves-souris ;
des jeunes filles, **des** jeunes gens ; **du** bon sens (*common sense*),
de la bonne volonté (*goodwill*), **des** bons mots (*witticisms*) ;
des petits garçons, **des** petits gâteaux, **des** petits pois (*green peas*).

(*b*) The article is used if the adjective follows the noun.

du lait chaud, **des** pois secs, **des** garçons intelligents.

(*c*) The article is always omitted after partitive **de** before **autre**(s).

J'ai **d'autres** amis. J'en ai **d'autres**. Donnez-moi **d'autre** vin.

(*d*) The article is omitted when the adjective qualifies, or is predicative to, **en** replacing a partitive noun.

Du vin, je peux vous en fournir ; j'**en** ai **d'**excellent.
J'**en** ai appris **de** belles sur votre compte ! *I have learnt fine things about you !*
On ferait beaucoup plus de choses si l'on **en** croyait moins **d'**impossibles.

But in colloquial style, frequently **du, de la, des**; this is largely a matter of idiom.

J'en ai vu, des livres, et **des** beaux.
J'ai du bon tabac dans ma tabatière ; . . . j'**en** ai **du** frais, j'en ai **du** râpé. . . .

(*e*) When a second adjective occurs with ellipsis of the noun, it takes or omits the article according to the construction of the first group.

Elle cueillit **des** fleurs rouges et **des** blanches.
Dans toute école on trouve **de** bons élèves et **de** mauvais.

2. A partitive noun governed by prepositional **de** (= *of, from, by, with,* etc.) may still be preceded by **un, une** or by an adjective, but not by the article **le, la, les.** Thus :

> **Nous** avons bu **un** verre **d'un** vin exquis, **de ce** vin, **de son** vin, un verre **d'excellent** vin.

But : Nous avons bu un verre **de** vin, *a glass of wine.*

The reason for this is obvious : the definite article must be reserved for its original function of particularizing the noun.

> Nous avons bu un verre du vin qu'il avait reçu au jour de l'an, *A glass of the wine which he had received . . .*

3. Thus the partitive noun is governed by prepositional **de,** the partitive article being entirely omitted :

(*a*) After many nouns denoting definite or indefinite quantity,

> une **bouteille** d'eau, une **livre de** thé, **trois ans de** guerre, **un grand nombre** (**une foule**) **de** personnes.

(*b*) After certain adjectives,

> une salle **pleine d'**invités, une garnison **dépourvue de** vivres.

(*c*) After many verbs and verbal phrases,

> **Munissons-nous de** provisions. Il faudrait **garnir d'**arbres toutes ces avenues. **Avez-vous besoin de** renfort ?

Note.—Thus also when **de** forms a part of a compound preposition,

> **Auprès de** maisons d'aspect misérable s'élève un magnifique hôtel.

4. The negative adverbs **ne pas, ne point** come under 3 (*a*) above, as **pas, point** were originally nouns, followed by prepositional **de** (§ 269). The other negative adverbs, **ne plus, ne guère, ne jamais,** had, for reasons relative to their etymology, the same construction, omitting the article.

> Il n'a **pas** (**point**) **d'**argent.
> Nous n'avons **plus de** ressources.
> Il n'y a **jamais de** représentations le dimanche.

Notes.—(*a*) If the negative adverb merely qualifies the verb, without affecting the partitive noun, the partitive article stands. Compare :

> Je ne vous donnerai pas **de** conseils, *I will give you no advice,*

and

> Je ne vous donnerai pas **des** conseils impossibles à suivre, *I will not give you advice which cannot be followed.*

> On ne peut pas faire **du** bien à tous, mais on peut témoigner **de la** bonté à tous.

(*b*) The article also stands after the adverb **ne . . . que** (*only*), which is affirmative as regards the following noun.

> On **ne** m'a donné **que des** conseils.

5. The article is omitted after the adverbs of quantity **beaucoup, peu, plus, moins, tant, autant, trop, assez, combien, que!** because the following **de** was originally prepositional.

> **Beaucoup de** paroles et **peu de** besogne. **Assez de** bêtises !
> **Combien de** gens qui ne savent pas cela ! **Que de** monde ici !
> Il a montré **plus de** crédulité que **de** bon sens.
> Il a montré **beaucoup trop de** crédulité et **assez peu de** bon sens.
> Je vous donnerai **autant d**'argent que vous voudrez.

(**But**: Je vous donnerai de l'argent **autant** que vous voudrez.)

Note.—The article stands after (*a*) **bien**, which is not an adverb of quantity, but is merely affective, being used to emphasize a statement, and (*b*) **la plupart**, which is really a superlative (=la plus grande partie).

(*a*) **Bien des** personnes m'ont assuré le contraire.
Il a passé par **bien des** dangers.
Mon grand-père avait eu **bien du** mal à élever sa famille.

(*b*) **La plupart des** invités étaient arrivés.
La plupart du temps il ne fait rien.

6. Partitive **de** is used before adjectives and nouns after the neuter and the indefinite pronouns **ceci, cela, que, quoi, ce qui, ce que, quelqu'un, quelque chose, personne, rien.**

> Son cas a **ceci de** particulier que sa réputation est sans tache.
> **Quoi de** nouveau ? **Que** savez-vous d'intéressant ?
> Dans tout **ce qui** m'arrive d'heureux, ou **de** triste, ma pensée se tourne vers ma mère.
> **Ce que** je sais **d**'intéressant, je le garde pour moi.
> Il me donna **ce qu**'il avait **d**'argent sur lui.
> Je me tirai d'affaire avec **ce que** je savais de français.
> Je ne sais **rien d**'intéressant.
> Y a-t-il **quelqu'un de** blessé ?
> J'ai appris **quelque chose** de très important.

7 Personal pronouns are not preceded by partitive de, but by **d'entre.**

> Les juges n'étaient pas d'accord. **Plusieurs d'entre eux** croyaient à l'innocence de l'accusé. *Several of them* . . .
> Les élèves sourirent, et **trois d'entre eux** rirent tout haut. *Three of them* . . .
> Y a-t-il **quelqu'un d'entre vous** qui puisse me prêter vingt francs ?

But one says either **L'un d'eux** or **L'un d'entre eux.** *One of them.*

8. The noun is, of course, never partitive when determined by numeral or indefinite adjectives.

> Quatre-vingts francs.
> J'ai parlé à plusieurs personnes.
> Attendez quelques minutes.

DEMONSTRATIVE ADJECTIVE

§ **172.**

cet enfant	**cet** homme	**cet** aimable enfant	*this, that.*
[1] **ce** livre	**ce** hasard	**ce** petit garçon	
cette édition	**cette** excellente édition		
ces livres	**ces** éditions	**ces** aimables enfants	*these, those.*

[1] **Cet** drops the **t** before a consonant or 'aspirate' **h.**

§ **173.** To stress the demonstrative adjective and differentiate between 'this' and 'that,' the adverbs **ci** and **là** are affixed to the noun or adjective (§ 313).

Je prends **ce** livre-**ci**, je vous laisse **ces** deux-**là**. *I'll take this book, I am leaving you those two.*

Cette édition-**ci** est la meilleure.

Notes.—1. In English, 'that,' 'those,' have both a particularizing and a generalizing function. The noun is particularized in :

Those *officers, who were with me, know that I am speaking the truth.*
Ces officiers, qui m'accompagnaient, savent bien que je dis vrai.

The noun is generalized in :

Those *boys who obtain* 80°/₀ *shall have a half-holiday.*

In French, the demonstrative never has a generalizing function, therefore the sentence above will appear as :

Les élèves qui obtiendront 80°/₀ [1] auront un demi-congé.
(*Or* **Tous ceux** qui obtiendront . . . *or* **Tout** élève qui obtiendra . . .)

2. For the use of **ce** in deferential address, see § **216**, note.

3. Note **ce dernier**, *the latter.*

POSSESSIVE ADJECTIVES

§ **174.**

mon père	**ma** mère	**mes** parents	*my*
ton père	**ta** mère	**tes** parents	*thy*
son père	**sa** mère	**ses** parents	*his, her, its*
notre père	**notre** mère	**nos** parents	*our*
votre père	**votre** mère	**vos** parents	*your*
leur père	**leur** mère	**leurs** parents	*their*

The masculine forms **mon, ton, son** are used also before feminine nouns and adjectives with initial vowel or 'mute' **h.**

mon amie	**mon** excellente amie
ton histoire	**ton** absurde histoire

Note.—In the third person the possessive does not, as in English, indicate the gender of the possessor.

son frère	*his or her brother*
sa sœur	*his or her sister.*

---

[1] Read "quatre-vingts pour cent" (§ 291.2).

§ **175.** The possessive adjective may be emphasized by the adjunction of **propre**, *own* :

Il me traite comme son propre fils,
Chacun de ces corps a ses qualités propres,

or by the adjunction of à moi, à toi, etc.

Ça, c'est mon affaire à moi ! *That's my business !*
Il avait chez eux sa chambre à lui. *His own room.*

Thus also : Je me confie en Dieu, notre Père à tous.

§ **176.** The possessive is frequently used in French before nouns in the vocative.

Arrive, mon enfant.—Oui, mon oncle.
Come along, child. —Yes, uncle.

This is the mode of address in the army, from inferior to superior :

Salut, mon capitaine. A vos ordres, mon colonel.

(The superior addresses an inferior as 'capitaine,' or as 'monsieur.')

§ **177.** Note the following constructions, in which French and English differ :

1. Jean est de mes amis.	*John is a friend of mine* (§ **118**, note).
C'est un ami à moi. C'est un de mes amis. Il est de mes amis.	*He is a friend of mine.*
2. Allons à sa rencontre.	*Let us go to meet him.*
Allons à son secours.	*Let us go to help him.*
3. Il est mon aîné.	*He is older than I.*
4. Dites-lui cela de ma part.	*Tell him that from me.*
Sauf votre respect.	*With all due respect to you.*

§ **178.** 1. Parts and attributes of the body are usually particularized in French not by the possessive, but by the definite article, when the commoner actions and states of daily life are referred to.

Le chien ouvre l'œil et dresse l'oreille. *Pricks up his ears.*
Pourquoi haussez-vous les épaules ? *Why do you shrug your shoulders ?*
Il grince des dents. *He gnashes his teeth.* (Literally : 'He gnashes *with the* teeth'; not : 'He gnashes *some* teeth.')
J'ai mal à la tête. *I have a headache.*
Plusieurs de ces malheureux perdirent la vie.

Notice that each of these lost his life, and that in this construction French has the singular.

2. This use of the article is sometimes extended to articles of clothing, etc., especially in nominative absolute constructions.

Il entra les mains dans les poches, le chapeau sur l'oreille, la cigarette aux lèvres.

3. A dative personal pronoun is often inserted to make the reference clearer.

Il **s'est** pincé le doigt. Je **lui** ai tiré les oreilles.
La tête **me** fait mal. Elle **lui** donna la main.

Distinguish carefully between

Elle **se** lave les mains and Elle **lui** lave les mains.

4. But the noun is determined by the possessive

(*a*) When the action is not one of the commoner ones of daily life.

Elle prit l'enfant sur **ses** genoux.
Il sacrifia **sa** vie.
Elle lui donna **sa** main. *She granted him her hand (in marriage).*

(*b*) If the noun is qualified by an adjective or adjective equivalent.

Le chien dressa **ses** oreilles **pointues**.
Elle leva vers moi **ses beaux** yeux bleus.
Elle leva vers moi **ses** yeux **qui souriaient à travers les larmes.**

Note.—The choice of the construction is largely optional.

Le Temps usera ses ongles sur ce que j'ai fait en huit jours. *Or:* Le Temps s'usera les ongles . . .
J'ai pu enfin me lancer dans l'azur, en plein soleil, avec devant mes yeux la route aérienne et fluide. . . . Des laboureurs me regardaient, avec, dans les yeux, une stupéfaction soudaine.—*L. Blériot.*

§ **179.** The article is used also in the construction

avoir, etc. + **noun object + predicative adjective.**

Ce chien a **les** oreilles pointues. *This dog's ears are pointed. This dog has pointed ears.*

Literally: 'has the ears pointed,' and not 'has the pointed ears.'

Je lui trouve **le** visage pâle. *He looks pale.*
Il a **la** digestion difficile. Il a **les** yeux bleus.
Vous avez **les** mains fiévreuses. *Your hands are feverish.*

This construction is much used, but it is quite correct to say:

Sa digestion est difficile. Vos mains sont fiévreuses
Ses yeux sont bleus. Il a des yeux bleus.

(Note that in the last example **bleus** is attributive, not predicative.)

§ **180.** The noun remains undetermined in certain adverb phrases.

Je tombai **à genoux.** *I sank to my knees.*
(But: Je tombai à **ses** genoux. *I knelt before him.*)

Also after changer de.

Il a **changé** d'avis, **de** souliers. *He has changed his mind, his shoes.*

§ **181.** When the possessor is inanimate, its relation to the thing possessed is often expressed by the genitive pronoun **en**, rather than by the possessive, when this can conveniently be done.

Nous avons visité la cathédrale, et **en** avons **admiré** les vitraux. . . . *and admired its stained glass.*
Le temps fuit ; la perte **en** est irréparable.
Je venais d'apercevoir l'entrée d'une église. Les portes **en** étaient grandes ouvertes.
Mon attention fut détournée par la cloche du dîner. **J'en** reconnaissais le son, **j'en** comptais les coups.

This construction, however, belongs rather to literature and 'careful' speech than to familiar intercourse, in which the possessive is generally used.

Note.—The possessive adjective frequently has an 'ethic' or affective value, as in English.

Et voilà **notre** homme qui se met à courir !
La voilà encore au lit avec ses migraines. *She is laid up again : those sick headaches* of hers.

INTERROGATIVE (AND EXCLAMATIVE) ADJECTIVE

§ **182.**

Quel livre ? *what book ?* **Quels** livres ? *what books ?*
Quelle maison ? *what house ?* **Quelles** maisons ? *what houses ?*
Quelle maison ! *What a house !*

Note that exclamative **quel** is not followed by an article as in English.

§ **183. Quel** may be used predicatively.

Quel est ce monsieur ? **Quels** sont ces messieurs ?

Note.—Compare Qui sont ces messieurs ? *Who are these gentlemen ?*
Que sont ces messieurs ? *What are these gentlemen ?*

'**Quels** sont ces messieurs ? ' is vaguer, and asks for general information without specifying whether '*who ?*' or '*what ?*' is meant.

§ **184. Quel** is also used in indirect questions and exclamations.

Dites-moi **quel** livre vous désirez.
Je vous demande **quels** sont ces messieurs.
Vous savez **quel** bruit il fait ! *You know what a row he makes !*

§ **185.** Quel is a relative adjective (used predicatively) in the expression **tel quel**.

Nous avons retrouvé la maison **telle quelle.** *We found the house just as we had left it* (*with nothing altered*).

DEMONSTRATIVE PRONOUNS

§ **186.** The demonstrative pronouns are

1. The stressed forms:

masc. **celui-ci**	*this one*		**ceux-ci**	*these*
fem. **celle-ci**			**celles-ci**	
masc. **celui-là**	*that one*		**ceux-là**	*those*
fem. **celle-là**			**celles-là**	

ceci (= ce ci) *this* } neuter and invariable
cela (= ce là) *that* }

In familiar speech **cela** is contracted to **ça.**

2. The stressed forms:

masc. **celui**	*the one, he, him*	**ceux**	*those*
fem. **celle**	*the one, she, her*	**celles**	

3. Unstressed **ce**, neuter and invariable.

§ **187. Celui-ci, celui-là,** stand for a noun previously expressed.

Vous n'avez pas de plume ? Prenez **celle-ci.**
Ces livres-ci sont à moi, **ceux-là** sont à mon frère.

Also: **Celui-ci,** etc. = *the latter.* **Celui-là,** etc. = *the former.*

Les chiens et les chats sont bien différents de caractère : **ceux-ci** s'attachent à la maison, **ceux-là** à leurs maîtres.

§ **188.** The neuter forms **ceci, cela (ça),** refer to facts, statements, or to objects which have not been previously specified.

Retenez bien **ceci** : Prudence est mère de la sureté.
Le voilà qui refuse, à présent ! Qu'est-ce que vous dites de **ça** ?
Montrez-moi **ça.** Qu'est-ce que c'est que **ça** ?
Ceci n'est pas à moi. C'est **ça,** allons-y. *That's it . . .*

§ **189.** As a neuter subject, standing for a previous statement, or, in dislocations, for the logical subject, **cela** is the pronoun to be used with any verb except **être.**

Partez en avant, **cela** vaudra mieux.
Être de retour pour dîner, **cela** me paraît impossible.
Cela ne vous a pas profité, **d'aller** dans le monde.

It is used occasionally with **être** ;

Voir égorger les bêtes, **cela** m'est pénible ;

and is even used instead of impersonal il as a provisional subject (§ 217).

Cela m'est très pénible de voir égorger les bêtes.

Note.—**Cela** also appears as a vague subject in such idiomatic uses as
Comment **ça** va-t-il ? *How are you ? How are you getting on ?*
Eh bien ! **ça** marche, les affaires ? — Oui, ça marche.

§ **190.** **Cela, ça** is also used familiarly, and often in a disparaging manner (affective uses), of people, things, already mentioned.

> Les enfants, c'est insouciant, **cela** ne pense guère à l'avenir.
> Avec un profond mépris elle dit : " **Ça** n'a pas seulement vingt-cinq ans ! "
> Regardez-moi ces gens-là ! **Ça** n'a pas le sou et ça vous parle d'un petit ton protecteur ! *They haven't a penny of their own, and they want to patronize you !*
> Que d'histoires ! Pour six cents francs ! . . . et ça va en Suisse ! . . . Carrossier ! . . .

§ **191.** **Ça** is often added in conversation to interrogative adverbs such as **où, pourquoi, comment,** in order to give a little more 'body' to the question.

> Je l'ai vu hier. — **Où ça ?**
> J'aime mieux rester ici. — **Pourquoi ça ?**
> Je m'arrangerai de façon à ne pas être reconnu. — **Comment ça ?**

§ **192.** As subject to the verb **être,** and corresponding to English 'that,' 'those,' pronounced with a stress, **cela** resolves itself into its elements when the predicate is completed by a noun or a clause.

> **C'**était **là** le secret de maître Cornille.
> **Ce** sont **là** des choses qui ne nous regardent pas.
> **C'**est **là** ce que je voulais dire.
> Est-**ce là** la foi que vous me devez ? Sont-**ce là** vos serments ?

But not before a predicative adjective.

> Cela est vrai.

Note.—An adjective qualifying **ceci, cela,** is always partitive. See § 171.6.

§ **193.** **Celui, celle,** etc., is completed by either (*a*) an adjective clause, or (*b*) an adjective equivalent (noun, adverb, infinitive) introduced by **de.**

(*a*) **Celui qui** mange peu dort bien.
L'honnête homme est **celui qui** fait tout le bien qu'il peut.
Nous pardonnons souvent à **ceux qui** nous ennuient, mais nous ne pouvons pardonner à **ceux que** nous ennuyons.
Ce n'est pas cette édition-ci qu'il me faut. Où est **celle dont** je me sers habituellement, **celle sur laquelle** j'ai fait des annotations ?

(*b*) Voici votre livre et **celui de** votre camarade.
Les médecins d'aujourd'hui sont plus habiles que **ceux d'autrefois.**
S'il nous faut une ambition, ayons **celle de** faire le bien.

Note.—Traditional grammar recognizes no constructions with **celui**, etc., except those given above. The following, however, are quite common :

(*a*) The complement to **celui**, etc., may be an appositive noun-clause.

L'un des arguments par lequel l'Allemagne socialiste a été entraînée à la guerre a été **celui que** la guerre était une lutte contre le tsarisme. (Que is a conjunction here.)

(*b*) Between **celui**, etc., and the adjective-clause or adjective equivalent, a qualifying adjective may be inserted.

Diverses expériences, notamment **celles très curieuses du** professeur Leduc . . .

La dynastie des Rourik, la seule véritable dynastie russe qui précéda **celle apocryphe** des Romanoff . . .

Je préfère les bons vins de France aux meilleurs que produit l'Italie, et même à **ceux tant vantés du** Rhin.

(*c*) The adjective clause is often represented elliptically by a present or past participle.

Les croix portant le nom d'une fille ou d'une veuve étaient nombreuses dans le cimetière ; **celles portant** le nom d'un garçon ou d'un homme l'étaient peu.

Il avait gagné toutes les batailles qu'il avait livrées en personne, mais sur **celles livrées** par ses lieutenants, il en avait perdu cinq.

And often assumes other forms, but always adjectival.

Tous **ceux porteurs** d'un uniforme quelconque étaient massés dans les casernes.

(**Porteurs**=qui portaient.)

Les rails en acier durent plus longtemps que **ceux en fer.**

(**En fer**=de fer.)

Sur la table du vestibule se trouvaient, à côté des lettres que venait de livrer le facteur, **celles à expédier.**

(**A expédier** is adjectival. *Cf.* § **102.1.*a*.**)

§ **194. Celui-là**, etc., is used for **celui**, etc., if the predicate to which it is subject precedes the adjective clause, as it naturally does if it is very short.

Celui-là est heureux **qui** a peu de besoins. *He is happy, whose needs are few.*

Celui-là a gagné, **qui** à la fin de la partie compte le plus de points.

Ceux-là seuls arrivent **qui** persistent jusqu'au bout.

§ **195. Ce** is used

1. As neuter antecedent to the relative pronoun (§ **210**).
2. As a neuter subject, real or temporary, to the verb **être** (**devoir être, pouvoir être**).

§ **196.** As subject to **être, ce** is used

1. To sum up a preceding subject (noun, pronoun, infinitive, noun clause) when a pause has been made after it in order that it may be fully stressed. (Dislocation.)

> **Paris, c'est** bien loin !
> **Celui** qui a raison, **ce** doit être vous.
> **Vouloir, c'est** pouvoir.
> **Le retrouver, ce** pourra être difficile. (Cp. § **217.**)
> **Ce qui m'afflige, c'est** de la savoir malade.
> **Que vous soyez fatigué, c'est** bien possible.

2. When the predicative complement or the logical subject to **être** is (*a*) a personal pronoun, (*b*) a noun preceded by a determining word.

In careful speech the verb becomes **ce sont** when the predicative complement is in the 3rd pers. plural.

> (*a*) Qui est là ? — **C'est moi. C'est nous. Ce sont eux.**
> (*b*) Quel est ce monsieur ? — **C'est mon père. C'est un ami.**
> **Ce** doit être un soldat. **C'est l'ami** dont je vous ai **parlé.**
> Quels sont ces messieurs ? **Ce sont mes amis.**
>
> In familiar speech : **C'est mes amis.**

Note.—The subject to **être** is personal if the noun is undetermined, *i.e.* adjectival (§ **170.5**) ; except in a disparaging sense (affective), as with **cela** (§ **190**) :

> **C'est** vicomte, on ne sait comment, et **ça** veut être plus **légitimiste** que nous . . . !

And **il, elle** are also very frequently used although the predicative noun is determined.

> La conscience ne nous trompe jamais ; **elle est le vrai guide** de l'homme.

There is a slight difference in meaning between **il est, elle est,** and **c'est,** in such sentences. **Ce** always retains some *demonstrative* value. The difference will be felt in such examples as

> Quel est ce monsieur ? — **C'est** mon père. *He is my father,* or *That's my father.*
> Je l'aime, car **il** est mon père. *I love him, for he is my father.* (Here we could not substitute 'For that's my father.')

3. As a neuter subject, representing a fact, statement, etc., when the predicative complement is adjectival or adverbial.

> Vous êtes bien négligent. — **C'est** vrai.
> Madame est servie. — **C'est** bien.
> Voilà cinq francs. — **C'est** peu.
> Je vous le vends cinq francs. **C'est** pour rien ! *Dirt cheap !*
> A qui le tour de jouer ? — **C'est** à moi.

Note.—**Il, elle,** etc., are of course used to represent a noun.

Que pensez-vous de la nouvelle ? — Elle est surprenante, **mais elle** doit être vraie.
Elle est très bien, cette jeune fille.
A qui ce parapluie ? — **Il** est à moi.

4. In the construction **c'est . . . qui, c'est . . . que,** which French employs to bring any given word into prominence (§§ 322–326).

Je lui ai acheté un chapeau.

C'est moi **qui** lui ai acheté un chapeau.
C'est à lui **que** j'ai acheté un chapeau.
C'est un chapeau **que** je lui ai acheté.

POSSESSIVE PRONOUNS

§ **197.**

Masc.	*Fem.*	*Masc.*	*Fem.*	
le mien	**la mienne**	**les miens**	**les miennes**	*mine*
le tien	**la tienne**	**les tiens**	**les tiennes**	*thine*
le sien	**la sienne**	**les siens**	**les siennes**	*his, hers*
le nôtre	**la nôtre**	**les nôtres**		*ours*
le vôtre	**la vôtre**	**les vôtres**		*yours*
le leur	**la leur**	**les leurs**		*theirs*

Je préfère votre plume à **la mienne.**
Nos parents et **les leurs** ne se connaissent pas.
Si vous n'avez pas votre livre, servez-vous **du mien.**

Note.—**Mien, tien,** etc., are occasionally used in their original adjective function.

Un **mien** ami, *a friend of mine.*
Il empruntait à d'autres des théories qu'il faisait **siennes.**

§ **198.** Idiomatic uses.

Il sera renié par **les siens.** *He will be disowned by his own people.*

And with partitive **du, des.**

Il fut convenu que ma camarade Sophie serait **des nôtres.** . . . *one of our party* (cp. § 118, note).
Il a encore fait **des siennes.** *He's been up to his tricks again.*
Il faut y mettre **du vôtre.** *You must contribute your share (of money, work, energy, etc.).*
La bienfaisance est une habitude de prendre **du sien** pour donner à autrui.

§ **199.** Predicative 'mine,' 'his,' etc., is oftenest expressed by **à moi, à lui,** etc.

A qui sont ces parapluies ? { Ils sont **à nous.** / Ce sont **les nôtres.** }

Ce chapeau est **à moi, à lui.** Ces livres sont **à eux.**

INTERROGATIVE PRONOUNS

§ 200. 1. Of persons, always **qui**, *who, whom.*

Qui vous a dit cela ? **Qui** désirez-vous voir ? **De qui** parlez-vous ! **A qui** pensez-vous ? **Qui** est venu ? **Qui** avez-vous vu ?

Note that interrogative qui is always treated as masculine singular, and that one cannot say : Qui **sont venus** ? Qui est **venue** ?

2. Neuter : **que** (unstressed), *what,* standing in either accusative or predicative relation to the verb to which it clings.

Que désirez-vous ? **Que** devenez-vous ?
Que faire ? **Que** penser ?

Thus also as logical subject.

Qu'est-il arrivé ?

Note : 'What,' subject of a verb, is expressed as shown in § **201** below.

Quoi (stressed), *what,* used (*a*) alone (interrogative or exclamative) ; (*b*) before partitive **de** (§ 171.6), (*c*) after prepositions.

(*a*) **Quoi ?** Que dites-vous ? **Quoi** ! c'est vous !
(*b*) **Quoi** de nouveau ?
(*c*) **De quoi** parlez-vous ? **A quoi** pensez-vous ?
Pourquoi (=Pour quoi) faites-vous cela ?

§ 201. Compound forms, much employed in conversation. The first pronoun is interrogative ; **est-ce** is followed by a relative pronoun or by the conjunction **que**.

Nom. subject.	**qui est-ce qui,** *who.*	**qu'est-ce qui,** *what.*
Accusative.	**qui est-ce que,** *whom.*	**qu'est-ce que,** *what*

Qui est-ce qui vous a dit cela ?
Qui est-ce que vous désirez voir ?
De qui est-ce que vous parlez ? (Que is a conjunction here.)
Qu'est-ce qui est arrivé ? *What has happened ?*
Qu'est-ce **que** vous voulez ?

and frequently :

A quoi est-ce **que** vous pensez ? (Que is a conjunction.)

Notes.—1. In conversation qui est-ce qui is frequently slurred into qu'est-ce qui.

Qu'est-ce qui vous a dit ça ?

2. Qu'est-ce que is used, not only as an accusative, but also as a predicative nominative.

Qu'est-ce que vous devenez ? Qu'est-ce que la grammaire ?

3. An affective adverb is frequently inserted before the relative pronoun.

Qu'est-ce **donc** que tout cet attirail (*finery*) ?
Qu'est-ce **enfin** que la douleur, sinon une illusion . . . *What is pain, after all . . .*

4. The tense of **être** may vary.

Qu'était-ce / **Que serait-ce** } que cette conquête sinon du brigandage ?

5. In conversation the form **qu'est-ce que c'est que** is also used.

Qu'est-ce que c'est que cet homme-là !
Qu'est-ce que c'est que ça ?

§ 202. Lequel, laquelle, lesquels, lesquelles, *which, which one.*

Lequel de ces chapeaux est le vôtre.
Je me sers d'un de ces livres. — **Duquel ?**
Auxquels de ces journaux vous êtes-vous adressé ?
A laquelle des deux donnez-vous la préférence ?

§ 203. In indirect questions

1. Personal **qui, qui est-ce qui,** etc., also **lequel,** remain.

Je voudrais bien savoir **qui** vous a dit cela.
Je ne sais pas **de qui** vous parlez.
Je ne sais pas **qui est-ce qui** vous a dit cela. (Colloquial.)
Dites-moi **lequel** de ces livres vous serait le plus utile.

2. Neuter **quoi** remains.

Je lui demandai **de quoi** il parlait.
Devinez **à quoi** je pense.
Dites-moi **de quoi** vous avez besoin.

Note.—Also, in careful speech :

Dites-moi ce dont vous avez besoin (§ 207).

3. Neuter **que, qu'est-ce qui, qu'est-ce que,** become **ce** + relative **qui, que.**

Dites-moi **ce qui** est arrivé.
Dites-nous **ce que** vous désirez.
On ne sait pas **ce que** vous devenez.

Except before an infinitive, in some idioms with **ne.**

Je ne savais **que** penser de tout cela.
Je n'ai **que** faire de vos souhaits. *I don't want your good wishes.*

RELATIVE PRONOUNS AND ADVERBS

§ **204. Qui.** 1. Nominative subject, *who, which.*

2. Accusative after prepositions, with a person as antecedent, *whom.*

1. Voici une phrase **qui** n'est pas française.
   Ceux **qui** ne sauront pas leur leçon resteront après les autres.
2. Voici la personne **à qui** je pensais.
   J'ai appris cela d'un voyageur **avec qui** je me suis trouvé.

Notes.—(*a*) **Qui** has no antecedent in many proverbs and phrases handed down from the past.

Qui dort dîne. **Qui** s'excuse s'accuse. Sauve **qui** peut !
Qui plus est. *Moreover.* **Qui** pis est. *What is worse.*

(*b*) **Qui** is an indefinite pronoun in the construction:

On se dispersa qui d'un côté, qui de l'autre. *We dispersed, some going one way, some another* (§ 251.4, note).

Also in:

Adressez-vous à qui vous voudrez. Invitez qui vous voudrez.

§ **205. Que** (unstressed). 1. Predicative nominative, *that.*

2. Accusative object, *whom, which, that.*

3. (Adverbial) accusative of measure, *which, that.*

1. Pauvre malheureux **que** je suis !
2. Montrez-moi le livre **que** vous avez acheté.
   Voici M. Dupont, **que** j'amène avec moi.
3. Je regrette les cinq francs **que** ce livre m'a coûté.

§ **206. Quoi** (stressed). Neuter accusative after a preposition, *which, what.*

Il m'a désobéi et il a menti, **en quoi** il est deux fois coupable.
Il exige que ses acteurs aient du talent, **ce en quoi** il a raison.
Ce à quoi j'occupe mon temps ne vous regarde pas.

§ **207. Dont = de qui, de quoi, duquel,** which it usually replaces.

C'est un homme **dont** (or **de qui**) on dit beaucoup de bien.
Voilà le livre **dont** j'ai besoin.
On va vous donner **ce dont** vous avez besoin.
Voici { ce dont il s'agit. / de quoi il s'agit (§ 203.2).
Celui qui n'est content de personne est précisément celui **dont** personne n'est content.

Notes.—(*a*) **Dont** must immediately follow its antecedent and cannot be used when the relative is dependent on a noun governed by a preposition.

Voici l'officier aux ordres de qui (*or* duquel) j'ai obéi.
Je reconnus la maison à la porte **de laquelle** j'avais frappé.

(*b*) The object noun never precedes the verb in French as it does in English when attracted by 'whose.'

Voici les élèves **dont** je vous ai montré **le travail.** *Whose work I showed you.*
Ils se cachèrent dans une salle de classe, **dont** ils fermèrent **la porte** à double tour.

(*c*) **Dont** is never interrogative.

Whose son are you ? De qui êtes-vous le fils ?
Whose book is this ? A qui est ce livre ?

§ **208. Lequel, laquelle, lesquels, lesquelles,** are the stressed forms corresponding to **qui, que.** They are used

1. Nearly always after prepositions when the antecedent is not a person.

Voici l'appareil **avec lequel** j'ai pris ces photographies.
Je lui laissai les adresses **auxquelles** il devrait m'écrire.

2. To stress the relative after a pause, especially in official and pompous language.

Ont comparu trois témoins, **lesquels** ont déclaré reconnaître l'accusé.

3. Always after **parmi** and **entre.**

Les deux messieurs **entre lesquels** je me trouvais assis.
Voilà les rois et les princes **parmi lesquels** on placera ce monarque.

4. To avoid ambiguity, as the compound relative gives a clear indication of gender and number.

Les soldats de César, par le courage **desquels** la Gaule fut vaincue, étaient peu nombreux.
Il épousa une sœur de Colin, **laquelle** le rendit très heureux.
J'ai écrit à un cousin de ma femme, **lequel** pourra me renseigner.
Il tient la barre du gouvernail, **laquelle,** pour être de niveau avec la main qui la dirige, rase le plancher de la poupe.

Note.—**Lequel,** etc., is occasionally used as a relative adjective.

Voici cent francs, **laquelle somme** vous était due par mon père.

§ **209. Où, d'où,** relative adverbs of place and time, *where, when, whence.*

> Le plateau **où** j'avais déposé ma lettre avait disparu.
> Voilà la maison **d'où** il est sorti, **où** il demeure.
> L'année où il fit si froid.
> Je me rappelle le jour **où** je le vis pour la première fois.

Notes.—1. The antecedent to où, when not otherwise specified, is là, which is, however, often omitted.

> **Là où** ont passé les sauterelles, il ne reste que la terre nue.
> Où vous irez, j'irai aussi.

2. **Que** is often used for **où**, as a relative adverb of time.

> L'année qu'il fit si froid.
> Je me rappelle le jour **que** je vous vis pour la première fois.

§ **210.** Neuter 'what' = 'that which,' and neuter 'which' with a clause as antecedent, have as French equivalents **ce qui, ce que,** etc.

Ce qui est très embarrassant, **Ce que** j'avais oublié, **Ce dont** je ne me souvenais pas, **Ce à quoi** je n'ai pas pensé,	c'est qu'il n'y a pas de trains le dimanche.

Il n'y a pas de trains le dimanche,	**ce qui** est très embarrassant. **ce que** j'avais oublié. **ce dont** je ne me souvenais pas. **ce à quoi** je n'ai pas pensé.

Notes.—(*a*) **Ce** is also required after **tout.**

> Faites **tout ce** que vous voudrez. *Do whatever you like.*

(*b*) **Ce** is sometimes omitted before **quoi.** *Cf.* § 206.

§ **211.** Note the important differences in the use of interrogative and of relative **qui, que.**

Interrogative	*Relative*
Qui. Nominative and accusative, of persons only.	**Qui.** 1. Nominative of all three genders. 2. Accusative, of persons, after prepositions.
Que. Object accusative neuter.	**Que.** Object accusative of all three genders.

PERSONAL PRONOUNS

§ 212. UNSTRESSED — STRESSED

SINGULAR

Persons.	*Nom. Subj.*	*Accus.*	*Dat.*	*Genit.*	*Nom. and Accus.*
1st	je	me	me		moi
2nd	tu	te	te		toi
3rd masc.	il	le }	lui, y }	en	lui
3rd fem.	elle	la }	lui, y }	en	elle
3rd neut.	il	le	y }	en	
3rd reflex.		se	se		soi

PLURAL

Persons.	*Nom. Subj.*	*Accus.*	*Dat.*	*Genit.*	*Nom. and Accus.*
1st	nous	nous	nous		nous
2nd	vous	vous	vous		vous
3rd masc.	ils	les	leur, y	en	eux
3rd fem.	elles	les	leur, y	en	elles
3rd reflex.		se	se		soi

§ 213. The Unstressed Pronouns. These cling to the verb, which as a rule they immediately precede (§ 329). The **subject** pronouns may follow the verb, in which case they take the stress when at the end of a word-group, with the exception of **je** (§ 313, note). The object pronouns also follow the verb in the imperative mood (§ 331), when they may also take the stress.

§ 214. Je, nous are used as in English. **Nous** is employed occasionally as a 'plural of majesty,' and as an 'editorial' plural. The concords are then in the singular.

> **Nous** avons **décrété** et **décrétons** par ces présentes . . .
> En présentant ce livre au public, **nous** sommes **convaincu** de son utilité.

§ 215. Tu, vous. Tu (toi, ton, tes, etc.) is the usual mode of address in the singular in speaking to young children, between near relatives, between intimate friends, between children attending the same school, between soldiers of the same unit, etc.

> **Tu** es un nouveau (*a new boy*), n'est-ce pas ? Comment t'appelles-**tu** ? Quel est **ton** professeur ?

Otherwise the usual form of address is **vous**, which has both plural and singular function, like 'you' in English, with corresponding plural or singular concords.

> **Vous** êtes bien **aimable**, monsieur. **Vous** êtes bien **aimables**, messieurs.

§ **216. Il, ils, elle, elles** are used of both persons and things, according to their gender.

La sentinelle voulut avertir ses camarades. **Elle** appela, mais **ils** n'entendirent pas.

Pourquoi cette porte est-**elle** ouverte ?

The third person is also used deferentially in addressing superiors.

Si **madame veut** bien attendre au salon.

Monsieur veut-il se donner la peine de s'asseoir ?

Quand elle me voyait lasse de coudre, elle disait en essayant de prendre un air hautain : " Puisque **Mademoiselle** n'aime pas la couture, **elle** n'a qu'à prendre le balai." (Ironical use.)

Note.—In this use, the plural of **monsieur, madame, mademoiselle**, is **ces messieurs, ces dames, ces demoiselles.**

Si **ces dames** veulent bien attendre.

Que prendront **ces messieurs** ?

§ **217. Il** is also used (*a*) as a neuter subject to impersonal verbs, and (*b*) as a provisional neuter subject to **être** when the logical subject is a clause following the predicate (§ 71).

(*a*) **Il** pleut. **Il** s'agit de vous. **Il** y a des plumes dans le tiroir.

Il est (*There are*) des pays où la vie est facile.

(*b*) **Il** est difficile **de travailler** pendant les vacances.

Il pourra être difficile **de le retrouver.**

Note to (*a*).—The impersonal verb is never attracted to the plural as is the case when the subject is **ce** (§ 196.2).

§ **218.** 1. **Le, la, les** are accusative objects.

Je connais Henri, je **le** verrai demain.

Cette maison, je **la** vois encore.

Ces abus, je suis décidé à **les** dénoncer.

2. **Lui, leur** are dative objects.

Je **lui** ai écrit et **lui** ai avoué la vérité.

Lorsqu'il (*or* elle) mourut, ce fut son frère qui **lui** succéda.

Voulez-vous **leur** permettre de m'accompagner ?

3. The pronouns **me, te, nous, vous, se** are either (*a*) accusative, or (*b*) dative objects.

(*a*) Il **m'**aime. On **te** voit. Il **se** vante.

Le maître **nous** a punis. Il **vous** invitera.

(*b*) Il **m'**a écrit et **m'**a avoué la vérité.

Je **te** permets de sortir.

Je **vous** donne ces dix francs.

Il est amusant, il **vous** imitera n'importe quel acteur (' Ethic ' dative).

§ 219. 1. The verb may govern two of the object pronouns given above, an accusative and a dative, **provided that the accusative is le, la,** or **les.** The accusative being thus clearly indicated, the other pronoun must be in the dative, and no ambiguity can arise.

Je **vous le** donne. Je **le lui** donne.
Il **nous les** prêtera. On **me l'a** dit.

Mon frère, je **vous le** présenterai volontiers. *I shall introduce him to you.*

Comme elle ne savait pas les cantiques, sœur Marie-Aimée me chargea de **les lui** apprendre.

2. If the accusative is not **le, la,** or **les,** a stressed pronoun (**§ 234**) governed by à takes the place of the unstressed dative.

Je **vous** présenterai **à lui.** (Not 'Je vous lui présenterai.')

Il **se** présentait **à elle** toutes les fois qu'elle passait. (Not 'se lui.')

Je ne **me** fie pas **à eux.** (Not 'me leur.')

Un hasard **nous** révèle **à nous-mêmes.** (Not 'nous nous !')

On **vous** avait montrée **à moi** comme une jeune fille vaniteuse et arrogante. (Not 'vous me,' or 'me vous.')

Notes.—1. An 'ethic' dative (affective) is, however, occasionally found with the indirect object.

La mule **vous lui** détacha un coup de sabot.

2. In addition to any one, or two, of the pronouns given above, **en** or **y** (§§ 224-230), or both, may occur before the verb.

J'étais au concert, mais je ne **vous y** ai pas vu. — Vous ne **m'en** aviez pas parlé. — Il **y en** aura encore un samedi, voulez-vous **nous y** accompagner ?

Votre bracelet, je vous **l'en** repêcherai, de la rivière.

§ 220. As a rule, when the verb has two objects, one is the accusative 'of the thing,' and the other the dative 'of the person.' It is only seldom that both objects are persons, as in **Je vous le présenterai, Je vous présenterai à lui,** and with a number of verbs the indirect object is always a stressed form governed by à when the direct object is a person, *i.e.* it ceases to have the value of an object, and takes on an adverbial function similar to that shown in § 237.1.

Le Seigneur l'avait envoyé **à eux** pour leur enseigner la loi divine. *Had sent him to them.*

(Although one would say : Ce lièvre, je **le leur** avais envoyé par un domestique. *Had sent it to them.*)

Lors même que Shakespeare représente des personnages dont la destinée a été illustre, il intéresse **ses spectateurs à eux** par des sentiments purement naturels.

§ **221.** A dative (of advantage, interest) is often used loosely in French where English would show quite different constructions.

Je ne **lui** savais pas tant de courage. *I didn't know he possessed so much courage.*
On **me** suppose de la fortune. *I am supposed to be well off.*
Vous sentez-vous les qualités nécessaires pour réussir ? *Do you feel that you possess the qualities requisite for success ?*
Je **lui** trouve mauvaise mine. *I don't think he looks well.*
Dès qu'il eut aperçu le roi, il **lui** tira une flèche. *He shot an arrow at him.*
Je fus surprise par un brouillard si épais qu'il **me** fut impossible de reconnaître mon chemin. *That I found it impossible.*

§ **222.** 1. **Le, la, les,** and 2. neuter **le** (invariable), are used not only as accusatives, but also as predicative nominatives (which must not be omitted, as they sometimes are in English).

1. Êtes-vous les parents de cet enfant ? — Nous **les** sommes. *We are.*
2. Êtes-vous fatigués ? — Nous **le** sommes. *We are.*
   Ceux qui sont amis de tout le monde ne **le** sont de personne.
   Nous n'étions pas riches, mais nous **le** sommes devenus.
   Les villages étaient presque abandonnés, les fermes **l'**étaient complètement.
   Voulez-vous être un moment satisfait ? vengez-vous. Voulez-vous **l'**être longtemps, pardonnez.

Note.—French grammarians insist on careful distinction between **le, la, les,** standing for a noun (example 1 above), and neuter **le** standing for an adjective or adjectival noun (examples 2). But both in colloquial and in written French there is a tendency to use neuter **le** in all cases.

Êtes-vous les parents de cet enfant ? — Nous **le** sommes.
Êtes-vous mère ? (*Are you a mother,* adjectival use) — Je **le** suis.
Êtes-vous sa mère ? — Je **le** suis.

§ **223.** 1. Neuter **le** is also used as an object or as a predicative complement standing for a clause.

Vous êtes fâchée, je **le** sais. *You are vexed, I know.*
Le lendemain matin il est vêtu comme il **l'**a désiré.
Il reviendra bientôt, je **le** sais.
Sois une lumière sans chercher à **le** paraître. (**Le** = être une lumière.)

In an answer, however, the use of **le** is optional.

Il reviendra bientôt. — Je **le** sais. Or: Je sais.

As also in the second term of a comparison.

Il est plus riche { que vous ne **le** pensez.
                   { que vous ne pensez.

2. On the other hand, with verbs such as **croire, juger,** followed by a predicative adjective, and an infinitive clause as object, French does not insert a pronoun to herald the object clause, as is done in English.

C'est une erreur que je **crois nécessaire** de signaler. *This is a mistake which I deem* it *necessary to point out.*

Je **jugeai prudent** de ne pas révéler mes projets. *I thought* it *wise not to disclose my plans.*

Note.—Compare also : Nous **entendons dire** assez souvent que l'ignorance est mère de l'adversité. *We hear* it *not seldom said that ignorance is the mother of adversity.*

§ **224. En** stands for (*a*) a **noun** governed by **prepositional de** ; (*b*) a **partitive noun** ; (*c*) a **clause** governed by **de** ; (*d*) **de là.**

(*a*) Vous avez appris la nouvelle ? — Oui, nous **en** parlions. (En = de la nouvelle.)

J'ai bien reçu la valise, mais je n'en ai pas la clef (§ **181**).

(*b*) Si vous n'avez pas de livres, on vous **en** prêtera. (En = des livres.)

Le duc d'Enghien eut autant de soin de les épargner qu'il **en** avait pris pour les vaincre.

Du pain, il y **en** a dans la corbeille.

Comment revenir ? De traces, il n'y **en** avait pas.

(*c*) Vous n'avez pas de fautes ? J'en suis fort heureux (En = de ce que vous n'avez pas de fautes.)

Vous remplacer, il n'en est pas capable.

(*d*) Vous avez été à Londres ? — Oui, j'**en** arrive. (En = de là, de Londres.)

Notes. To (*b*).—Partitive en may stand as logical subject to a verb.

Me voilà inondé de violettes. Il **en** coule sur ma table, sur mes genoux, sur mon tapis. Il s'**en** glisse dans mon gilet, dans mes manches.

To (*c*).—En also stands for a clause not introduced by **de,** when le cannot be used because the main verb already has a direct object.

Thus, on the one hand :

Je ne suis pas l'offenseur ; je **le** déclare hautement. (Le = que je ne suis pas l'offenseur. § **223.1.**)

But, on the other hand :

Je ne suis pas l'offenseur ; j'**en** prends mes camarades à **témoin.** (En = (de ce) que je ne suis pas l'offenseur. Neuter 'le' cannot stand for the clause, because 'prends' has already a direct object : 'mes camarades.')

Je lui rendrai raison (*I shall give him satisfaction, shall fight*), je vous **en** donne à tous ma parole d'honneur. (En = que je lui rendrai raison.)

§ **225. Partitive en** always replaces a noun when the latter is omitted after (*a*) qualifying adjectives; (*b*) adverbs or other expressions of quantity, including numerals; (*c*) indefinite adjectives.

(*a*) La pauvreté n'est pas un vice, mais la colère **en** est un grand.

(*b*) Si vous avez peu de patience, moi j'en ai beaucoup.
Faut-il du thé ? — Oui, achetez-**en** deux livres.
Il me faut des gants, achetez-m'**en** deux paires.
Jules a six ans, Pierre **en** a quatre.
Il me faut au moins cinq francs. — Tenez, **en** voici dix.

(*c*) Prenez ce crayon; j'**en** ai un; j'**en** ai un autre; j'**en** ai plusieurs.

Note.—J'en ai. *I have some.* J'en ai un(e). *I have one.*

§ **226.** The use of **en** to replace a partitive noun extends to persons.

Des amis, j'en ai beaucoup.

With regard to nouns denoting a person, governed by **prepositional de,** usage varies. The tendency is to use a stressed pronoun governed by **de.**

J'ai reçu **d'elle** une lettre charmante.

But the unstressed form is often preferred, especially if the person has just been mentioned.

Il rencontra la fille d'un seigneur. Il **en** devint amoureux et l'épousa.

§ **227.** For **en** replacing the possessive, see § 181.

§ **228. En** has an adverbial function, = **pour cela, à cause de cela,** in comparative clauses.

Vous auriez cent mille francs de rente, **en** seriez-vous plus heureux ? *Would you be the happier* on that account, any *the happier.*

Pense deux fois avant de parler une, et tu **en** parleras deux fois mieux.

§ **229. Y** stands for (*a*) a **noun** governed by **à, dans, en, sous,** etc.; (*b*) a **clause** governed by **à**; (*c*) **là** (= either *to* or *at* a place).

(*a*) Quel terrible accident! J'**y** pense sans cesse. (Y = à cet accident.)
Prenez ce miroir et regardez-vous-**y**. (Y = dans ce miroir.)
Jean s'était senti tout de suite sous le charme. Il **y** était encore. (Y = sous le charme.)

(*b*) Il me fallait tuer les poules et les lapins. Je ne pouvais m'**y** décider. (Y=à les tuer.)
Rien ne m'empêchera de parler, de les dénoncer . . . quand (§ 388, note) je devrais **y** perdre ma place. (Y=à parler, à les dénoncer.)

(*c*) J'aime la campagne. **J'y** vais demain. **J'y** demeure volontiers.

§ **230.** **Y** is used with reference to persons only after a few verbs, such as **penser, songer, croire, se fier, s'intéresser à** qqn, and even with these only when a stressed form (noun or pronoun) has been used immediately before, and it is not desirable to repeat the stress.

Pensez-vous quelquefois **à lui** ? Mais oui, j'**y** pense, et je m'**y** intéresse.
Cet homme-là, vous savez, ne vous **y** fiez pas.

§ **231.** The pronouns **en, y,** and neuter **le** are used in many idiomatic phrases in which the noun which they replace has remained unexpressed, or was lost sight of long ago.

Il m'en veut. (En=du mal.) *He bears me ill-will, a grudge.*
Il en a fait de belles ! *He has been up to fine tricks !*
Où **en** sommes-nous ? *How far have we got (in the reading, etc.) ?*
Ne vous **en** prenez pas à moi. *Don't blame me.*

Je vous **y** prends ! *I've caught you in the act !*
Il **y** va de notre vie. *Our lives are at stake.*
La brave petite chevrette, comme elle **y** allait de bon cœur ! *How heartily she enjoyed herself !*
On n'**y** voit pas ici. *One cannot see here.*

Vous **le** prenez de bien haut ! *You are very peremptory !*
Ce fut la prudence qui l'emporta. *Prudence carried the day.*

Note.—**En** also serves to differentiate the impersonal construction **il en est de . . .** '*it is with . . .*' from **il est**=**il y a.**

Il en est des vers comme des melons : s'ils ne sont pas excellents ils ne valent rien. *It is with poetry as with melons . . .*
(**Il est des vers comme des melons** would mean '*There is poetry which resembles melons*' ; *i.e.* **des** would be understood as partitive.)
Il en fut de lui comme **de** ses camarades. *He suffered the same fate as his comrades.*
En est-il vraiment ainsi ? *Is it really so ?*

§ **232.** The **accusative** pronouns, partitive **en,** and adverbial **y** are also governed by the prepositions **voici** and **voilà,** which have a verbal origin (' vois ici,' ' vois là ').

Me voici. **La** voilà. Du pain, **en** voilà.
Nous **y** voilà enfin ! *We've got there at last !*

§ **233.** For the uses of **se,** see pronominal verbs, § **70.**

§ 234. The Stressed Pronouns.

moi	toi	lui	elle	soi
nous	vous	eux	elles	

The stressed forms are used

1. When the pronoun cannot cling to the verb, *e.g.* (*a*) when it is used alone ; (*b*) when it is the second term of a comparison ; (*c*) when it is limited by **ne . . . que** ; (*d*) when it is the antecedent of a relative pronoun ; (*e*) when it is governed by a preposition ; (*f*) when it is predicative after **c'est.**

(*a*) Qui est là ? — **Moi.**
(*b*) Je suis plus âgé que **toi,** que **lui,** qu'**eux.**
(*c*) On n'entend que **toi** !
(*d*) **Toi** qui le connais, va le voir.
(*e*) Nous sommes arrivés **avant eux.**
Ce livre est **à moi** (§ 199).
(*f*) **C'est moi, c'est toi, ce sont eux** (§ 196.2).
C'est lui qui a raison.

Note to (*d*).—A relative pronoun cannot have an unstressed personal pronoun clinging to the verb for its antecedent. In such a sentence as '*He hates me who am not so brave as he,*' the object pronoun must be duplicated.

Il me hait, **moi** qui ne suis pas aussi brave que **lui.**

2. When it is desired, or necessary, to stress the subject or object. If the pronoun is of the first or second person, or an object of the third person, the stressed form is nearly always additional to the corresponding unstressed pronoun. (Duplication, § 323.)

If the pronoun is a subject of the third person, it need not be duplicated.

Subject pronouns.

Toi, tu as raison. Tu as raison, **toi.**
Vous, vous avez raison.
Moi, j'étais en arrière, mais **lui** a tout entendu.
Lui seul peut me sauver.
Il était évident que **lui aussi** était séduit par la physionomie franche et ouverte du conscrit.
Le vieux bûcheron, qui croyait les enfants bien endormis, s'en alla à la messe de minuit. Mais **eux** s'étaient levés aussitôt après son départ.

A double subject is always stressed.

Lui et son père sont là. **Lui et elle** m'ont écrit.
Vous et moi nous y arriverons bien. *Shall manage it.*

Object pronouns.

Vous **m'**accusez, **moi** !
Lui, je **le** connais. Je **le** connais, **lui**. *Him I know.*
Vous **me** dites cela, **à moi** ! (§ 325.1.)

There is no duplication when an alternative is presented.

Parlez-vous **à moi ou à lui** ?

§ **235. Moi, toi** are used as objects in the positive imperative except before **y** and **en**. (But *cf.* § 331, note *b.*)

Donnez-le-**moi**. Assieds-**toi**. Montrez-**moi** ça.
Donnez-**m'en**. Va-**t'en**.
Tiens, voilà une chaise libre. Assieds-**t'y** bien vite !

§ **236.** 1. The stressed forms may be strengthened by the adjunction of **même**=' self,' and are then called emphatic pronouns.

Je l'ai fait **moi-même**. *I did it myself.* **Eux-mêmes** l'ont entendu
Parlez à **lui-même**. C est à **nous-mêmes** qu'il a parlé.
Martine me poussa sur un banc, et **elle-même** alla s'asseoir sur celui qui était devant moi.

2. In the plural the pronoun is often strengthened by the adjunction of **autres**. This applies especially to **nous** and **vous**.

Je sais que **vous autres**, jeunesses d'à présent, vous ne croyez plus aux fées.
Mais, dit le paysan, vous êtes soldats, **vous autres** ; ils me pendront, **moi**, s'ils me prennent avec vous.
Nous ne buvons guère de thé, **nous autres** Français.

§ **237.** A person is represented by the stressed form of the pronoun, governed by **à** :

1. When its relation to the verb is that of an adverb equivalent answering the question " whither ? " (Cp. § 220.)

J'allai **à lui** sans hésitation.
Laissez venir **à moi** les petits enfants.

Note.—But the dative is used if there is no motion in space. (Cp. § 221.)

L'ennui **lui** vint. Cette robe ne **me** va pas.
C'est une heureuse idée qui **m'**est venue d'aller le trouver.

Also, very frequently with **revenir**.

Ah ! Je savais bien que vous **me** reviendriez !

(In all of which **me** is a dative of advantage, and not to be taken as adverbial.)

2. After **être**, to indicate possession (§ 199).

Cette maison est **à eux**.

Note.—But : Cette maison **leur** appartient.

3. **As** indirect object to pronominal verbs (§ 219.2).

Ne vous fiez pas **à eux.**

4. As indirect object to certain verbs and verb-phrases, such as **penser, songer ; avoir recours, avoir affaire, prendre garde.**

Je ne les ai pas oubliés ; je pense souvent **à eux.**
Je me permets d'avoir recours à toi.
Encore une sottise de ce genre, et vous **aurez affaire à moi.**

§ **238.** The stressed forms are used chiefly of persons; with reference to things, they are avoided as much as possible. Thus, English 'it,' governed by a preposition, is often replaced in French by an adverb.

Voici une boîte, mais il n'y a rien dedans. *Nothing in it.*
Sur le quai il y avait une malle, et un voyageur à côté. *Beside it.* Au bout d'un instant il s'assit dessus. *On it.*
Une rangée de pupitres avec des chaises derrière. *Behind them.*

§ **239. Soi.** The stressed reflexive pronoun **soi**, according to traditional grammar, may be used only with reference to a subject which is indefinite. It is thus used (*a*) as an accusative ; (*b*) as a nominative, either predicative or forming the second term of a comparison.

(*a*) On doit rarement parler **de soi.**
Chacun **pour soi** et Dieu pour tous.
Il ne faut pas toujours penser à **soi** en ce monde.

(*b*) Viennent la fortune et les honneurs, il faut rester **soi.**
On a souvent besoin d'un plus petit que soi.

Note.—As a matter of fact, **soi** is constantly used, alternatively with **lui, elle,** referring to a subject which is quite definite.

Compare :

(*a*) Il jette **autour de lui** un coup d'œil craintif.
L'artiste qui doute souvent **de lui-même,** est fort ; **l'artiste qui** ne croit jamais **en lui** est perdu.

And :

(*b*) Un sans-le-sou qui inspecte **autour de soi** le pavé.
Mais aussitôt il se cligna malicieusement de l'œil **à soi-même.**
Un sacrifice volontaire laisse toujours **après soi,** dans l'âme qui se l'impose, quelque chose de fortifiant.

§ **240. Soi** may be strengthened by the adjunction of **même** (*cf.* § 236.1).

Pour s'assurer qu'une chose sera bien faite, il faut la faire **soi-même.**

INDEFINITE PRONOUNS, ADJECTIVES, AND ADVERBS

Under this heading are traditionally gathered various words of manifold function, some of which might equally well be classified as demonstratives, and others as words indicating number; while on the other hand the 'indefinite article' properly belongs here.

§ **241. On,** unstressed pronoun subject, clinging to a verb always singular: *one, people, we, you, they,* used in a vague sense.

As an elegance, French often has **l'on,** especially to avoid 'hiatus.'

> **On** ne fait pas toujours ce qu'**on** veut.
> Que dira-t-**on**, si **l'on** vient à le savoir?
> **On** ferme les grilles à neuf heures. *The gates are closed at nine o'clock.*
> Eh bien, Juliette, a-t-**on** été sage aujourd'hui?

Notes.—1. Predicative nouns and adjectives agree according to the sense.

> On n'est pas toujours jeune et belle, madame.
> Encore, **on** serait seuls, on risquerait la partie.

Note also the following nominative absolute:

> On porta le cadavre, têtes nues, sur la grande table de la salle basse.

(Here, tête nue would imply that the *body* was bare-headed.)

2. The oblique case corresponding to on is generally **vous**; the possessive, **son, sa, ses**; the reflexive pronoun **se**.

> Il en est de l'amitié comme de toutes choses: **on** n'en reconnaît le prix exact que lorsque le sort **vous** l'arrache.
> On ne peut pas toujours agir à **sa** guise.
> Je pense qu'on a bien tort de **se** quitter.
> On croit toujours que **sa** fille **vous** ressemble.—*H. Bataille.*

§ **242. Quelque, quelqu'un, quelques-uns,** etc.

1. **Quelque(s),** adjective: *some, some little, a few.*

> J'ai eu **quelque** difficulté à résoudre ce problème.
> **Quelques** centaines de personnes furent blessées.
> Il y a **quelques** années qu'il est mort. *He died a few years ago.*

Compare: Il y a des années qu'il est mort. *He died years ago* (with affective stress on des années, *years*).

2. **Quelque,** adverb and invariable, modifies numeral adjectives.
Quelque deux cents personnes furent blessées. *Some two hundred . . .*

3. **Quelqu'un,** masculine pronoun: *some one, somebody.*
Je connais **quelqu'un** qui pourra vous conseiller.
Quelqu'un de haut placé l'aida à faire son chemin (§ 171.6).

Note.—**Quelqu'un** with feminine **quelqu'une** occurs only before a partitive noun.
Quelqu'une de ses amies lui aura raconté l'affaire. *One or other of her friends.*

4. **Quelques-uns, quelques-unes,** pronoun: *some, a few.*
Quels beaux fruits! Achetons-en **quelques-uns.**
Quelques-unes de nos amies vont venir.

5. **Je ne sais qui:** *some one or other, I forget who(m).*
Je ne sais qui disait un jour que tous les hommes sont des ânes.
Il s'est adressé à **je ne sais qui.**

Also used as a noun:
Il passe son temps avec des **je ne sais qui.**

6. **N'importe qui,** *anyone.*
Adressez-vous à **n'importe qui. N'importe qui** vous renseignera.

§ **243. Quelque chose, autre chose,** etc., neuter pronouns.

1. **Quelque chose:** *something.*
Quelque chose me dit qu'il viendra aujourd'hui.
Nous avons appris **quelque chose de** curieux (§ 171.6).

2. **Autre chose:** *something else.*
Je n'aime pas ça, donnez-moi **autre chose.**
Nous avons appris **autre chose de** curieux.

3. **Pas grand'chose:** *not much.*
Je n'ai **pas grand'chose** à vous apprendre.
Qu'est-ce que vous faites à cette classe? — **Pas grand'chose d'**intéressant (§ 171.6).

4. **Peu de chose:** *little.*
Peu de chose me suffira.
J'ai **peu de chose d'**intéressant à vous apprendre.

5. **Je ne sais quoi:** *something or other.*
On lui a raconté **je ne sais quoi d'**assez stupide (§ 171.6).

§ 244. Plusieurs, certain, maint, etc.

1. **Plusieurs**: *several*, (*a*) adjective, (*b*) pronoun.

(*a*) Je l'ai vu **plusieurs** fois.
(*b*) **Plusieurs** l'ont vu. J'ai parlé à **plusieurs** de vos amis.

2. **Certain(s)**: *certain*, (*a*) adjective, (*b*) pronoun.

(*a*) C'est (une) **certaine** personne haut placée qui me l'a assuré. Cette règle est sujette à (de) **certaines** exceptions.
(*b*) **Certains** affirment que la légende dit vrai.

Note.—**Certain**, in stressed position (*i.e.* following the noun), and when predicative, is a qualifying adjective.

Je vous apporte des nouvelles **certaines**. *Reliable news.*
Il va pleuvoir, c'est certain.

3. **Maint**, adjective: *many a*, an old word used only in literary French.

Il lui rendit service en **mainte** circonstance.
C'est arrivé **mainte(s)** et **mainte(s)** fois.

Note.—In normal speech, **plus d'un(e)** is used instead of **maint**.

Il lui a rendu service en **plus d'une** circonstance.
C'est arrivé **plus d'une** fois.

4. **Différents, divers**, adjectives: *different, diverse, various.*

J'en ai parlé à **différentes** personnes, à **diverses** personnes.

Note.—When predicative, or in stressed position, these are qualifying adjectives.

On rencontre cette légende sous les formes **les plus diverses**.
Je vous trouve **tout différent**, aujourd'hui.

§ 245. Personne, rien, etc.

1. **Personne**, pronoun masculine singular: *any one, no one.*

(*a*) **Affirmative** in meaning, but used (in preference to **quelqu'un**) when a negative answer is expected or implied.

Personne a-t-il jamais songé à cela !
Si seulement je connaissais **personne** à qui m'adresser !

(*b*) **Negative**, with **ne** expressed or understood, or with **sans**.

Personne n'est venu ? — **Personne**. Absolument **personne**.
Je **n'**ai rencontré **personne** d'assez aimable pour me renseigner (§ 171.6).
Il est parti **sans** prévenir **personne**.

Note.—This pronoun, always masculine, must be distinguished from **la personne**, *person*, always feminine.

Je m'assis auprès d'une **personne** longue et maigre que les enfants appelaient "mon oncle."

2. **Rien,** pronoun neuter singular: *anything, nothing.*

(*a*) **Affirmative** (see **personne** above).

Avez-vous jamais **rien** vu d'aussi drôle (§ 171.6)?

(*b*) **Negative.**

Rien ne l'intéresse. Qu'est-ce que vous faites? — **Rien.**
Il est parti **sans rien** dire.
Il **ne** peut y avoir **rien** de parfait.

Notes.—(*a*) **Rien** usually precedes the past participle and the **infinitive**, losing its stress. See the examples above, and also § 333.3.

(*b*) **Rien** is used without **ne** in many phrases.

C'est pour **rien**! *That's dirt cheap!*
Sa fortune est réduite **à rien.**

(*c*) **Rien que** is used to modify a verb in the infinitive (§ 271, note).

Rien qu'à le voir on le devine notaire. *Only to see him you can tell him for an attorney.*

(*d*) **Rien** is also a noun, = *trifle.*

Il se fâche pour un rien. Il s'occupe **à des riens.**

§ 246. Chaque, chacun.

1. **Chaque,** adjective, singular: *each.*

Donnez-nous aujourd'hui notre pain de **chaque jour.**
Chaque élève apportera une contribution.

2. **Chacun,** pronoun, singular: *each* (*one*).

Chacune de ces lignes contient une vérité profonde.
Voici un gâteau pour **chacun** de vous.

Note.—**Chaque** may be used familiarly for **chacun** in the **construction**

Ces poulets coûtent trois francs **chaque.**

§ 247. Tout, tous, adjective, pronoun, and adverb.

1. Adjective. (*a*) The noun (singular) is not otherwise determined: *any and every.*

Le travail est la loi de la vie, la loi de **toute** création et de **tout** progrès. **Toute** profession honnête est honorable.

(*b*) The noun is particularized in the singular: *the whole, all.*

J'ai dépensé **tout mon** argent.
Je l'ai attendu **toute la** journée.

(*c*) The noun is particularized in the plural: *all, every.*

Il vient **tous les** jours. **Tous ces** livres sont à moi.
La nature est un livre ouvert à **tous les** yeux.

Note.—The article is, or may be, omitted in a few phrases of long standing.

Nous étions enveloppés **de toutes parts.**
Il y avait là des personnes **de toutes sortes.**
Des mouches **de toutes couleurs** tournaient autour de moi.
On vous a cherché **de tous** (les) côtés. Venez **tous** (les) **deux.**

2. Pronoun, stressed. (*a*) Singular neuter: *all, everything.*

Votre silence, votre confusion, **tout** vous accuse.
Voilà **tout** ce que je sais (§ **210,** note *a*).

Note.—Neuter **tout** generally precedes the past participle and the infinitive, losing its stress (§ 333.3).

Laissez-moi **tout** vous dire. Je lui ai **tout** raconté.

(*b*) Plural: *all.* The masculine is pronounced [tuːs].

Ils sont **tous** là. Elles sont **toutes** là.
Tous étaient venus à ma rencontre.

Note.—Used occasionally in the singular masc. or fem.

L'âme d'un gourmand est **toute** dans son palais (*palate*).

3. Adverb: *quite, entirely, very.*

Maître Sylvain disait qu'il (*i.e.* son frère) était **tout** le portrait de leur mère. *The very image.*
Et **tout** là-bas, à l'autre bout du dortoir, il y avait Colette.
Ses cheveux sont **tout** blancs. Elle était **tout** émue.

But: Elle était **toute** petite. For this concord, see § **418.**

Notes.—1. **Tout** may not be followed by a partitive pronoun, as is done with 'all' and 'both' in English.

Nous l'avons **tous** entendu, or Nous **tous** l'avons entendu. *All* of us *heard it.*
Il y allait de leur bonheur **à tous.** *The happiness of all* of them *was at stake.*
Nous avions **tous les deux** des larmes aux yeux. *The eyes of both* of us *were wet.*

2. For neuter **tout** = *all, everything,* a stronger form **toutes choses** is sometimes used. Cp. the use of 'all things' in English.

Toutes choses deviennent possibles pour celui qui les considère comme telles.
Par-dessus **toutes choses,** soyez bons.

3. 'Everyone' = **tout le monde.**

Tout le monde se plaint de sa mémoire et personne ne se plaint de son jugement.

To avoid ambiguity, one nearly always expresses 'the whole world' as **le monde entier.**

§ 248. Aucun, nul, etc.

1. **Aucun**, pronoun and adjective. (*a*) **Affirmative**: *some, any.*

  Aucuns prétendent qu'il est encore en vie.
  Avez-vous **aucune** intention de faire ce voyage ?

(*b*) **Negative**, with **ne** expressed or understood, or **sans**: *no, none.*

  De tous ces élèves, **aucun n'a** répondu.
  Quelle réponse a-t-il faite ! **Aucune.**
  J'ai dit cela **sans aucune** intention de vous blesser.

2. **Nul, nulle**, pronoun and adjective, negative: *no, no one.*

  Nul n'est prophète dans son pays.
  Il **n'**avait **nulle** cause de se plaindre.

Note.—**Nul** is also a qualifying adjective.
  Le testament fut déclaré **nul**. *Null and void.*
  C'est une partie **nulle**. *A drawn game, a draw.*

3. **Pas un(e)**, pronoun and adjective : *not one.*

  Pas une amie **ne** lui reste. **Pas un ne** répondit.

Note.—Also used in familiar speech in the construction
  Il connaît Paris comme **pas un**. *His knowledge of Paris is unique.*
  Elle chante comme **pas une**. *She's a rare singer.*

§ 249. Tel, un tel, pareil.

1. **Tel, telle.** (*a*) Pronoun : *such* (*a one*).

  Tel qui rit vendredi, dimanche pleurera.

(*b*) Adjective: *like, such, such and such.*

  Tel père, **tel** fils. **Telle** fut sa réponse.
  Son avarice est **telle**, qu'il vole la pâtée à son chien.
  On me dit de me rendre à **tel** endroit, et de faire **telle** et **telle** chose.

2. **Un(e) tel(le)**: *such, such a, so and so.*

  Je n'ai jamais ressenti **une telle** douleur. *Such a pain.*
  De tels sentiments vous font honneur.
  J'arrive : on me présente à M. **un tel**, puis à Mme **une telle.**

3. **Pareil, pareille**, adjective : *such a,* when spoken with indignation or other strong feeling.

  A-t-on jamais vu { une conduite **pareille**! / une **pareille** conduite! }

Note.—**Pareil** is also a qualifying adjective = *similar, like.*
  Vous ne trouverez nulle part une étoffe **pareille** à celle-ci.

§ **250. Même,** adjective, neuter pronoun, and adverb.

1. Adjective preceding the noun, or in the predicate: *same.*
   Nous avons la **même** leçon qu'hier.
   Riches ou pauvres, ils furent toujours les **mêmes**.

2. Adjective following the noun or pronoun: *very, self.*
   La probité s'effarouche de l'ombre **même** d'un soupçon.
   Les ennemis **mêmes** de Napoléon ne pouvaient lui refuser le génie.
   C'est cela **même**! *That's the very thing!*
   Nous l'avons vu nous-**mêmes** (§ 236.1).

3. Neuter.
   Cela revient au **même**. *It comes to the same thing.*

4. Adverb: *even.*
   Ceux **même** qui le connaissaient le mieux ne le comprenaient pas. Il en fit un secret **même** à ses amis.

Note the predicative phrases **être, mettre qqn, à même de faire qqch.**
Il n'est pas encore **à même de** gagner sa vie. *Not yet fit, ready, to earn his living.*
Le père doit mettre ses enfants **à même d'**apprendre un état. *Should give the children the opportunity to learn a trade.*

§ **251. Un, autre, autrui,** etc.

1. **Un, une, l'un, l'une** are used as pronouns, especially

(*a*) With a dependent partitive noun.
   Prêtez-moi **un** de ces livres.
   C'est (**l'**)**un** de vos amis qui me l'a dit.

(*b*) In conjunction with **l'autre.**

Note.—**Un, une,** used as adjectives, are called the 'indefinite article' (§ 169).

2. **Autre,** pronoun and adjective: *other.*
   Dites cela à d'**autres**!
   Je vous dirai cela une **autre** fois.

Note.—For **autres** used in apposition to a personal pronoun, see § 236.2.

3. **Autrui,** pronoun, always stressed: *others,* in a general sense.
   Il vaut mieux se tromper soi-même que de tromper **autrui**.
   Ne convoitez pas le bien d'**autrui**.

Note.—**Autrui** is not used as a subject, except when referring to **autrui** already used in the accusative.

Ne pas faire à autrui ce que nous ne voudrions pas qu'**autrui** nous fît, voilà la justice.

But referring to **autrui**, we may also use **il**.

Faire pour autrui, en toute rencontre, ce que nous voudrions qu'il fît pour nous, voilà la charité.

4. **L'un(e), l'autre ; les un(e)s, les autres,** pronouns : *the one, the other, some, others.*

L'un affirme que c'est vrai, **l'autre** que c'est faux.
Ils s'en allèrent **les uns** par ci, **les autres** par là.
Bouilleron se mit à les injurier tous **les uns** après **les autres.**
Vous parlerez **l'un** après **l'autre.**

Note.—**Qui . . . qui** (204, note *b*) are also used as indefinite pronouns in this construction.

Ils s'en allèrent **qui** par ci, **qui** par là.

5. **L'un(e) et l'autre** : *both* ; **les un(e)s et les autres** : *all and sundry.*

L'un et l'autre sont venus me voir.
Je me suis adressé en vain **aux unes et aux autres.**

6. **L'un(e) ou l'autre** : *either* ; **ni l'un(e) ni l'autre** : *neither.*

Comme **l'une ou l'autre** me rendrait heureux ! *How happy could I be with either !*
Je ne les connais **ni l'un ni l'autre, ni les uns ni les autres.**

7. **L'un(e) l'autre, les un(e)s les autres** : *each other, one another.*

L'un is appositive to the subject, **l'autre** is in the accusative, the two pronouns frequently being used as adjuncts of a reciprocal verb.

Ils se flattent **l'un l'autre.** Ils se nuisent **les uns aux autres.**
Elles se moquent **les unes des autres.**
Elles marchaient serrées **les unes contre les autres.**

§ 252. Quelconque, quiconque.

1. **Quelconque,** adjective, following the noun : *any whatever.*

Décrire un cercle passant par trois points **quelconques.**

2. **Quiconque,** pronoun equivalent to two subjects, or to object and subject : *whoever, who(m)soever.*

Quiconque s'éloigne de la sagesse s'éloigne du bonheur.
Je le protégerai contre **quiconque** l'attaquera.

Note.—**Quiconque** is sometimes used in the sense of **qui que ce soit** (253.3, note).

Je pense qu'il me défendra mieux que **quiconque** (*anyone*).
Elle ne parlait jamais à **quiconque** de cette manie de griffonner.

§ **253.** **Quel que, quelque que, qui que, quoi que** ; so-called 'concessive' adjectives, pronouns, and adverbs, always followed by the subjunctive mood denoting concession (§ 383).

1. **Quel que**, adjective, predicative with **être** : *whatever.*

   Quelles que soient vos aptitudes, il faut y joindre le travail.

2. **Quelque . . . qui** (or **que**). (*a*) Adjective : *whatever.*

   Quelque passion **qui** l'agite, il paraît toujours calme.
   Quelques aptitudes **que** vous ayez, il faut y joindre le travail.

(*b*) Adverb modifying a predicative adjective or adverb : *however.*

   Quelque agitées **qu'**elles soient, elles paraissent calmes.
   Quelque heureusement douées **que** vous soyez, il faut travailler.

Note.—Thus also **si . . . que**, with subjunctive, and **tout . . . que**, usually with indicative.

   Si agitée **qu'**elle fût, elle paraissait calme.
   Tout agitée **qu'**elle était, elle paraissait calme.

3. **Qui que**, pronoun : *whoever, whomever.*

   Qui que vous soyez, parlez.
   Soyez poli, à **qui que** vous parliez.

Note.—Hence is derived the phrase **qui que ce soit**, *anyone.*

   Soyez poli en parlant à **qui que ce soit**.

4. **Quoi qui** (or **que**), neuter pronoun : *whatever.*

   Quoi qui survienne, restez calme.
   Quoi que vous entendiez, ne dites rien.

Notes.—(*a*) Hence is derived the phrase **quoi que ce soit**, *anything whatever.*

   Puis-je vous servir en **quoi que ce soit**?

(*b*) Distinguish between **quoi que** and **quoique** (§ 311.2).

§ **254.** The following are the more important indefinite adverbs, additional to those reviewed above:

Vous trouverez cela **partout**. *Everywhere.*
Vous ne trouverez cela **nulle part**. *Nowhere.*
Allez vous faire pendre **ailleurs**. *Elsewhere.*
Cherchez asile **autre part** que chez moi. *Elsewhere.*
J'ai oublié mon parapluie **quelque part**. *Somewhere.*
Nous étions enveloppés **de toutes parts**. *On all sides.*
Vous trouverez cela **n'importe où**. *Anywhere.*
Venez **n'importe comment**. *Anyhow, just as you are.*

And the 'concessive' **où que** (*cf.* § 253) : *wherever.*

   Soyez poli, **où que** vous alliez.

NUMERAL ADJECTIVES AND NOUNS
MEASUREMENT OF TIME, SPACE, ETC.

§ **255.** The **cardinal numeral adjectives** are

1 **un(e)**	11 **onze**	
2 **deux**	12 **douze**	20 **vingt**
3 **trois**	13 **treize**	30 **trente**
4 **quatre**	14 **quatorze**	40 **quarante**
5 **cinq**	15 **quinze**	50 **cinquante**
6 **six**	16 **seize**	60 **soixante**
7 **sept**	17 **dix-sept**	70 **soixante-dix**
8 **huit**	18 **dix-huit**	80 **quatre-vingts**
9 **neuf**	19 **dix-neuf**	90 **quatre-vingt-dix**
10 **dix**		100 **cent**
	1000 **mille**	0 **zéro**

§ **256.** 1. The old Gallic or Celtic numeration by scores instead of tens has survived from 61 to 99. But 70, **septante,** 80, **octante,** 90, **nonante,** are used in Switzerland and in the adjoining parts of France ; and **septante, nonante,** are used in Belgium.

2. Units are joined to tens by a hyphen, except when joined by **et** (§ 13.3).

3. **Et** is used only in 21, 31, 41, 51, 61, 71.

4. **Cent** and **mille** are not preceded by **un** as in English 'one hundred.'

5. **Vingt** and **cent** take plural **s** when multiplied by a preceding numeral, and not followed by another numeral (§ 422).

6. Cardinal numbers are therefore written and spoken as follows :

21 **vingt et un**	22 **vingt-deux**
23 **vingt-trois**	24 **vingt-quatre**
25 **vingt-cinq**	26 **vingt-six**
27 **vingt-sept**	28 **vingt-huit**
29 **vingt-neuf**	31 **trente et un**
32 **trente-deux**	61 **soixante et un**
69 **soixante-neuf**	71 **soixante et onze**
72 **soixante-douze**	75 **soixante-quinze**
81 **quatre-vingt-un**	82 **quatre-vingt-deux**
92 **quatre-vingt-douze**	99 **quatre-vingt-dix-neuf**
101 **cent un**	121 **cent vingt et un**
122 **cent vingt-deux**	200 **deux cents**
250 **deux cent cinquante**	1001 **mille un**

666,666 **six cent soixante-six mille six cent soixante-six**

§ **257.** In legal documents, which require the date to be written in full, the form **mil** is used in dates of our era, instead of **mille.**

l'an mil neuf cent dix-huit.

But 1918 is generally spoken : **dix-neuf cent dix-huit.**

Note that **cent** is not omitted as in English ' nineteen eighteen.'

§ **258.** **Ordinal Numbers.**

Premier, second *or* **deuxième, troisième, quatrième, cinquième, . . . neuvième, dixième, onzième . . . dix-neuvième, vingtième, vingt et unième** (*not* premier !), **vingt-deuxième . . . centième, cent unième . . . millième.**

Je suis le **premier** de ma classe (§ 280, note), Henri est le **troisième.** *I am first in my class . . .*

Je suis **le onzième** (note the absence of elision).

§ **259.** **Nouns of Number.**

1. **Le million, le billion,** etc.

Deux millions d'hommes étaient rangés en bataille.

Note.—**Million,** etc., become adjectival when not used as a round number.

Deux millions cinq cent mille hommes.

2. Nouns in **-aine** denoting approximate numbers.

Une **huitaine,** *about a week* ; une **quinzaine,** *a fortnight.*
Une **douzaine** d'œufs. *A dozen eggs.*
Une **dizaine** (**z,** *not* **x** !), **une vingtaine,** une **centaine,** un **millier.**
Il y avait une **trentaine** d'invités. . . . *about thirty guests.*
Des **milliers** de combattants.

3. Fractional numbers.

$\frac{1}{2}$ **la moitié,** $\frac{1}{3}$ **le tiers,** $\frac{1}{4}$ **le quart,** $\frac{1}{5}$ **le cinquième,** and thereafter the **ordinals** do duty as **fractionals.**

$\frac{1}{3}+\frac{1}{4}=\frac{7}{12}$. Un tiers plus un quart égalent sept **douzièmes.**

Note.—The only fractional adjective is **demi,** *half.* Compare :

Une demi-heure. Un quart d'heure.

4. Multiplicatives.

Le **double,** le **triple,** le **quadruple,** le **quintuple,** le **sextuple, etc.**
La Triple Alliance.

These are used adverbially with **à.**

Il m'a rendu **au quadruple** ce que je lui avais prêté.
He returned fourfold what I had lent him.

§ **260. Cardinal** numbers are used instead of **ordinals,** with the exception of **premier,** (*a*) in titles of sovereigns ; (*b*) in dates ; (*c*) frequently as in English in giving volume, page, chapter, or verse.

(*a*) Henri Ier, Henri **premier.** Louis XIV, Louis **quatorze.**
(*b*) Le **cinq** mars 1870. Le **premier** avril.
(*c*) Nous allons lire au chapitre **trois,** page **trente-cinq.**

Note.—In the above cases, **vingt** and **cent** never vary (§ 422).
L'année dix-neuf **cent.** La page quatre-**vingt.**

§ **261. Common Measurements.**

1. **Time.**

Son discours a duré **vingt minutes, une demi-heure.**
Il a parlé **pendant** vingt minutes. . . . *for twenty minutes.*
J'ai étudié en France **pendant** deux ans. . . . *for two years* (past time).
Je m'en vais en France **pour** deux ans. . . . *for two years* (future time).
Je l'ai vu **il y a** cinq ans. . . . *five years ago.*
Il y a cinq ans **que** je suis ici.
Voilà cinq ans **que** je suis ici. } *I have been here for five years.*
Je suis ici **depuis** cinq ans.
Il arrivera (est arrivé) **jeudi.** . . . *on Thursday.* See also § 168.5.
Je le reverrai **dans** deux ans. **Dans** expresses point in time.
J'ai fait ce devoir **en** vingt minutes. **En** expresses **extent** of time (284.1.*b*).

2. **Time of day. Quelle heure est-il?**

Il est **midi, minuit.** (*Never* douze heures!)
Il est **une heure** (du matin), **deux heures** (de l'après-midi).
Il est **midi et demi, deux heures et demie.**
Il part **à midi un quart, à trois heures un quart, à quatre heures moins un quart** (*or* moins le quart).
Il arrivera **à midi dix, à six heures vingt, à huit heures moins vingt.**

Notes.—(*a*) In official language, *e.g.* in railway time-tables:
Le train part **à une heure quinze, à une heure trente.**
Il arrive à huit heures cinquante-cinq.

(*b*) Railway time in France is now divided into 24 hours, starting from midnight. Thus:
L'express de Bordeaux part à 20 h. 40.
The Bordeaux express starts at 8.40 *p.m.*

3. **Dates.**

C'est aujourd'hui { **mardi, le deux juin.** / **le mardi deux juin.**

Ce sera demain **le huit, le onze.** (Cp. § 258.)

Je suis né **le 1er décembre** 1906.
Il mourut **en** (**l'année**) 1793.
(In official language: **en l'an** 1793.)
As heading to a letter: **Mardi, six mai, 1919.**

4. **Age. Quel âge avez-vous?**

J'ai dix-huit ans. } *I am eighteen.*
Je suis âgé **de** dix-huit ans. }

Ans is never omitted as in English.

J'ai quinze ans et mon frère **en** a douze (§ 225).
J'ai trois ans **de plus que** lui.
Je suis plus âgé que lui **de** trois ans (§§ 158.5 ; 279.1.*e*).

5. **Price.**

Ce ruban coûte **deux francs le mètre.** . . . *two francs* a *yard.*
Je l'ai payé deux francs. *I paid two francs* for *it.*
J'achète mon vin en barriques de 200 litres, que je paye 150 fr. ; il me coûte donc 0 fr. 75 c. le litre. Il me revient à 0 fr. 75 c.

(Read: Il me coûte, il me revient à, soixante-quinze centimes.)

Note the use of **sou** in familiar speech.

C'est du vin qu'on n'achèterait pas au détail à **quinze sous** le litre. On le paierait au moins vingt sous (*i.e.* un franc).
Prêtez-moi **une pièce de cent sous** (*i.e.* une pièce de cinq francs).

6. **Length,** breadth, etc. **Quelle est la longueur de la classe?**

La classe a 6 mètres **de long.** *Is* 6 *metres long.*
Elle **a** 5 m. de large et 4 m. 50 (cm.) **de haut.**
Elle a 6 m. de long **sur** 5 m. de large.
Nous étions dix sur un banc **long de** trois mètres.

Less frequently:

La classe a 6 m. **de longueur** et 5 m. **de largeur.**
La classe est **longue de** 6 m. et **large de** 5.

But these latter constructions are the only ones used with **profond(eur), épais(seur).**

A cet endroit la rivière a trois mètres **de profondeur**, *or* est **profonde de** trois mètres.
Les murs avaient un mètre **d'épaisseur.**
Le mur, **épais d'**un mètre, était percé d'ouvertures très étroites.

ADVERBS, PREPOSITIONS, AND CONJUNCTIONS

§ **262.** In French as in English there are no strict lines of demarcation between these three parts of speech.

Thus the following have both **adverbial** and **conjunctive** functions :

aussi, ainsi, cependant, d'ailleurs.

Il est **aussi** (*adv.*) grand que moi, **aussi** (*conj.*) me prend-on souvent pour le plus jeune.
Ainsi (*conj.*) c'est entendu, vous nous accompagnez ?
Ainsi (*adv.*) mourut ce grand homme.

And the following have both **adverbial** and **prepositional** functions :

après, avant, avec, contre, depuis, devant, derrière (§ 238), **voici, voilà.**

Après la pluie vient le beau temps.
Récitons d'abord la leçon ; les devoirs viendront **après.**
Je ne l'ai pas vu **depuis** jeudi.
Je l'ai vu jeudi, mais pas **depuis.**
Voilà Henri. Garçon ! — **Voilà !** *Coming !*

§ **263.** Those double functions, however, are not so numerous in French as in English. Thus :

Many prepositions are differentiated from the adverb by the adjunction of **de** :

près de, loin de, autour de, hors de.

{ Votre ami demeure tout **près.**
{ Il demeure **près d'**ici, **près de** nous.
{ Des soles frites, avec des tranches de citron **autour.**
{ Regardez **autour de** vous.

And subordinating conjunctions are mostly formed by the adjunction of **que**

(*a*) To **adverbs** : **lorsque, aussitôt que, tant que,** bien que, **non que,** etc.

(*b*) To **prepositions** : **dès** que, **pendant** que, **après** que, **avant que, jusqu'à ce que,** sans que, pour que, etc.

(*a*) { Je lui fis signe, et il se leva **aussitôt.**
{ Il se leva **aussitôt que** je lui fis signe.
(*b*) { Il est levé **dès** l'aurore.
{ Il s'avança **dès qu'**il m'aperçut.
{ Il sortit **après** mon discours.
{ Il sortit **après que** j'eus parlé.

A few adverbs, on the other hand, are formed from prepositions by prefixing **de** :

dedans, dessous, dessus (from an old prep. **sus**). *Cf.* § 238.

§ **264.** For the prepositions and prepositional phrases corresponding to subordinating conjunctions, and governing the infinitive, see § 405.

ADVERBS

A detailed account of the adverbs belongs to the study of the vocabulary and of idiom. The formation of adverbs of manner has already been described, as also the chief functions of adverbs of quantity and degree.

There remain to be studied the adverbs used in affirmation and negation.

Affirmation

§ 265. Affirmation, in answer to a question, is most commonly expressed by the adverb **oui.**

Savez-vous votre leçon ? — **Oui** monsieur.

But in answer to a question put in negative form, it is expressed by **si,** or more politely, by **pardon.**

Est-ce que vous ne savez pas votre leçon ? — **Si** monsieur.
Vous n'étiez pas à la fête hier ? — **Pardon,** mademoiselle.

These affirmations are frequently strengthened or modified by the adjunction of some other word (affective uses).

Vous le saviez ? — **Mais oui** [mɛ wi] ! **Dame oui** !
Vous ne le saviez pas ? — **Mais si** ! **Que si** [kə si] ! **Si fait** [fɛt] !

Qualified affirmation is expressed by

Mon Dieu oui. Mon Dieu si.

Other forms of affirmation are :

(*a*) **Certainement, parfaitement, en effet, naturellement.**

(*b*) In careful speech :

Certes, oui certes, oui vraiment.

(*c*) In colloquial and familiar speech :

Bien sûr, pour sûr, bien sûr que oui, bien sûr que si.

(*a*) C'est à moi que vous osez dire cela ! — **Parfaitement.**
(*b*) Vous pensez qu'il en aura le courage ? — **Oui certes.**
(*c*) Ce qu'on s'embête ici ! — **Pour sûr !** *Of all the slow places ! — Rather !*

Note.—In polite speech, **oui, non, si, pardon,** should always be followed by **monsieur, madame, mademoiselle, docteur, ma sœur** (to a nun), etc.

'Oui mademoiselle' is not a vulgarism like 'Yes, Miss' in English.

§ 266. Oui and **si** often replace a subordinate clause, especially after **croire, dire, répondre, assurer.**

On a commandé la voiture ? — Je crois **que oui** [kwi].
Vous n'en viendrez jamais à bout. — Je vous assure **que si** [kəsi].
Je crois que si [ksi].

Negation

§ **267.** Negation is expressed, (*a*) by the stressed form **non**; (*b*) by the unstressed form **ne**, which clings to the verb, or to other unstressed adjuncts of the verb (§ 330).

§ **268.** **Non** is used

1. As the equivalent of a clause, like **oui, si.**

   Savez-vous votre leçon ? — **Non** monsieur.

   Thus also: **Mais non! Dame non! Que non! Non vraiment.**
   Mon Dieu non (qualified negation).
   Bien sûr que non.
   Je pense **que non.** Je vous assure **que non.**
   Que vous veniez ou **non,** cela nous est égal.

2. To negative members of the sentence other than the verb.

   Non loin de la ville se trouve un château.
   Il est fâché, **non** sans raison.

Note.—**Non,** like **ne,** may be strengthened by the adjunction of **pas, point.**

Il nous faut des amis sincères, et **non pas** des flatteurs.

§ **269.** To negative a statement, the unstressed form **ne** is attached to the verb as a proclitic (§ 328). At an early stage of the language, **ne** was strengthened by the adjunction of various nouns, such as **pas, point, goutte, mie** (*crumb*), **mot,** as is usual in most languages. Thus in English: 'He answered *not a word*.' 'He doesn't mind *a bit*.'

Of these, **pas** and **point** have remained in common use, and assumed adverbial function.

Il **n'**entrera **pas.** Je **n'**en ai **point** entendu parler.
On **n'**est **pas** moins injuste en **ne** faisant **pas** ce qu'on doit faire qu'en faisant ce qu'on **ne** doit **pas** faire.

Notes.—1. The normal negation is **ne pas.** As for **ne point,** very common in the seventeenth century, it is used to-day chiefly in dialect, in literature by those who affect the 'classical' style, and in many phrases, proverbs, etc., of long standing. The statement found in many French grammars that **ne point** denies more strongly, is more emphatic, than **ne pas,** is no longer, if it ever was, true.

The emphatic forms of negation to-day are: **certainement pas, pas du tout, nullement.**

Je ne le ferai **certainement pas.** Ce n'est **pas du tout** cela.

2. **Goutte, mie, mot,** survive in a few familiar expressions such as

On **n'y** voit **goutte** ici. *You can't see a thing here* (*i.e.* it is too dark).

La chimie, je **n'y** entends **goutte**. *I know nothing about chemistry.*

Il **ne** répondit **mot**. *He answered never a word.*

3. To indicate the answer 'yes' or 'no' which he expects to his question, the speaker may put it as an affirmative or negative statement followed by the invariable phrase **n'est-ce pas,** = 'is he?' 'isn't he?' 'will you?' 'won't you?' etc. etc.

Vous venez avec nous, **n'est-ce pas** ? — Oui, *or* Non.

Vous ne le ferez plus, **n'est-ce pas** ? — Si, *or* Non.

In familiar speech, **dis, dites** are often used for **n'est-ce pas.**

Tu reviendras, **dis** ?

4. With many groups of verb + infinitive, French, like a number of other languages, negatives the head verb rather than the dependent infinitive.

Il **ne** faut **pas** faire cela. = Il faut | ne pas faire cela.

Pour ne point calomnier il **ne** faut **jamais** médire. = Il faut | ne jamais médire.

Je **ne** pense **pas** le revoir. = Je pense | ne pas le revoir.

Je **ne** veux **plus** le revoir ! = Je veux | ne plus le revoir !

But the sense may not allow of this transposition of **ne pas.** Thus the following are quite different in meaning :

Je **n'**espère **pas** le revoir.

J'espère **ne pas** le revoir.

§ 270. Other negative forms in common use are

1. The adverbs **ne guère, ne nullement, ne aucunement, ne jamais, ne plus, ne pas encore, ne nulle part, ne pas non plus.**

Vous **n'**avez **guère** de courage ! *You haven't much pluck !*

Je **ne** m'oppose **nullement** à votre départ.

Il **ne** répond **jamais**. **Jamais** il **ne** répond.

Je **n'**ai **plus** d'argent. *No more money, no money left.*

Ne partez **pas encore**. *Not yet.*

On **ne** le rencontre **nulle part**. **Nulle part** vous **ne** rencontrerez de plus jolis visages (§ 254).

Je **n'**avais **pas** oublié **non plus** le coup de poing que j'avais reçu de Madeleine, lorsque je m'étais accrochée à sa jupe. *Not either.*

2. The conjunction **ne ni . . . ni.**

Je **n'**ai **ni** femme **ni** enfants.

Ce **n'**est **ni** vrai **ni** vraisemblable.

Je **n'**y consentirais **ni** pour or **ni** pour argent.

3. The adjectives and pronouns **ne aucun, ne nul, ne pas un, ne personne, ne rien** (§§ 245, 248).

Je **n'**ai **aucune** envie de le revoir.
Pas un des élèves **ne** répondit.
Je **ne** vois **personne**. **Personne n'**est venu.
Je **n'**ai **rien** dit. **Rien ne** l'arrête.

4. Combinations of the above, such as :

ne plus ni . . . ni, ne plus jamais, ne plus guère, ne plus personne, ne plus rien, ne jamais personne, ne jamais rien, ne jamais ni . . . ni.

Je **n'**ai **plus ni** foyer **ni** patrie.
On **n'**entendit **plus jamais** parler de lui.
Les habitants **ne** se voient **plus guère** hors des villes.
Il **n'**y a **plus personne**. Je **ne** dis **plus rien**.
On **ne** voit **jamais personne** aux fenêtres.
Vous **ne** répondez **jamais rien**.
Il **n'**a **jamais ni** livre **ni** cahier. *Either . . . or.*

Note.—**Sans** and **sans que**, which have negative force without the adjunction of **ne**, also combine with the above.

Il travaille **sans aucun** intérêt.
Il se tira d'affaire **sans** le secours de **personne**.
Des mois ont dû se passer **sans que rien** se gravât **plus** dans ma tête.

§ 271. Ne que, = **seulement**, negative in form, is restrictive in meaning. **Que** immediately precedes the member of the sentence which is restricted.

Je **n'**ai **que** dix francs sur moi.
De sa famille je **ne** connais **que** lui.
Je **ne** le connais **que** depuis huit jours.

As **que** always follows **ne**, it cannot be used to restrict the subject of the sentence, unless the latter is made the object of **y avoir.**

Seul, l'auteur pourra nous renseigner.
L'auteur **seul** pourra nous renseigner.
Il **n'**y a **que** l'auteur qui puisse nous renseigner.

Nor can **que** restrict the verb, unless the latter is turned into an infinitive dependent on **faire**.

Qui a brisé ce vase ? — Je l'ai **seulement** touché, et il est tombé.
Je **n'**ai **fait que** le toucher, et il est tombé.
Loin d'abattre les protestants, la Saint-Barthélemy **ne fit que** les irriter.

Note.—But if the verb is in the infinitive, it is usually restricted by **rien que** (§ 245.2, note *c*).

Rien qu'à le voir, on se sent attiré vers lui. ***Only to see him . . .***

§ **272.** **Ne que** combines with **plus, jamais, guère.**

> **Il ne** me reste **plus que** vingt francs.
> **Il n'y** a **plus qu'à** masser les réserves à proximité du front.
> Je **ne** bois **jamais que** de l'eau.
> Ce mot **n'est guère** usité **que** dans la langue littéraire.

Note.—Also with **pas**, a neologism which has become established in spite of adverse criticism.

> A Rome il n'y avait **pas que** les esclaves (*not only the slaves*) qui fissent le métier de gladiateurs.

§ **273.** All the above are used negatively without **ne,** when the verb is not expressed.

> **Pas** de tapage ! **Personne** ici ?
> Qu'a-t-il répondu ? — **Rien.**
> Le peuple donne sa faveur, **jamais** sa confiance.
> **Plus que** trois jours avant les vacances ! *Only three days left . . .*
> Ensuite on avait entendu quelques plaintes. Puis, **plus rien.**
> Il me faudrait un millier de francs. — **Que cela !** *Is that all?* (Literally : *Only that!*)

§ **274.** In literary French and elegant speech, **ne** may be used without the adjunction of **pas**

1. **In** clauses of any type

(*a*) With **pouvoir, savoir, cesser, oser**+**infinitive** expressed or **understood.**

> Je **ne puis** m'expliquer cet accident.
> Je **ne sais** s'ils viendront.
> Je **ne savais** comment expliquer cela.
> Je restai toute seule, **ne sachant** où aller.
> Pendant la veillée, les chiens **ne cessèrent** d'aboyer avec fureur.
> Appeler, faire du bruit, je **n'osais.**

(*b*) In ' rhetorical ' questions introduced by **qui, que,** or by **adverbial que**=pourquoi.

> **Qui ne** connaît cette œuvre célèbre ?
> **Que ne** ferait-il pour vous plaire ?
> **Que ne** m'avez-vous dit cela plus tôt ?

(*c*) Before partitive **d'autre . . . que.**

> Je **n'ai d'autre** désir **que** celui de vous plaire.

2. **In** dependent clauses

(*a*) Of consequence, when the head clause is negative, etc. (§ 387).

> **Il n'est pas si** stupide **qu'il ne comprenne** ces allusions.

(*b*) Introduced by **si**.

C'était en 1849, **si je ne me trompe.**
S'il n'était venu à mon secours, je me noyais.

(*c*) In compound tenses of verbs dependent on **il y a . . . que, voilà . . . que.**

Voilà six mois que je ne l'ai vu. *It's six months since I saw him* (= *I haven't seen him for six months*).
Comme il y a longtemps **que je ne t'ai vue** !

(*d*) Adjectival, if the antecedent is negatived or put in doubt (§ 384).

Il ne lui reste pas / Lui reste-t-il / S'il lui reste } un ami auquel il **n'ait** déjà emprunté de l'argent.

§ **275.** In all the above, **pas** *may* be inserted, and its insertion is the rule in colloquial French.

Mais vous **ne pouvez pas** rester là, voyons !
Je n'osais pas la regarder de peur de la fâcher.
Je ne sais pas s'ils viendront.
Je n'aime pas les enfants qui **ne** savent **pas** se tenir **tranquilles.**
Qui est-ce qui ne connaît pas ça ?
Je n'ai pas d'autre beurre que celui-ci, madame.
Il n'est pas si stupide qu'il **ne** comprenne **pas** ces allusions.
Si vous n'étiez pas venu à mon secours, qu'est-ce que je serais devenu ?
Il y avait bien deux mois qu'elle **n'était pas** sortie de sa chambre.

Note.—With **pouvoir, ne pas** is always used in the double negation **which** is the only equivalent in French to 'cannot but.'

Le jour où, pour un méchant mot, il rompit avec Desportes, éclata une querelle qui **ne pouvait pas ne pas éclater.**

§ **276.** **Pas** is always omitted in a few expressions and constructions of long standing, most of which savour of 'literary' style. Thus:

Il n'eut garde de leur confier le secret. *Took good care not to.*
N'importe. *No matter.*
A Dieu ne plaise ! *God forbid !*
Qu'à cela ne tienne ! *By all means !*
Je ne sais que faire. *I don't know what to do.*
Je n'ai que faire de vos excuses. *I don't want your excuses.*
N'eût été mon désir de vous revoir, je ne serais pas rentré si tôt à Paris.
De ma vie je n'ai entendu pareil discours. (= Jamais je n'ai entendu.)
Nous n'avons trouvé âme qui **vive.**
(In which **âme qui vive** is a strengthened equivalent to 'personne,' 'qui que ce soit.'

Thus also **Je ne saurais** = *I cannot* (§ 84.2.*a*).

Je ne saurais vous permettre cela.
On ne saurait excuser une pareille conduite.

§ **277.** In literary French a superfluous **ne**, due originally to a vague desire to express that a thing should *not* be done, is also used in certain dependent constructions (mostly in the subjunctive mood). This **ne** is seldom inserted in colloquial French; even in literary style the present tendency is to dispense with it, and it will probably soon be considered archaic. Instances of its use and omission:

1. After verbs, nouns, conjunctions, expressive of **fear.**
   Je crains que vous **ne** preniez froid. (*Don't catch cold!*)
   Fermez la porte, de crainte qu'on **ne** nous entende.
   J'ai peur qu'on te fasse du mal.
   J'ai bien peur que ce temps-là nous amène des loups.

2. After **empêcher, éviter, prendre garde.**
   Évitons que l'élève **ne** se trompe, de peur qu'il **ne** prenne de mauvaises habitudes.
   Tâchez d'éviter que la nouvelle se répande avant son départ.

3. After **s'en falloir de peu.**
   Peu s'en fallut que la voiture **ne** versât. *The carriage came very near being overturned.*
   Il s'en faut de peu que le compte y soit. *That's very nearly the right amount.*

4. After **ne pas douter, ne pas nier.**
   Je ne doute pas qu'il **ne** vous reçoive.
   On ne nie pas que je **ne** sois dans mon droit.
   Je ne doute pas que cette affreuse guerre en soit la cause.

5. After **à moins que, avant que.**
   Restez ici à moins qu'on **ne** vous appelle.
   Ne sortez pas avant que l'heure **ne** sonne.
   Il arrivera avant que nous soyons prêts.
   Il ne doit rien en savoir encore, à moins qu'on lui ait envoyé une dépêche.

6. In a clause forming the **second term of a comparison,** after **plus, moins, mieux,** etc., **autre, autrement.** (Here the mood is the indicative.)
   Il est plus vigoureux qu'il **ne** le paraît.
   Il est plus intelligent que vous le pensez.
   Je ne sais pas me faire autre que je **ne** suis.
   Il agit autrement qu'il **ne** parle.
   Il était autrement riche, il y a quelques années, qu'il l'est aujourd'hui.

§ **278.** In colloquial French, even among educated people, **ne** is constantly omitted, the negation being reduced to **pas.**

Non! . . . **C'est pas** une idée qui me viendrait. *Gyp.* (A viscount is speaking.)
Tu feras pas mal de répéter ta scène avant de t'en aller.
Aie pas peur. *H. Lavedan.* **C'est pas** la même chose.
Mirette de Beauvais? **Connais pas.** *I don't know her.*

PREPOSITIONS

A detailed account of the prepositions and of their uses belongs to the study of the vocabulary and of idiom. Only those are dealt with here which are of special importance in the construction of the sentence.

§ **279. De.** The most important preposition in French is **de**, the chief functions of which are

1. To form **adverb phrases,** expressing

(*a*) A point of departure in space or time.

Il vient **de Paris.** Il demeure à deux lieues **d'ici.**
Il travaille **du matin** au soir.
Il y a **de cela** cinq cents ans passés.
Je reviendrai **d'aujourd'hui** en huit.

And by extension of this use :

J'ai appris cela **de mon père.**
Nous sommes près **de sa maison.** (Reckoning the distance *from* his house.)
Je vous l'ai dit plus **d'une fois.** (**Une** is taken as the point of departure.)
Il pleure **de joie.** (The cause is taken as point of departure.)
Je suis Anglais **de naissance.** Des vins **d'Espagne.**

(*b*) A time only vaguely indicated.

Il ne reviendra pas **de longtemps.**
Il partit **de nuit, de grand matin, de bonne heure.**
(Cp. Il partit **à trois heures, à Pâques.**)
Du temps des anciens chevaliers s'étendait ici une vaste forêt.

(*c*) The agent, means, or instrument.

Il est accompagné, respecté, **de ses amis** (§ 67.3).
J'ai fait cela **de ma main** (§ 287, note 1).
Je le frappai **de mon bâton.**

Note.—But several prepositions have this function.

Cette correction a été faite **par** le maître, **de** sa main, **à** l'encre rouge, mais **avec** une mauvaise plume.

(*d*) The manner.

Il me regarda **d'un air fâché.**
Comment pouvez-vous agir **de la sorte ?**

(*e*) Measure.

Je suis âgé **de seize ans.**
Ma montre retarde **de dix minutes.**

2. To form adjective phrases, expressing

(*a*) Possession (Genitive equivalents).

Le livre de Pierre.

(*b*) Material.

Un pont de bois. Une robe de soie.

(*c*) A distinguishing mark.

Une dame de haute taille.
Le journal d'hier. La route de Paris.
Le train de Boulogne.

(Ambiguous, like 'the Boulogne train' in English, *i.e.* either 'the train *to*' or 'the train *from* Boulogne.')

Plus tard seulement mes visions d'enfant prirent figure.
Childish visions.

3. Partitive function.

Un verre de vin. Beaucoup de paroles.
Une livre de café. Il y a eu dix hommes de tués.
Nous allons manger quelque chose de bon.

4. To introduce (*a*) the subject, or (*b*) the object of the action, in relation with nouns denoting a verbal activity (subjective and objective genitive equivalents).

(*a*) **L'arrivée des invités.**
(*b*) **Le partage de la succession.**

(Sometimes ambiguous, but for the context: **L'amour de Dieu** may mean either '*God's love for us*' or '*our love for God.*')

§ **280.** **De** has also taken on many uses in which its meaning, although derived from the functions described above, can hardly be classified. Thus it is used

1. To introduce the object of indirectly transitive verbs.

J'ai changé d'avis. Jugez de ma surprise.

2. To form such adverbial phrases as

Venez de ce côté. Il ne reviendra pas de longtemps.
De ma vie, je n'ai entendu pareil discours.

Note.—**De** is often used where English has 'in,' 'at.'

Le meilleur élève de la classe. In *the class.*
Les rues de Paris sont larges.
Les petits oiseaux des bois célèbrent le printemps.
Il reçut le roi dans sa maison de Vaux. *His house* at *Vaux.*

§ 281. De has also taken on some non-prepositional functions, *i.e.* uses in which it ceases to govern the accusative case.

1. It serves as a mere link between an infinitive and some other member of the sentence. (Compare the use of 'to' in English.)

Il est honteux **de** mentir.
Je crains **d'**être en retard.
Je n'ai pas le temps **de** m'occuper de vous.
Il tempêtait, vociférait, et la foule **de** rire! ('Historical' Infinitive, §§ 89, 109.)

2. It serves as a partitive particle, which does not govern a case. Thus the partitive noun is in the nominative in:

De braves gens se trouvaient là.
Du vin était répandu sur la table.
Des amis sincères ont blâmé sa conduite.
Vous êtes **des** ingrats.

While in

Je bois **de** l'eau. Je m'adresserai **à des** amis,

the accusative is governed by **boire**, by **à**, and not by partitive **de**.

3. It may introduce an apposition to the head-noun, or a predicative complement.

La ville **de** Paris. Le mois **de** juin.
La comédie **du** Misanthrope.
Il fut traité **de** lâche.

§ 282. A. The preposition **à** serves

1. To form adverb phrases denoting

(*a*) **Motion toward** a point in space, time, or number.

Je vais **à** l'école, **à** Paris.
Remettons cela **à** demain.
Il travaille du matin **au** soir.
Il y eut de 300 **à** 400 morts.

(*b*) **A point in** space or time.

Je suis **à** l'école, **à** Paris. Nous jouons **au** jardin.
Des nuages noirs s'amassent **au** ciel.
Les fermes riaient **au** soleil.
Il demeure **à** deux lieues d'ici.
Il avait un révolver **à** la main.
Il vivait **à** l'époque de Louis XIV.
Les vacances commencent **au** mois de juillet.
Tâchez d'arriver **à** l'heure.

(*c*) Manner.

Parlez à haute voix. Marchez au pas.
Je me promène à pied, à cheval, à bicyclette.
Il s'est meublé à l'anglaise.
Il ne faut jamais faire les choses à moitié.
Ici, les pommes de terre se vendent au poids, ailleurs elles se vendent au boisseau.
La grandeur des aspirations humaines se mesure à l'inspiration qui les fait naître.

Including the ideas of distribution, ratio, price, rate.

Nous marchons deux à deux.
Je prendrai un taxi à l'heure.
Deux est à trois comme quatre est à six.
A quel prix vendez-vous cela ?
Voici du drap à huit francs le mètre.

(But : Je vends ce drap huit francs le mètre.)

Je volais à quatre-vingts à l'heure.

2. To introduce the indirect object (Dative equivalent).

J'ai donné une pomme à Pierre.
J'emprunterai de l'argent à un ami (§ 123.1).
Je trouve à votre frère assez mauvaise mine (cp. § **221**).
Cette nouvelle fut agréable à tout le monde.
Je me fie à vous.

3. To form adjective phrases denoting

(*a*) Purpose.

Une tasse à thé. Un moulin à blé.

(*b*) Instrument.

Un moulin à vent. Une machine à vapeur.

(*c*) A distinguishing mark.

Un piano à queue. Un chapeau à plumes.
Un homme à barbe noire.
Un enfant aux yeux bleus.
Un jeune garçon à l'intelligence éveillée.

(*d*) Possession.

Ce livre est à Pierre. (Cp. § 279.2.*a*.)
Il a deux maisons à lui.
C'est un cousin à moi qui m'a dit ça.
Ce n'est pas de ma faute, à moi, si vous êtes en retard !

§ 283. A is also used to introduce an infinitive, generally with a well-marked idea of tendency toward a goal. See §§ 99-102.

§ **284. En,** less determinate than **dans,** generally introduces a noun not particularized. It is thus used:

1. To form adverb phrases denoting

(*a*) Place within which . . ., or into which . . .

On était en pleine mer.
Il était en prison. Il fut mis **en prison.**
(But: Il fut détenu **dans la prison** du Temple.)

J'ai vécu en France, en Amérique.
(**But**: Cela se passait **dans la France** de l'ancien **régime.**
Il a fait sa fortune **dans l'Amérique du Sud.**)

(*b*) Time within which . . .

Je suis né **en 1905.** Il y fait très froid **en hiver.**

And extent of time.

On fait la traversée **en cinq jours.**
J'ai fait mon thème **en une demi-heure.**

(Point in time is expressed by **dans** or **à.**

Je pars **dans cinq jours.** Je pars **à six heures.**
J'aurai fini **dans une demi-heure.**)

Note.—**En été, en automne, en hiver**; but: **au printemps.**

(*c*) State, manner.

L'école, c'est le monde **en petit.**
Laissez-moi vivre **en paix.** Travaillez **en silence.**
On était alors **en guerre.** Nous vivions **en famille.**

Including manner of dress.

Il était **en uniforme.** Je m'habillai **en Suédoise.**
Pour son premier bal elle était **en blanc.**

(*d*) Change, collection, or division into.

Aussitôt l'ogre se changea **en souris.**
Les ouvriers réunissent les lignes **en pages.**
Traduisez cela **en français.** La forêt finit **en pointe.**
Il se promenait de long **en large.**
On partagea les vivres **en trois portions.**
Tragédie **en cinq actes.**

2. To introduce a predicative complement of manner (118.1.*b*).

Il s'est conduit **en honnête homme.**
Il mourut **en héros.**

3. To form adverbial gerund clauses (§§ 113.3, 410).

J'ai fait cela en m'amusant.

4. To form adjective phrases denoting
   (*a*) Material: Une montre **en or.** Un escalier **en bois.**
   Pour la reliure des livres il y a des couvertures **en carton, en toile, en parchemin.**
   (*b*) Manner: Une fenêtre **en ogive.** Un escalier **en spirale.**

Notes.—1. Only feminine names of countries may be governed by **en**; masculine names are governed by **à** + definite article.

Il est né **en** France, **en** Normandie.
Il est né **au** Japon, **au** Canada, **au** Mexique.

Thus also:

Il revient **de** France (§ 168.1, note *c*). Il revient **du** Canada.

2. 'To,' 'at,' or 'in' a town are expressed by **à**.

Je l'ai rencontré **à** Paris. *I met him* in *Paris.*

§ **285. Dans,** *in, into,* introduces a noun which is clearly determined, to form adverb phrases of time and place.

Il demeure **dans la ville.** Nous entrons **dans la classe.**

(Compare:

Il demeure **en ville.** *In town.* Nous entrons **en classe.**)

Il reviendra **dans huit jours** (§ 284.1.*b*).
Il entre **dans sa dixième année.**

Note.—**En** is used for **dans** before a noun determined by the article, etc., in a few expressions dating far back in the language.

En l'absence du colonel, le plus ancien des officiers préside.
Cela s'est fait **en mon absence.**
Pourquoi regardez-vous **en l'air**?
Cela se passait **en l'an** 1800 de notre ère.

§ **286. Par.** 1. Relations of time and space.

Il a sauté **par la fenêtre.** Entrez **par ici.** *This way.*
On se rend à Paris **par Douvres** ou **par Newhaven.**
C'était **par une belle journée** de juin.

2. Agency, means, motive.

Il a été puni **par le maître.**
Il est arrivé **par le train** de huit heures.
Je vous demande cela **par simple curiosité.** *Merely out of curiosity.*

Note.—For the use of **de** and **par** denoting the agent, see § 67.

3. Distributive.

Les prisonniers défilaient **par centaines.**
Le laitier vient deux fois **par jour.**

4. With the infinitive. See § 104.

§ **287. Avec,** *with*; **sans,** *without.*

J'irai avec vous, sans vous.
Il marche avec des béquilles (*crutches*), sans béquilles (§ 170.10).
Il travaille avec courage (§ 152, note), sans courage.

Notes.—1. **De** and **avec** are both used to denote the 'instrument.' **De** denotes the more obvious and habitual instrument used in performing an action; **avec,** that which is not so obviously indicated.

{J'ai signé ce document **de** ma propre main.
{Je l'ai signé **avec** une plume à réservoir.

{Il lance la pierre **d'**une main habile.
{Il lance la pierre **avec** une fronde.

{Regarde **de** tous tes yeux!
{Il regarde tout **avec** des lunettes couleur de rose.

{On combla **de** pierres les tranchées ravagées.
{On combla la tranchée **avec** des cadavres.

2. **Sans** also corresponds to *but for.* Sans vous, je tombais.

§ **288. Avant,** *before*; **après,** *after.* Relations of time.

Il est arrivé avant moi, après moi.

Note.—**Après** also has the meaning *in contact with,* after certain verbs. In every case **à** might equally well be used.

Elle épinglait ses draps et ses couvertures après (*or* à) son matelas.
La chatte fit un bond formidable et s'accrocha après (*or* à) un rideau, tout en haut d'une fenêtre.

§ **289. Devant,** *before, in front of*; **derrière,** *behind.* Relations of space.

Nous causions devant l'école, derrière l'école.
Il parut devant ses juges.
Son chien trottait derrière lui.

§ **290. Chez,** *at the house of, with.* Always governs a noun or pronoun denoting a person, or people.

Il est en pension chez un de ses professeurs.
Je l'ai trouvé chez lui.
Je vais passer les vacances chez un camarade.
Je voudrais bien avoir un chez moi. *A home of my own.*

By extension of meaning: *in, among.*

Cherche les vertus chez les autres et les vices chez toi.
Vous trouverez cette expression chez (*or* dans) Lamartine.
Il y avait chez (*or* en) lui de la prudence mêlée à de l'audace.
On goûte beaucoup les sports chez les Anglo-saxons.

§ 291. **Pour.** 1. Relations of space and time.

Le voilà parti **pour** l'Amérique.
Je suis à vous **pour toute la vie.**
Je pars en vacances **pour huit jours** (261.1).

2. Derived relations.

Cette lettre est **pour vous.**
Je répondrai **pour vous.** *In your stead.*
Il est mort **pour la patrie.**
Œil **pour** œil, dent **pour** dent.
J'ai placé (*invested*) la somme à quatre **pour cent.** *Per cent.*

3. With the infinitive. See § 106.

§ 292. **Contre.** Relation of space, with derived moral relation.

Ne vous appuyez pas **contre le mur.** *Against the wall.*
Tout le monde est **contre moi.**
Il est fâché **contre vous.** *Angry with you.*

§ 293. **Depuis,** *since, from*; **jusqu'à, jusque,** *until, as far as.* Relations of space and time. The usual form is **jusqu'à**; **jusque** is used before another preposition, and before **ici, là.**

Il n'y a rien de nouveau **depuis hier.**
Jusqu'ici, on n'a rien appris de nouveau.
J'ai été malade **depuis Newhaven jusqu'à Dieppe.**
Il courut **jusque chez lui.**
Depuis quand êtes-vous ici ? (§ 73.1).
Depuis le matin jusqu'au soir on l'avait attendu.

(But when less emphatic : **de . . . à :**
Il travaille **du** matin **au** soir (§§ 279.1, 282.1).

§ 294. **Dès,** *as early as, no later than.*

Il est levé **dès six heures.**
Je me mettrai au travail **dès ce soir.**

§ 295. **Sur, sous.** Relations of space and time.

Le chat est **sur, sous,** la table.
Le chat sauta **sur, sous,** la table.
Il prit un verre **sur la table** (§ 123.4).
Je n'ai que cinq francs **sur moi.**
Il est arrivé **sur les neuf heures.** *About nine o'clock.*
Il vécut **sous le règne** de Henri IV.

§ **296. Vers,** *toward.* Relations of space and time.

Il se dirigea **vers la porte.**
Il viendra **vers trois heures.**

§ **297. Envers,** *toward, to.* Moral relation.

Soyez respectueux **envers vos maîtres.**
Il a été très aimable **envers moi,** *or* **pour moi.**
Ne soyez pas cruels **envers les animaux,** *or* **aux animaux.**

Note.—Whether **envers, pour,** or **à** should be used depends partly on the adjective, partly on the balance of the sentence.

§ **298. Entre,** *between.* Relations of space and time.

J'étais assis **entre deux grosses dames,** qui étaient elles-mêmes **entre deux âges.**
Si jamais il me tombe **entre les mains !**
Je vous attends **entre cinq** (heures) **et six.**

By extension of meaning, **entre,** in a few idioms, implies more than two persons.

Mes cousines et moi, nous causions **entre nous.**

For **d'entre,** partitive, see § 171.7.

§ **299. Parmi,** *among.*

Parmi les assistants, on remarquait plusieurs **prêtres** mondains.

§ **300. Pendant, durant,** *during.* **Durant** follows the noun in a number of phrases, in the sense of *during the whole of.*

J'ai fait du français **pendant,** *or* **durant, mes vacances.**
Neuf années durant, il élabora sa théorie.
Il lui acheta sa bibliothèque, mais lui en laissa la jouissance **sa vie durant.**

§ **301. Selon,** *according to* ; **d'après,** *according to, (copied) from.*

Selon lui, *or* **D'après lui,** la nouvelle serait fausse.
Évangile **selon saint Luc.**
Un tableau **d'après nature, d'après Rembrandt.**

§ **302. Malgré,** *in spite of.*

Je pleure **malgré moi.**
Je lui écrirai, **malgré la défense** qu'on m'en a faite.

§ **303. Outre,** *besides, in addition to* ; literally *beyond.*

Il a plusieurs dettes, **outre son terme** (*term's rent*) **qui n'est** pas payé.
Les pays d'outre-mer.

§ **304. Hors,** *except* ; **hors de,** *outside of.*

Il y a remède à tout, **hors la mort.**
Hors d'ici, misérable ! Il demeure **hors de Paris.**

Note.—**Hors** is used alone, in the sense of *outside of*, in a number of phrases.

Il fut mis hors la loi. *He was outlawed.*

§ **305. Près de,** *near.*

Il s'assit près du feu, près de **moi.**
Il demeure près de Paris.

Note.—**Près** is used alone in a number of phrases, especially with the name of a place, used to locate another place, in official style.

Il mourut à Asnières, près Paris.
Grande propriété à vendre, sise à **Marchezais, près Dreux.**

§ **306. Auprès de,** *close to, in comparison with.*

Il s'assit **auprès de moi, auprès de** la fenêtre.
Vos ennuis sont peu de chose **auprès de** ce que j'ai **souffert.**
L'art est toujours grossier **auprès des créations** de la nature.

§ **307. Quant à,** *with regard to, as for.*

Quant à moi, je n'en ferai rien (§ 323.2).
Quant à rester jusqu'à samedi, cela me serait impossible.

§ **308. Voici,** *here is, are* ; **voilà,** *there is, are.* Of verbal origin (§ 232). Unstressed pronouns are proclitic to these prepositions.

Voilà Henri. — Oui, **le voilà.**
Où êtes-vous ? — **Me voici.**
Sa harangue finie, **nous voilà** tous **à** nous regarder, assis en rond.
C'est ce que nous montre la petite histoire **que voici.** *The following little story.*

May govern a clause in the indicative. (Affective uses.)

Mes amis, **voici que** nous **commençons** véritablement **notre traversée.**
Ah ! mon Dieu, **mais voilà qu'il est une heure !**

Governs the infinitive in the phrase **voici venir.**

> **Le régiment défile, et voici venir le grand drapeau aux trois couleurs, que porte un officier.**

May be followed by a predicative adjective, and is then equivalent to **être.** (Affective use.)

> **Vous voilà bien malade !**
> **Nous voilà obligés de rentrer à pied !**

Note also the colloquialism **voilà-t-il.**

> **En voilà-t-il, du monde !**
> **Voilà-t-il pas, pauvre homme, que j'ai peur de le voir rentrer !**

§ 309. Many prepositional phrases may be governed by **de,** especially such as are formed with **avec, chez, derrière, entre, sur, sous.**

> **Chaque année on séparait les agneaux d'avec leur mère.**
> **Je sors de chez lui.**
> **La jeune sœur (*nun*) me fit asseoir sur une chaise qu'elle tira de derrière le rideau.**
> **La gêne s'en était allée d'entre nous.**
> **Elle leva les yeux de sur son dessin.**
> **Il sortit tout penaud de sous la table.**

CONJUNCTIONS

§ 310. The following are used to co-ordinate or to correlate multiple subjects, objects, or adjuncts of a clause :

1. Co-ordinating : **et, ainsi que, ou, ni.**

> Henri **et** Pierre sont là.
> Les juges **ainsi** que le public lui donnèrent raison.
> Il y a malice, erreur **ou** distraction dans la manière dont on a lu la pièce.
> Il arriva sans argent **ni** bagages.

Note.—Sans argent **ni** bagages. *Without money* or *luggage.*

2. Correlating : **et . . . et, ni . . . ni, non seulement . mais encore, ou . . . ou, soit . . . soit.**

> **Et** les juges **et** le public lui donnèrent raison.
> L'accomplissement du devoir, voilà **et** le véritable but de la vie **et** le véritable bien.
> **Ni** Henri **ni** Pierre ne sont là.
> **Non seulement** le public, **mais encore** les juges lui donnèrent raison.
> Ils exigeaient des paysans **ou** du blé **ou** de l'argent.
> **Soit** aujourd'hui, **soit** demain, il arrivera un accident.

Note.—The correlative constructions belong for the most part to literary style.

§ 311. The following are used to join clauses:

1. Co-ordinating:

et, ou, ni; mais, cependant, pourtant, néanmoins; donc, car, ainsi, aussi; puis;
and such phrases as: **ou bien, en effet, c'est pourquoi, d'ailleurs.**

> Christophe était mortifié, **et** il avait le cœur gros.
> Il ne mange **ni** ne boit.
> Frappe, **mais** écoute. Je pense, **donc** (dɔ̃k) je suis.
> Je suis venu en courant, **car** je me croyais en retard.
> Ce fut comme un coup de tonnerre, **puis** il se fit un grand silence.
> Prenez un train du soir, **ou bien** restez ici jusqu'à demain.
> Il jeta sur l'horizon un regard inquiet, **en effet** la brise fraîchissait.

Notes.—1. *He* neither *eats* nor *drinks*: Il ne mange **ni ne boit. Ni** is not used before both verbs.

2. **Ni** is never used to introduce a clause, like 'nor' in English. *I will not apologize,* nor *will I admit that I am wrong.* Je ne ferai pas d'excuses, **et** je n'admets pas **non plus** que je sois dans mon tort.

3. **Donc** introducing a clause is pronounced [dɔ̃k]; but in its affective use after verbs, as in Mais venez donc! **Allons donc!** it is pronounced [dɔ̃].

2. Subordinating:

These conjunctions consist of simple words such as **que, comme, si, quand**; of compounds spelt as one word, such as **puisque, lorsque, quoique,** and of phrases formed with **que,** introducing clauses

(*a*) In the indicative mood:

alors que, dès que, pendant que, **à** mesure que, **tant que, après que, depuis que, à peine . . . que, parce que, vu que, tandis que, selon que**; etc.

(*b*) Usually in the subjunctive mood:

avant que, jusqu'à ce que, en attendant que;
non que, loin que, sans que;
en cas que, à moins que, pourvu que, supposé que;
bien que, encore que;
afin que, pour que, de peur que, de crainte que, etc.

(*c*) In either mood:

de sorte que, de façon que, de manière que, etc.

(*d*) To which must be added:

quand (même), au cas où, dans le cas où, lors même que,

which are regularly followed by a verb in the future-in-the-past tenses of the indicative (§ 388, note).

The uses of most of the above are shown in §§ 385-389.

Notes.—1. **Où,** and not **quand,** heads a clause qualifying a noun which expresses a definite time (§ 209).

That day when *I met you in London.* Le jour **où** je vous ai rencontré à Londres.

The summer of 1911, when *it was so hot.* L'été de 1911, **où** il fit si chaud.

He lived there until 1875, when *he settled in Paris.* Ce fut là qu'il résida jusqu'en 1875, **époque où** il se fixa à Paris.

If the time is indefinite, the time clause is introduced by **que.**

One day, when *I was strolling through the woods.* Un jour **que** je me promenais à travers bois.

2. **Quand** never has the continuative function which is assumed by 'when' in such sentences as:

His first voyage was made in 1492, when *he reached the West Indian Islands.* Son premier voyage eut lieu en 1492, **et** il atteignit **alors** les Antilles.

3. In literary style the components of **lorsque** are often separated by **même, donc. Lors** is then pronounced [lɔr].

Lors même **qu'il** pleurait, son aspect avait quelque chose de comique. *Even when he wept . . .*

Lors donc **qu'il** fut arrivé à la conclusion de son discours . .
When therefore . . .

PART II

SENTENCE CONSTRUCTION

Stressed and Unstressed Elements of the Sentence

§ **312.** Every spoken sentence consists of one or more **word-groups,** each of which contains **one,** or **two, stressed** elements, and a number of unstressed elements which ‘ cling ’ to, or ‘ lean ’ upon, those which bear the stress.

In the following sentences the stresses are indicated in heavy type, and the word-groups separated:

I am **glad** | that you **spoke** to him.
There is the **sugar,** | beside the **milk-jug.**
How **beautiful** the country is!

In French:

Je suis **content** | *que* vous *lui* ayez **parlé.**
Voilà *le* **sucre** | *à* côté *du* pot *à* **lait.**
Comme *la* campagne est **belle!**

It will be noticed that in English the position of the stress within the word-group is not fixed. In French it occurs regularly at the end of the word-group, and there may also be an initial stress.

Note the constant end-stress in the following series:

Je **sais.**
Je le **sais.**
Je ne sais **pas.**
Je ne le sais **pas.**
Je ne le sais pas **bien.**
Je ne le sais pas assez **bien.**
Je ne le sais pas assez bien pour **ça.**

§ **313.** In the series and the examples given above, certain words are printed in italics. These words are of such a nature that they can *never* bear the stress ; they ‘ cling ’ to some word of greater sonority, with which they stand in close syntactical relation, and such unstressed members of the sentence are always proclitic in French, *i.e.* they always precede the word to which they cling.

Many of these unstressed forms have a corresponding strong form capable of bearing the stress.

The following is a list of the more important proclitic forms:

	Unstressed Forms, proclitic.	*Corresponding Stressed Forms.*
Articles.	le, la, les, du, des, au, aux.	
Adjectives.	ce, cet, cette, ces.	ce . . . -ci ; ce . . .-là.
	mon, ma, mes ; ton, etc.	mien, mienne ; tien, etc.
Pronouns.	je, tu, il, ils.	moi, toi, lui, eux.
	on.	
	me, te ; le, la, les ; se.	(à) moi, (à) toi ; lui, elle, eux, elles ; (à) soi.
	y, en.	
	que ; ce.	quoi ; ceci, cela.
Adverbs.	ne ; y, en.	non ; là, de là.
Prepositions.	de, à, en, etc.	
Conjunctions.	et, que, si, etc.	

Note.—The pronouns **le, la, les** take the stress when at the end of the word-group in the imperative ; **le** is then fully pronounced [lə], approximating to a short [lø] : **Prenez-le.**

Tu, il, ils, on, following the verb, also take the stress at the end of a word-group : **Viens-tu ? Pourquoi s'en va-t-il ?**

But never **je**, which remains [ʒ]. Thus : **Que dis-je ! = [kə diːʒ].**

§ **314.** Some words may either take the stress or cling to other words, without alteration in form, but frequently with a change of function. Such are : **un, une ;** the pronouns **elle, nous, vous ; qui ; tout, rien ; lui, leur ;** parts of the verbs **être, avoir, faire, aller, devoir,** etc., when used as auxiliaries.

§ **315.** Unstressed particles are usually repeated in French before each of the words with which they stand in close syntactical relation. Thus :

(*a*) Articles, demonstrative and possessive adjectives.

Le père et **le** fils sont associés. *The father and son are in partnership.*

Donnez-moi **du** lait et **du** sucre.

Mon frère et **ma** sœur sont ici. *My brother and sister.*

(*b*) Prepositions, especially **de, à, en.**

Voici les devoirs **de** Jean et **de** Henri.

En été et **en** hiver.

Nous nous promenons **par** monts et **par** vaux. *We wander over hill and dale.*

(*c*) Object pronouns.

Je l'aime et **le** respecte.

§ **316.** The determinants of the noun (*a* and *b* above) are not repeated when two or more nouns have long stood united to form a collective whole.

On invitera les parents et amis.
Il est ingénieur des ponts et chaussées.
Je restai orphelin avec mes frères et sœurs.

Nor are they repeated before a second noun synonymous with and explanatory of the former.

Un député ou représentant du peuple.
Une majuscule ou lettre capitale.

Again, it is obvious that one will say:

La grande et la petite classe (two class-rooms),

and:

Une grande et belle classe (one class-room).

But in the plural this distinction is not always observed. Thus:

Les lois divines et humaines.

PRINCIPLES OF WORD-ORDER

§ **317.** From the law governing the distribution of the stresses in the French sentence may be derived the following general principles:

1. Since the end of the sentence bears the principal stress, this 'strong position' should be occupied by some word or phrase of special importance. Thus, the question

Quand attendez-vous votre frère?

will be answered:

Nous l'attendons à Londres jeudi prochain.

And the question

Où comptez-vous retrouver votre frère?

will be answered:

Nous l'attendons jeudi à Londres.

2. The word or phrase at the end of the sentence or word-group should be of sufficient sonority to bear the stress, and not be overshadowed by what precedes. Thus the ear would not tolerate

Il revient d'un voyage long;

but will be satisfied by

Il revient d'un voyage prolongé.

3. The beginning of the sentence, which may take an initial stress, is often occupied by one or more important words or phrases.

> **Moi,** je n'aime pas les égoïstes.
> **Le quatre août,** l'Angleterre déclarait la guerre.
> **Chose remarquable, à Paris** l'on ne savait encore rien de ce qui s'était passé.

4. The verb, partaking largely of the nature of a copula, tends to occupy a central position in the word-group.

> Je ne **sais** pas. De qui **parlez-vous** ?
> Votre père **viendra-t-il** ? L'expérience **rend** sage.
> Devant la maison **s'étendait** une large pelouse (*a lawn*).

Note.—The capacity of the verb for occupying the stressed position depends on its relative importance and picturesqueness in the sentence. We cannot say :

> Devant la maison une pelouse **était** (*or* **se trouvait**),

because **être** and **se trouver** are 'empty of content.' But

> Devant la maison { une pelouse **se déroulait**,
> { **se déroulait** une pelouse,

are both possible, according as we wish to stress **pelouse**, or the 'picturesque' verb **se dérouler**. Thus again :

> Nous regardions l'horizon, que le soleil couchant **embrasait** (*all aglow with the setting sun*).

But not :

> Nous regardions l'horizon, où un soleil embrasé **se couchait.**

Embrasé is the important word, and we must have

> . . . où **se couchait** un soleil embrasé.

The question is always one of the *relative* importance of words ; even the verb **être** *may* assume first importance.

> Dieu dit : Que la lumière **soit.** Et la lumière **fut.**

5. It is logical, in the unfolding of ideas, to proceed from the known to the unknown ; therefore any new person, thing, or fact which is brought to our notice generally has the end-stress. Thus, after describing the reign of Edward VII, we proceed :

> Edward VII was succeeded by **King George V.**

And also in French,

> A Édouard VII succéda **le roi Georges V,**

not

> Le roi Georges V succéda à Edouard VII.

In a history of Cæsar we shall write :

> Peu après, César conquit **la Gaule.**

In giving an account of Gaul we should write :

> Peu après, la Gaule fut conquise **par César.**

§ 318. The principles explained above refer to 'normal' speech. In affective speech the stress is frequently regressive, both in individual words and in the word-group. Thus we say, with principal stress on the syllables italicized:

> Mais c'est *par*faitement vrai! C'est im*pos*sible!
> C'est ab*so*lument faux! Mais c'est *épou*vantable, une *ac*tion pareille!

In the same way the principal stress may shift to the beginning of the sentence or word-group, the end then taking a secondary stress. Thus, in

> **Grande** fut sa surprise. **Jamais** je n'y consentirai,

the principal stress shifts to the words **grande, jamais** (*ja*mais), and may be much more pronounced than in the 'normal' constructions

> Sa surprise fut grande. Je n'y consentirai jamais.

Hence the further principle that

In affective speech a word may head the sentence in order to receive the principal stress.

§ 319. The principles enumerated above point to considerable freedom in the arrangement of the word-group and of the sentence. This freedom is limited, however, by the following consideration: French, like English, having almost entirely lost its original case-endings, a fixed and commonly accepted word-order is often the only means of indicating clearly the interrelation of the different members of the sentence, *i.e.* of achieving lucidity.

Thus the statement

> Petrus amat Paulum. Paulum amat Petrus. Petrus Paulum amat, etc.,

admits in French and English of no other order but

> Pierre aime Paul. *Peter loves Paul.*

Thus again, the subject may be placed in 'strong position' in

> A Édouard VII succéda **Georges V,**

the subject being clearly distinguished from the prepositional object; but we could not say

> La Gaule (*object*) conquit César (*subject*)

instead of

> La Gaule fut conquise par César.

§ **320.** Lucidity, absence of any ambiguity, is an essential feature of the French language, and has constantly to be taken into consideration in the arrangement of the sentence. Thus the following are not sufficiently clear to satisfy the French mind:

Il arriva chez des amis sans argent. Ces détonations firent naître l'idée d'un combat dans mon esprit. Le général donna les ordres nécessaires aux chefs de ces trois armées.

Recast as follows they leave no doubt as to the meaning:

Il arriva sans argent chez des amis. Ces détonations firent naître dans mon esprit l'idée d'un combat. Le général donna aux chefs de ces trois armées les ordres nécessaires.

§ **321.** The sentence should be not only lucid, but well balanced, easy to speak and pleasing to the ear, in accordance with the dictum of Flaubert: "Une phrase est née viable (*capable of life*) quand elle correspond à toutes les nécessités de la prononciation. Je sais qu'elle est bonne lorsqu'elle peut être lue tout haut."

Thus in the sentence

Je rappellerai tout à l'heure ce qu'a été l'attitude du Japon, | depuis le début de cette formidable lutte,

the first half, when spoken, leaves us out of breath; by a slight dislocation the author obtains a better arrangement in three word-groups:

Ce qu'a été l'attitude du Japon, | depuis le début de cette formidable lutte, | je le rappellerai tout à l'heure.

Thus again, to balance the sentence, a lengthy direct object will follow, instead of preceding, the prepositional object.

Dieu a donné sa grâce | à toutes les créatures humaines.
Dieu a donné | à toutes les créatures humaines | sa grâce divine et fortifiante.

Note.—In literary style a pleasing balance is often achieved by the artifice known as chiasmus.

Ce que *chantaient* les rhapsodes, les acteurs le *déclament*.
Ce qu'on *tolère* devient intolérable, incorrigible ce qu'on ne *corrige* pas.
Profond était le *silence*, la *mer* brillante, mais seule, monotone.

§ **322.** A well-balanced French sentence is a compromise between the two necessities (1) of achieving lucidity, and (2) of bringing into 'strong position' those words on which we wish to lay the stress.

This compromise can be achieved in a number of ways. Suppose we wish to express in French: 'Henry gave me this book.' As the stress may be placed in English on any member of the word-group, the sentence above embodies five different statements, according as we say:

1. *Henry* (not *John*) gave me this book.
2. Henry *gave* (did not *lend*) me this book.
3. Henry gave *me* (not *you*) this book.
4. Henry gave me *this* (not *that*) book.
5. Henry gave me this *book* (not this *knife*).

These five statements may be rendered in French as follows :

1. (*a*) Ce livre m'a été donné par **Henri.**

Passive construction, bringing **Henri** into strong position.

(*b*) **C'est Henri** | qui m'a donné ce livre.

The sentence is broken up into two word-groups, again bringing Henri into a strong position. The construction **c'est . . . qui, c'est . . . que** is a common and powerful means of bringing a word into prominence.

2. Ce livre, | Henri me l'a **donné.**

By a dislocation, **donné** is brought into a strong position, in which we may give it full vocal stress. Note that the dislocation involves a duplication of the object.

3. **C'est à moi** que Henri a donné ce livre.

Availing ourselves of the construction **c'est . . . que.**

4. Henri m'a donné **ce livre-ci.**

Using the stressed form **ce . . . -ci** of the demonstrative adjective (§ 313).

5. **C'est ce livre** que Henri m'a donné.

If we content ourselves with the statement **Henri m'a donné ce livre,** the word **livre** is, of course, in strong position, but as we are using merely the 'normal' word-order, the stress will not be so apparent (§ 318) as in the more powerful construction **c'est . . . que.**

§ 323. The **subject** of the sentence may be stressed :

1. Merely by using the stressed form of the personal pronoun (in the 3rd person only, § 234.2).

Lui l'a fait.

2. By isolating the subject at the beginning of the sentence (dislocation, involving duplication).

Moi, je l'ai vu. **Quant à moi, je** l'ai vu.
La guerre, ce serait la ruine (§ 196.1).
Ces maladies-là, ça dure longtemps (colloq., § 190).
Que vous soyez si affairé, cela me surprend un peu (§ 189).

This is the usual construction when the subject is an infinitive clause.

Bien commencer, c'est déjà beaucoup.
Partir sur-le-champ, cela offrait quelques difficultés.

3. By isolating it at the end of the sentence (dislocation, involving duplication).

Je l'ai vu, moi.
Elle ne savait que répondre, la pauvre enfant.
En plein soleil, c'était sinistre, ce pillage.
C'est gentil, de s'aider les uns les autres (colloq.).

In literary style, without dislocation.

Il m'est doux de parler de ce livre admirable.

4. By a simple inversion.

Au beau milieu de notre joie arriva **Mathieu.**

5. By a change to the passive construction.

César conquit la Gaule. La Gaule fut conquise **par César.**

6. By the construction **C'est . . . qui.**

C'est moi qui l'ai vu. **Ce fut César** qui conquit la Gaule.

§ **324.** The **direct object** of the sentence may be stressed:

1. By isolating it at the beginning of the sentence (dislocation, involving duplication).

De l'argent, je n'en ai pas. *Money I have none.*
Les cigares, je ne les aime pas.
Quant aux cigares, je ne les aime pas.
Les cigares, je n'aime pas ça (colloq.).
En parler à mes parents, je ne l'osais pas.
Qu'il sorte seul, je ne le permets pas.

2. By isolating it at the end of the sentence (dislocation, involving duplication).

Je ne les aime pas, vos cigares.
Je n'aime pas ça, les cigares (colloq.).

3. By transposing any member of the sentence which would otherwise follow the object, in order that the latter may occupy the 'strong position.'

A cette observation il ne fit aucune **réponse.**

4. By the construction **C'est . . . que.**

Ce n'est pas de l'argent que je désire.

§ **325.** The **prepositional object** may be stressed:

1. By isolating it at the beginning or at the end of the sentence (dislocation, involving duplication).

If isolated at the beginning of the sentence, it requires no preposition.

If isolated at the end of the sentence, it takes the preposition. Thus:

'Il ne songe guère à vos conseils' becomes
Vos conseils, il n'**y** songe guère.
Il n'**y** songe guère, **à vos conseils.**

Thus also:

Vos menaces, il s'**en** moque bien.
Il s'**en** moque bien, **de vos menaces.**
Moi, ça **m**'est bien égal.
Ça **m**'est bien égal, **à moi.**

2. By the construction **C'est . . . que** (conjunction), **c'est . . . à qui, dont,** etc.

{ **C'est à vous que** je dois mon salut.
{ **C'est vous à qui** je dois mon salut.

{ **C'est de vos amis que** je parle.
{ **Ce sont vos amis dont** je parle.

§ **326.** The construction **c'est . . . qui, c'est . . . que** (either relative pronoun or conjunction) may be used to stress not only the subject or object, as in the examples above, but also (*a*) the adverbial adjuncts and (*b*) the predicative complements of the verb.

(*a*) **C'est demain** qu'il part. **C'est là** que nous habitons.
C'est ainsi qu'on l'appelle.
C'est en parlant une langue qu'on apprend à la parler.

(*b*) **Ce fut un homme étrange** que Robespierre.
C'est un drôle de petit bonhomme que cet enfant.
C'est déjà beaucoup que de bien commencer.

Notes.—(*a*) Upon this all-important construction **c'est . . . que, qui,** are based the expressions **est-ce que, qui est-ce que, qui est-ce qui,** etc., which have also such a wide use in French (§ 340.4).

(*b*) In exclamations, **c'est** may be replaced by **quel,** or may be entirely omitted.

Quel personnage **que** le vent pour un marin ! C'est **de lui** qu'on s'entretient le plus le long des jours, c'est **à lui** qu'on pense sans cesse.

Drôles de gens que les Anglais !

Fameuse canaille (*A regular scoundrel*) **que** ce vieux père Mathieu !

THE NORMAL WORD-ORDER

§ **327.** English and French have the same fundamental word-order.

Subject.	*Verb.*	*Direct Object.*	*Prepositional Object.*
Pierre	écrit	une lettre	à son père.
Peter	*is writing*	*a letter*	*to his father.*

Subject.	*Verb.*	*Direct object.*	*Predicative Complement.*
Son frère	était resté		garçon.
His brother	*had remained*		*a bachelor.*
Les soldats	appelaient	Napoléon	le Petit Caporal.
The soldiers	*called*	*Napoleon*	*the Little Corporal.*

§ **328.** The following is an essential difference between the two languages:

In English the verb is followed by its unstressed adjuncts.

I saw *you*. He gave *me* a book.

In French, all unstressed adjuncts, whether of noun or verb, are **proclitic** (*i.e.* cling to following noun or verb), in conformity with the law of end-stress.

Le père, **cet** enfant, **mon** ami.
Il me voit. **Je vous en** donnerai.

§ **329.** The unstressed adjuncts of the verb precede it in the following order:

Subject	*Object Pronouns*			*Pronouns and Adverbs*		*Verb*
je	me					
tu	te					
il, elle / on, ce	se	le, la	lui	y	en	
nous	nous					
vous	vous					
ils, elles	se	les	leur	y	en	
Il	me	le				donnera
Je		le	leur	y		ai envoyé
Nous	vous				en	aurions prêté
Ils	s'				en	vont
On	vous			y		mènera

§ **330.** In the negative adverbs **ne pas, ne jamais, ne plus,** etc., **ne** is also unstressed ; it precedes the verb, and the object pronouns if any.

The sentence then assumes the following typical order :

Subject (stressed or unstressed)	*Ne*	*Unstressed pronouns and adverbs*	*Verb or Auxiliary*	*Pas, jamais, etc.*	*Past participle*	*Stressed objects*
Le roi	n'		avait	pas		d'argent
Pierre	ne	leur	avait	pas	rapporté	l'argent
Je	n'	en	parlerai	jamais		
On	ne	nous en	a	pas	parlé	
Il	n'	y en	a	pas		pour moi
Nous	n'	en	avons		parlé	à personne
	Ne	vous en	occupez	plus		
	Ne	t'en	va	pas		
	Ne	le	dites	pas		à tout le monde
	Ne	le	dites			à personne

§ **331.** In the **positive imperative** the pronominal adjuncts follow the verb, and may take the stress (§ 313, note), **me, te,** becoming **moi, toi,** if not followed by **y** or **en.** The word-order is as follows :

Le, la, les,	before	**moi, toi, lui, leur,**	before **y, en.**
Nous, vous,	before	**le, la, les,**	

But : **m'y, t'y ; m'en, t'en.**

Donnez-**moi** un livre.
Assieds-**toi.** Asseyez-**vous.**
Prenez-**le.** (§ 313, note.)
Donnes-**en** aux autres. Vas-**y.** (§ 23.7.)
Donnez-**m'en.** Va-**t'en.** Allez-**vous-en.**
Vous avez une serviette ; servez-**vous-en.**
Donnez-**le-moi.** Donnez-**le-lui.** Donnez-**nous-les.**

Notes.—(*a*) In colloquial speech, constantly, Donnez-**moi-le.** One sometimes hears also : Donnez-**les-nous.**

(*b*) In the construction **laisser + infinitive,** each verb retains its own adjuncts, without elision between the pronouns.

Laissez-**le y** réfléchir. Laissez-**moi y** réfléchir.
Laissez-**moi en** parler à cœur ouvert.

§ 332. The position of the unstressed object pronouns with the verbs of §§ 92–94, 97, requires special attention.

1. With the group **faire + infinitive**, the unstressed pronouns cling to **faire** or its auxiliary, no matter **to** which of the verbs they stand as objects.

> Je **le fais** venir. **Faites-le** venir. (**Le** object to **faire**.)
> Son déjeuner, je **le lui fais** porter. } (**Le**, **lui**, objects to
> **Faites-le-lui** porter. } **porter**.)
> Sœur Marie-Aimée **me fit** appeler près d'elle.
> Ce matin, la supérieure **m'a fait** demander. *Sent for me.*
> Est-ce que madame la supérieure ne **vous a** pas **fait** demander ?

2. The groups **voir, entendre,** sentir, **laisser, envoyer + infinitive** have the same construction, but, as has already been said (§ 93), the combination is a looser one, and alternative constructions are possible.

> Mes camarades blessés, je **les avais vus** partir pour un voyage long et mystérieux. (**Les** object to **avais vus**.)
> Je me rappelai le fermier, et je tournai à gauche comme je **le lui avais vu** faire. (**Le** object to **faire**, **lui** object to **avais vu** ; double accusative avoided.)
> *Or :* . . . et je tournai à gauche comme je **l'avais vu le faire**. (Each verb has its own accusative ; colloquial construction.)
> Il **les envoya** réveiller par son valet. (**Les** object to **réveiller**.)
> *Or* Il envoya son valet **les réveiller**.

> But always : Je **l'ai envoyé** chercher. *I sent for him.*
> **Envoyez-le** chercher.

> Miss Lydia **se sentit saisir** d'une tristesse profonde. (**Se** object to **saisir**.)
> Cette histoire, je **vous la laisse** raconter. (**Vous** is in the dative.)
> Cette histoire, je **vous** laisse **la** raconter. (**Vous** is in the accusative.)

Note.—For the sentences

> (*a*) Quand elle **la** voyait **m'**embrasser, } elle rougissait de dépit,
> (*b*) Quand elle **me** voyait **l'**embrasser, }

one could *not* say :

> Quand elle **me la** voyait embrasser . . .

Standing for (*a*), this would constitute a double accusative.
Standing for (*b*), this would constitute the dative + accusative, but this construction applies to the dative of the 'person' + the accusative of the 'thing,' and is not available when, as here, both objects are persons.

Thus also in : Madeleine **m'**envoyait **la** chercher.

3. With the groups **falloir, vouloir, devoir, pouvoir, savoir, oser, aller, venir, + infinitive,** in the XVIIth century the pronoun object was very frequently prefixed to the head-verb. To-day it usually clings to the infinitive.

XVIIth century use	*Present use*
Il **le faut** faire.	Il faut **le faire.**
Vous **y devriez** courir.	Vous devriez **y courir.**
J'ai cru **le devoir** faire.	J'ai cru devoir **le faire.**
Vous **en avez pu** entendre parler.	Vous avez pu **en entendre** parler.
Je ne **vous le saurais** permettre.	Je ne saurais **vous le permettre.**
Je **le vais** souvent voir.	Je vais souvent **le voir.**
Il **se vient** plaindre.	Il vient **se plaindre.**
Il **se veut** aller pendre.	Il veut aller **se pendre.**

The XVIIth century construction is not used to-day in colloquial French, but many writers continue to favour it as a literary elegance. The following examples are recent:

Il **se les faut** concilier par des dons.
Si je **l'ose** avouer.
Il **s'est venu** plaindre à moi.
Enfin, je me décidai à **l'aller** chercher.
(Here, perhaps to avoid the awkward 'hiatus' à **aller le** chercher.)

Note.—In the compound tenses of pronominal verbs, the auxiliary verb changes with the construction.

Il s'est voulu pendre. Il **a** voulu **se** pendre.

§ **333.** 1. **Adverbs** regularly (*a*) follow the verb, and (*b*) precede the adjective or adverb, which they qualify.

(*a*) Il **vient souvent** chez nous.
Je **vois quelquefois** votre ami Dupont.
Il **viendra demain.**
Il ne **viendra pas** s'il fait mauvais temps.

(*b*) Voilà un garçon **bien** aimable!
Vous êtes **trop bonne,** madame!
Il agit **fort prudemment.**
Il ne viendra **certainement pas.**
Nous n'avons **presque plus** de charbon.

Note.—Except, of course, interrogative, exclamative, and relative adverbs, which always head the clause.

Comment dites-vous? **Comme** il fait froid!
Il était monté sur un rocher, **d'où** il me faisait signe.

2. In (*a*) compound tenses, and (*b*) the construction **verb + infinitive,** the adverb usually precedes the past participle or infinitive, but follows if it ought to take the stress, as is the case. for instance, with such words as

hier, aujourd'hui, demain, ici, là,

and frequently with adverbs in -ment.

(*a*)	Il est **souvent** venu chez nous.	Il est venu **ici hier.**
	Je l'avais **déjà** rencontré.	Je l'avais rencontré **là.**
	Vous avez **bien** agi.	Vous avez agi **sagement.**
(*b*)	Il faut **souvent** se taire.	Il faut vous taire **ici.**
	Je le fais **quelquefois** appeler.	Je le ferai appeler **demain.**
	J'espère **bientôt** la revoir.	

3. The adverbs **bien, mieux, mal, trop, peu,** and also **the indefinite pronouns tout, rien,** used as objects, frequently lose all stress, and cling to the **infinitive** so closely that they may be inserted either before or after an unstressed object pronoun.

Il faut **mieux vous** conduire *or* Il faut **vous mieux** conduire.
Je vais **tout vous** dire *or* Je vais **vous tout** dire.
Il aperçut l'oiseau bleu, et s'en approcha pour **le mieux** regarder.
Nous bien conduire est un devoir envers nous-mêmes et envers les autres.

§ 334. But the rules governing the position of adverbs are by no means rigid. Among the examples given above, the following might equally well show the adverb in stressed position :

Je l'avais rencontré **déjà.** Je le fais appeler **quelquefois.**
J'espère la revoir **bientôt.** Il faut vous conduire **mieux.**

(And thus also : Je vais vous dire **tout.**)

Note also the place of the adverb in the following:

Ce moment fugitif est resté dans ma mémoire, gravé **ineffaçablement.**
Presque il baisa la terre dans son empressement de courtoisie.
Elle est **toujours** remuante, avec **toujours** les mains derrière le dos.

§ 335. Adverb phrases and equivalents, on account of their greater length and sonority, usually take the end-stress.

Il est venu ici **tout à l'heure.** J'espère vous revoir **d'ici peu.**
Il est arrivé hier **à huit heures.**

But no absolute rules can be given : Thus :

Il reçut une dépêche d'un ami qui **depuis la veille** l'attendait à Paris.
Il vaut mieux lire **deux fois** un bon ouvrage qu'**une fois** un mauvais.

§ **336.** In compound tenses, adverb phrases and other members of the sentence which are of secondary importance, or parenthetical, are frequently inserted between the auxiliary and the past participle.

Ils avaient conscience d'avoir, **pendant une heure**, vécu d'une pensée commune.

Deux provinces furent **cependant, sous ce règne,** ajoutées au royaume.

La Corse nous fut, **en 1768,** abandonnée par Gênes.

Thus also parenthetical clauses.

Vous n'êtes pas, **je vous connais,** venu de Portsmouth ici sans avoir essayé de le faire parler.

Aurait-il, **s'il avait vécu,** été un obstacle à la fortune de Bonaparte ?

Thus also appositive pronouns or adjectives.

M. de Humboldt a **le premier,** je crois, constaté ce fait.

Ils se sont **l'un et l'autre** dévoués à la science.

Ils avaient, **eux aussi,** écrit à leurs parents.

§ **337.** When the adverb is a '**sentence-qualifier,**' *e.g.* when it expresses a personal opinion or feeling of the writer or speaker, it may occupy almost any position, provided that it does not separate proclitics from the word to which they cling, and it occurs very frequently at the beginning of the sentence.

{ **Pourtant** elle se savait aimée.
{ Elle se savait **pourtant** aimée.
{ Elle se savait aimée, **pourtant.**

Tout à l'heure je vous raconterai une histoire.

{ **Heureusement** l'accident n'eut pas de suites.
{ L'accident n'eut **heureusement** pas de suites.
{ L'accident n'eut pas de suites, **bien heureusement.**

C'étaient des jours affreux et sublimes comme **peut-être** la terre n'en avait point vu.

. . . comme la terre **peut-être** n'en avait point vu.

. . . comme la terre n'en avait **peut-être** point vu.

. . . comme la terre n'en avait point vu **peut-être.**

§ **338.** The direct object noun precedes the infinitive and participle in a number of phrases dating far back in the language.

Ils entrèrent dans la ville sans **coup** férir.

Il m'a raconté cela **chemin** faisant.

Apart from these cases, the accusative noun can only precede the verb through a dislocation of the sentence, involving duplication (§ 324), or when it is introduced by an interrogative adjective.

§ **339.** The transpositions of the prepositional objects have been dealt with in §§ 321, 325.

INTERROGATIVE WORD-ORDER

§ **340.** There are four interrogative constructions.

1. The subject precedes the verb, the question being indicated

(*a*) By voice-pitch alone.

Vous venez ? Vous ne viendrez donc pas ?

(*b*) By the fact that the subject is an interrogative word or word-group.

Qui vous a dit cela ?
Quels élèves ont plus de trois fautes ?

2. The subject follows the verb or auxiliary ('simple' inversion):

(*a*) If it is an unstressed pronoun (je, tu, etc. ; on, ce).

Venez-vous ? Vous en a-t-il parlé ?
Qu'en dira-t-on ? Est-ce vrai ?

(*b*) If the question is headed by an interrogative adverb or pronoun. The subject then takes the end-stress.

Comment va votre frère ? Quand arrive le train ?
Où demeure votre ami ? Quel est ce monsieur ?
De quoi se compose le mobilier de la classe ?
A qui pensait la jeune femme ?

(*c*) Always when the direct object is interrogative que (since que clings to the verb).

Que signifie tout cela ? Qu'a répondu le maître ?
Que prendront ces messieurs ? (§ 216, note.)

3. A stressed subject is duplicated, the verb being enclosed between noun (or pronoun) and personal pronoun ('pronominal' inversion):

(*a*) If the sentence does not begin with an interrogative word, or if it begins with pourquoi.

Votre ami viendra-t-il ? Madame désire-t-elle quelque chose ? Quelqu'un a-t-il vu mon livre ?
Cela vous va-t-il ? *Does that suit you ?*
Pourquoi votre frère ne nous accompagne-t-il pas ?

(*b*) In opposition to 2 (*b*) above, if the verb has a noun object or other complement, so that the subject cannot take the end-stress.

Quand votre famille a-t-elle su la nouvelle ?
Comment une pareille idée est-elle venue à ces messieurs ?

(*c*) **Optionally,** in careful speech and literary style, **in sentences** of the type 2 (*b*) above.

> Quand **le train** arrive-t-il ?
> Où **votre ami** demeure-t-il ?
> De quoi **le mobilier de la classe** se compose-t-il ?
> A quoi **la jeune femme** pensait-elle ?
> En quoi **ceci** nous interesse-t-il ?

(But this construction is not possible with predicative **quel, qui** ; always :

> **Quel** (*or* **Qui**) est **ce monsieur** ?)

And **necessarily,** when lucidity demands this construction. We cannot say :

> Quels ennemis vainquirent les Romains ?
> Qui a interrogé le professeur ?

if we mean :

> Quels ennemis les Romains vainquirent-ils ?
> Qui le professeur a-t-il interrogé ?

Note.—The pronominal inversion was originally a dislocation: **Votre ami, viendra-t-il ?** in which the order could be varied : **Viendra-t-il, votre ami ?** forms which are still used colloquially. But in normal French the construction is now close-knit, there being neither comma nor pause between the two elements of the subject and the verb.

The construction has grown out of the natural tendency to give the verb the central position which ensures both lucidity and the balance of the sentence. A sentence of the type : **Tua le chasseur le lion ?** would be ambiguous, and would lack balance, since the two stressed elements would be brought together. In the forms : **Le chasseur tua-t-il le lion ?** or **Le lion tua-t-il le chasseur ?** the meaning is clear and the ear is satisfied. Compare also : **Quand reviendra votre ami de Paris ?** (Does this mean 'from Paris,' or 'your Paris friend'?) and the correct construction : **Quand votre ami reviendra-t-il de Paris ?**

4. In colloquial French, the varied constructions given above are generally avoided by the inversion of the construction **c'est . . . que, qui** (§§ 322.1, 326, note), followed by the normal word-order.

> **Est-ce que** vous venez ? **Est-ce que** vous ne viendrez pas ?
> **Est-ce qu'il** vous en a parlé ? **Est-ce que c'est vrai ?**
> Quand **est-ce que** le train arrive ?
> **Est-ce que** quelqu'un a vu mon frère ?
> **Est-ce que** le lion tua le chasseur ?
> Qui **est-ce qui** vous a dit ça ?
> Qui **est-ce que** le professeur a interrogé ?
> Qu'**est-ce qu'on** en dira ?
> Qu'**est-ce que** le maître a répondu ?

§ **341.** In **dependent** questions, (*a*) the unstressed subject is not inverted ; (*b*) there is usually simple inversion of the noun subject, (*c*) unless the verb is followed by a stressed object or other complement.

(*a*) Je ne sais pas quelle heure **il est.**
Dites-moi ce que **vous désirez.**
Il raconta comment **il m'avait trouvé** la veille.

(*b*) Je ne sais pas à quelle heure **arrive le train.**
Dites-moi ce que **désire votre protégé.**
Je vis une fois de plus combien vive **était leur intelligence.**
Je demandai à ma gouvernante d'où nous **était tombé ce pauvre petit homme.**

(*c*) Je ne sais pas pour quelle heure **ces dames ont commandé la voiture.**
Dites-moi de quoi **votre protégé désire m'entretenir.**

And with the dependent question as logical subject:

(*a*) Il vous sera demandé si **vous chassez.**
(*b*) Il me fut demandé qui j'étais et quelle **était ma profession.**
(*c*) Il n'a jamais été publié où et comment **ce fait a eu lieu.**

INVERSION OF SUBJECT AND VERB IN NON-INTERROGATIVE SENTENCES

The tendency to balance the sentence by keeping the verb in a central position in the word-group will account for the greater number of the following constructions.

§ **342.** Simple inversion of **any subject** occurs

1. In clauses beginning with stressed **ainsi,** *thus.*

Ainsi dit-il. Ainsi mourut ce grand homme.

Note.—No inversion after **ainsi** used as a conjunction (=*so*).

Ainsi vos amis ne viendront pas ? *So your friends aren't coming?*

2. In the parenthetical use of **dire, répondre, s'écrier,** etc.

Très bien, **répondit le** professeur.
J'aurais, **dit-il,** beaucoup d'objections à vous faire.
Comment ! **s'écria Pierre,** c'est encore vous !
Boudet était un brave homme, **ai-je dit.**

§ **343.** **Simple** inversion of the **noun** subject (or of a **stressed** pronoun) occurs

1. In official style, when the subject is of great length.

   Seront admis à se présenter à l'examen oral **tous les candidats qui aux épreuves écrites auront obtenu une moyenne d'au moins cinquante pour cent.**

   Ont assisté à la cérémonie : **le maire, ses adjoints, et les membres du conseil municipal, le sous-préfet et le commandant de la garnison . . .**

And, generally speaking, whenever the verb is quite overshadowed by the subject. Thus especially with the verbs **suivre, venir, rester, arriver.**

   Suivit **une scène indescriptible.**
   Venaient ensuite **deux éléphants de grande taille.**
   Voilà deux obstacles de surmontés. Reste **un troisième.**
   On gagne beaucoup à être poli. **Est** bien naïf **celui qui ne s'en aperçoit pas.**

2. In wishes **not** introduced by **que** (initial stress, affective).

   Vive la France ! Périsse **le tyran !**

3. In sentences introduced by adverbs and adverb-phrases, especially those of time and place, *e.g.* **bientôt, déjà, alors, aujourd'hui, hier soir, ici, là** ; provided the subject can, and ought to, take the stress.

   Bientôt viendra **la nuit.**
   Alors commença **une discussion confuse.**
   Aujourd'hui sont arrivés **deux bataillons de renfort.**
   Hier soir s'est répandue **une nouvelle des plus inattendues.**
   Ici commence **la grande plaine septentrionale.**
   De là découlent **des conséquences inattendues.**

4. When a predicative adjective heads the sentence, with an affective stress.

   Profond était **le silence.**
   Radieux est **le spectacle**, aux approches du soir.

5. In dependent clauses (*a*) adjectival, (*b*) introduced by **c'est . . . que,** (*c*) forming the second member of a comparison, (*d*) introduced by **quand, lorsque,** etc. ; provided the verb has no stressed object or other stressed complement.

   (*a*) C'est un homme **que** ne respecte **personne.**
   Scylla était un rocher menaçant, au pied **duquel** se trouvaient **des cavernes souterraines.**
   (*b*) **C'est** aux cœurs hardis **que** sourit **la fortune.**
   (*c*) Il est **plus** intelligent **que** ne le pense **son maître.**
   Vous répondez **comme** le ferait **un enfant.**
   (*d*) **Quand** viendra **le printemps,** la terre reverdira.

Notes.—1. But compare the following, in which the subject could not take the end-stress :

(*a*) Charybde était un gouffre dans lequel **la mer s'enfonçait en tournoyant.**
(*b*) C'est aux cœurs hardis que **la fortune accorde** ses **faveurs.**
(*c*) Il est plus intelligent que **son maître** ne nous l'**avait donné à entendre.**
(*d*) Quand le **printemps ramènera la chaleur,** la terre reverdira.

2. Inversion in these dependent clauses is largely a matter of taste. Many writers avoid it if the subject does not overweight the verb.

L'esprit se nourrit et se fortifie par les sublimes vérités que **l'étude lui fournit.**
Ce devait être au commencement de mon second hiver, à l'heure triste où **la nuit vient.**
Notre maison était restée telle que **ma grand'mère** l'avait **arrangée.**

6. In the concessive clauses dealt with in § 383.

Quelles que soient **vos raisons,** il ne vous écoutera pas.

And in certain assumptive constructions shown in § 388.

Vienne **le printemps,** la terre reverdira.

§ **344. Pronominal** or **simple** inversion, according as the subject is a **noun** or an **unstressed pronoun,** occurs

1. In clauses introduced by **encore** (=*nevertheless*), **aussi** (=*so*), **peut-être, au moins, à plus forte raison, à peine,** etc.

En admettant que votre absence fût justifiée, **encore aurait-il** fallu nous prévenir.
Peut-être y a-t-il encore de l'espoir.
Il y avait eu erreur, **aussi** { nous fit-**on** des excuses. / les agents nous firent-**ils** des excuses. }
A peine étions-**nous** sortis / **A peine la compagnie** fut-**elle** sortie } qu'il se mit à pleuvoir.

2. In the following asyndetic construction of assumptive clauses (dislocation, originally question and answer).

M'aurait-**on** invité, je n'aurais pas pu accepter.
Le roi m'aurait-**il** invité, je n'aurais pas pu accepter.

Note.—Many of the inversions shown above belong to literary and academic style, and are avoided in familiar speech. Thus :

La nuit va bientôt venir.
Cet homme-là, personne ne le respecte.
Il est plus intelligent que son maître le pense.
Peut-être qu'il y a encore de l'espoir.
Il y avait eu erreur, aussi, on nous a fait des excuses.
On m'aurait invité que je n'aurais pas pu accepter.

POSITION OF THE EPITHET ADJECTIVE

§ **345.** The position of the attributive adjective is not fixed; almost any adjective may be found either preceding or following the noun. Their relative position is a question primarily of which of the two ought to take the stress, but also largely of use and wont.

§ **346.** In normal French the governing principle is to place the adjective after the noun if it is entitled to take the stress, *i.e.* if it serves to distinguish the object under consideration from others of its kind, if it is a **distinguishing mark**. Thus:

> Donnez-moi de l'**encre rouge.** *Red ink, not black!*
> Buvez tous les matins un verre d'**eau froide.** *Not hot!*

Adjectives denoting shape, colour, and other physical qualities, those denoting a nationality or religion, etc., are most commonly used as distinguishing marks, and usually follow the noun; and all adjectives used in a technical and scientific sense naturally follow.

> **l'acide sulfurique, un angle droit, un nombre impair.**

§ **347.** On the other hand, very common adjectives, of wide connotation, such as **grand, gros, petit, bon, mauvais, gentil, méchant, jeune, vieux, joli, vilain,** are usually unstressed, and precede the noun.

> **des petits enfants, un bon garçon, un vieil ami** de la famille,

and in many cases tend to form a compound with the noun:

> **des petits pois** (*green peas*), **mon petit-fils** (*grandson*), **un jeune homme, une jeune fille, le Nouveau Monde, le bonheur, le gentilhomme.**

Note.—That the connection between adjective and noun is much closer than that between noun and adjective is proved by the fact that 'liaison' always takes place between the former and, in prose, never between the latter. Thus, **un savant aveugle** is either

> [œ̃ savɑ̃ avœ:gl], *a blind scientist,*
> or [œ̃ savɑ̃t avœ:gl], *a learned blind man.*

When Gaston de Presles asks Hector to act as his second in a duel:

> Tu ne me comprends pas, toi, mon témoin naturel, **mon second obligé ?**

he pronounces: [mɔ̃ zgɔ̃ ɔbliʒe], **second** being the noun,
while [mɔ̃ zgɔ̃t ɔbliʒe]
would mean 'the second person whom I have obliged,' **obligé** being the noun.

§ **348.** But even the commonest adjectives may in certain contexts have the value of a distinguishing mark, and **follow** the noun, taking the stress.

Ce serait déchirer le vêtement neuf, sans que la pièce neuve s'accorde avec le **vêtement vieux.** *Luke* v. 36.

Un genre de plantes caractérisées par leurs **feuilles petites** et jaunâtres.

Pour endurer ce climat il faut des **hommes jeunes.**

Le roi de Prusse recherchait les **hommes grands** pour **les** enrôler dans sa garde.

§ **349.** If the adjective denotes some quality which is **already implied in the connotation of the noun,** it is obviously not a distinguishing mark, and will precede the noun. Compare the positions in the following groups of sentences :

La mère avait mis sa **robe blanche.** *Not her blue or her green dress!*

La mère caressait de sa **blanche main** les cheveux du petit garçon.

A lady's hand is white, by implication. Here, **sa main blanche** would be absurd ; blanche would be a distinguishing mark, and this would suggest that her other hand was of some other colour.

Nous avions alors une **domestique normande.**

Nous ne pouvions rien contre la **normande obstination** de notre domestique.

The peasants of Normandy are proverbially obstinate.

L'Angleterre protestante était rangée d'un côté, les **catholiques** de l'autre.

La **protestante** Angleterre soutenait les huguenots.

L'Angleterre protestante: that part of England which was Protestant.

La protestante Angleterre: England, that Protestant country.

Nous avons fait le voyage avec **une famille parisienne.**

Les dames de la ville se sentaient éclipsées par **la très** parisienne élégance des nouvelles venues.

Compare also :

une rue étroite	une étroite amitié
de l'eau froide	la froide raison
un voisin riche	un riche seigneur
une famille noble	un noble seigneur
un ruban noir	la noire verdure des cyprès
un temps sombre	un sombre désespoir
un train rapide	ses rapides progrès

§ **350.** The adjective may denote an attribute implied, not in the noun, but in what has come before ; in this case also it will precede the noun.

{ Pas d'excuses **timides**, montrez de l'assurance !
{ Ces **timides** excuses furent à peine écoutées.

We have just read them, and know them to have been timid.

{ Je distribuerai cet argent à des **amis malheureux.**
{ Mon **malheureux** ami mourut peu après.

We have just heard his unhappy story.

§ **351.** It will be noticed that in most of the examples given above, the adjective preceding the noun has an affective value, being used to express some feeling, or to 'adorn the discourse.' We may say, therefore, that as a rule **adjectives precede the noun in affective speech.** They may, of course, take an affective stress.

§ **352.** Many adjectives, however, are always used affectively, *e.g.* **énorme, terrible, redoutable, délicieux, sublime,** and as there is no danger of their being interpreted as distinguishing marks, they may be placed either before or after the noun, with stress in either position. Here, balance of the sentence is the chief consideration. If the noun has a prepositional complement, the adjective will generally come first, in order that noun and complement may remain in close proximity.

La Prusse était pour la Pologne une **redoutable voisine** *or* **une voisine redoutable.**

{ Mme X portait une **robe délicieuse.**
{ Mme X portait une **délicieuse robe** en crêpe de Chine.

{ On faisait de la force un **emploi continuel.**
{ Il fallut renoncer au **continuel emploi** de la force.

The ear must always be satisfied.

On entendit un **long rugissement** *or* un **rugissement prolongé,**

but *not* **un rugissement long** (§ 317.2).

§ **353.** In a number of compounds dating back to a time when the principles stated above had not yet come into being, the adjective precedes the noun though it is a distinguishing mark.

le bas Rhin, la rue des **Blancs-Manteaux,** un **blanc-bec** (*greenhorn*), **le moyen âge, le Saint-Siège.**

But **les Pays-Bas, la Terre Sainte.**

§ 354. Past participles usually follow the noun, being distinguishing marks.

> une porte fermée, une fenêtre ouverte.

But the rule is not absolute, *i.e.* the participle may be affective.

> Vous n'êtes pas chargé de corriger mes prétendues fautes d'orthographe !
> C'est un rusé compère.

§ 355. Proper nouns are of course preceded by the adjective,

> L'excellent M. Leblanc. L'antique Cérès.
> L'ancienne Agrigente, qui est la moderne Girgenti.

Except in the rare cases when the adjective is a distinguishing mark.

> Fromont jeune et Risler aîné.
> Je voyais devant moi un monsieur Forain vieux et cassé, fort différent de celui que je m'étais imaginé.
> La Rome antique (as distinct from modern Rome).

§ 356. Numeral and indefinite adjectives precede the noun.

> Il est venu trois fois, plusieurs fois, mainte et mainte fois.
> Le vingtième siècle. Le premier acte.

But the numeral may be a distinguishing mark.

> Louis quatorze. Voyez à la page douze.
> Acte premier, scène deux.

Note also the position of quelconque.

> Adressez-vous à un ami quelconque.

§ 357. Many adjectives have different meanings according to their position, differences which belong to the study of the vocabulary rather than of grammar, but which can for the most part be deduced from the general principles laid down above. Thus, certain indefinite adjectives may become distinguishing marks.

On m'a raconté certaines choses.	C'est une chose certaine (*beyond doubt*).
J'ai vu diverses personnes.	On m'a donné des conseils très divers.
Je n'ai nulle envie de le revoir.	C'est un homme nul (*of no account*).

Compare also :

Un mauvais calcul (*wrong, mistaken*).	Des calculs mauvais (*evil*).
Un méchant écrivain (*worthless*).	Un auteur méchant (*ill-natured*).
Le pauvre homme ! *Poor man !*	Un homme pauvre (*not rich*).
La dernière semaine du mois.	La semaine dernière (*last week*).
Il y a un seul Dieu (*one God*).	Dieu seul peut nous secourir (*God alone*).

§ **358.** The position of the adjective is not affected by short adverbs such as **très, plus, si,** etc.

> **C'est une très (fort, bien, assez) bonne personne.**
> **Nous avons fait une si belle promenade !** (. . . *such a fine walk !*)

But it naturally follows the noun if it is qualified by an adverb of some length (§ 317.2).

> **Un très riche** seigneur, *but* Un seigneur **excessivement riche.**
> **Un trop long** discours, *but* Un discours **beaucoup trop long.**

The adjective also follows whenever it has a prepositional complement.

> Une **riche** contrée, *but* Une contrée **riche en vins.**
> Une **bonne** chose, *but* Une chose **bonne à manger.**

§ **359.** If the noun is qualified by two adjectives,

1. The noun and one of the adjectives may form a whole which is qualified by the other adjective :

> Une petite fille | intelligente.
> Une gentille | petite fille.
> De beaux | arbres fruitiers.
> Une vilaine | petite boîte | de carton.

2. Or the two adjectives may stand in similar relation to the noun ; they are then joined by a conjunction :

> Une grande et belle maison.
> Une intelligence forte et éclairée.

§ **360.** The appositive adjective has no fixed position.

> **Souriante,** la mère écoutait les questions que faisaient les enfants.
> La mère, **souriante,** écoutait les questions . . .
> La mère écoutait, souriante, les questions . . .
> **Triste,** je gagnai les ponts.
> Suzon, **très grave,** tricotait un bas de laine bleue.

§ **361.** Prepositional complements of the noun always follow.

> Un homme de bien. *A righteous man.*
> Une tasse à thé. Une petite boîte de carton.
> **Une armée en déroute.** Un soldat pour rire.

THE SIMPLE SENTENCE

§ **362.** **Statements** and **questions** have the verb in the **indicative** mood.

Il **fait** froid. Je **n'aurais** pas cru cela. **Venez-vous** ?

Notes.—1. In literary style only, the past perfect subjunctive is found instead of the future perfect in the past.

Il en **eût été** (aurait été) fort embarrassé.

2. The subjunctive is used, with an implication of doubt, in the expression **je ne sache pas que.**

Je ne sache pas qu'on ait jamais fait mieux.

3. A statement may also be in the historical infinitive. See § 109.

§ **363.** Ellipsis of a verb which can be easily supplied, and especially of **être, y avoir,** is frequent.

(*a*) In statements.

Heureux les peuples sans histoire.
Région étrange que celle-là.
Dans le bourg, rien d'intéressant.
Rien de sinistre et formidable comme cette côte de Brest.

Ellipsis is especially common in descriptive passages.

Le Colysée apparaît . . . Personne dans l'intérieur ; un profond silence ; rien que des blocs de pierre, des herbes pendantes, et, de temps en temps, un cri d'oiseau.

And is the rule in answers to questions.

Avez-vous faim ? — Oui.
Quel âge avez-vous ? — Dix-sept ans.

(*b*) In questions.

Quoi de neuf ? A quand votre réponse ? A qui le tour ?
De qui cette lettre ?
Êtes-vous satisfait ? — Pourquoi non ? *or* Pourquoi pas ?

§ **364.** Ellipsis of the subject occurs in a few cases.

Ainsi fut fait. A Dieu ne plaise ! *God forbid !*

§ **365.** **Commands** have the verb, (*a*) in the first and second persons, in the **imperative** mood ; (*b*) in the third person, in the **subjunctive** (introduced by **que**), according to the general principles governing the use of the subjunctive (§ 371).

(*a*) **Ouvrez** la fenêtre. **Asseyez-vous.**

(*b*) **Qu'il fasse** vite. **Qu'elle ait** bien soin de tout cela.
Que monsieur **m'écoute** un instant.

Note.—Commands are frequently 'softened' by the use of the verb **vouloir** (bien).

> **Voulez-vous bien** m'aider ? **Veuillez** (bien) vous asseoir.

And may be further softened by the use of the future in the past (§ 84.2).

> **Voudriez-vous bien** ouvrir la fenêtre ?
> Monsieur **voudrait-il bien** m'écouter un instant ?

§ **366.** Ellipsis is frequent.

> Silence ! A boire ! Feu ! Aux armes !
> Garçon, deux potages.

§ **367. Wishes and desires** have the verb in the **subjunctive,** (*a*) in the present tense (with future value), if it is hoped that the wish may be realized ; (*b*) in the past tenses if the wish is beyond realization. The conjunction **que** is sometimes expressed, but more usually omitted, in favour of simple inversion of subject and verb.

> (*a*) **Que** Dieu nous **soit** en aide !
> **Puissé-je** arriver à temps !
> (*b*) **Plût** à Dieu **qu'il fût arrivé** à temps !
> **Pût-il** être arrivé à temps ! *Would that he might . . . !*

Note.—Wishes are also introduced by **que ne**+indicative :

> **Que ne suis-je** resté dans mon village ! *Why didn't I . . . !*

by **si**+past descriptive or past perfect :

> Ah ! **si j'étais (j'avais été)** encore jeune ! *If only . . . !*

by **que** or **comme**+future in the past :

> **Que (Comme)** nous **boirions** bien un verre de bière !

In the two latter constructions the compound tenses may be in the subjunctive in literary style.

> **Si** j'**eusse été** encore jeune !
> **Comme** il **eût** volontiers **renoncé** aux grandeurs !

§ **368.** Ellipsis is frequent :

> Bon voyage. Bonne chance !
> Grand bien vous fasse ! *Much good may it do you !*

§ **369. Exclamations** may be in effect statements, questions, commands, or wishes.

1. Exclamative statements are usually introduced by **que, comme, combien,** and have the verb in the **indicative.** The predicative adjective is not transposed as in English.

Comme vous **êtes** désagréable aujourd'hui ! *How crusty you are . . . !*
Comme (Qu') il **fait** chaud ! *How warm it is!*
Combien je **regrette** de vous avoir dérangé !

They may take the inverted order.

Est-elle méchante ! *Isn't she naughty!*

They may be introduced by **quel,** with ellipsis of the verb.

Quelle chaleur ! Quel bel enfant !

Note.—Quel may be replaced by the definite article if the noun has a preceding adjective (which then takes an affective initial stress).

Le bel enfant ! **La sotte** réponse !
L'aimable enfant que cette petite !

2. Exclamative questions are generally emphasized by some affective adverb.

Venez-vous, **à la fin** ?

3. Thus also exclamative commands.

Mais venez **donc** !

Often in interrogative form.

Voulez-vous bien vous taire ! (Affective stress on **voulez**; cp. English, *Will you hold your tongue !*)

4. Wishes. The constructions studied in § 367 are all exclamative and affective.

THE COMPLEX SENTENCE

§ 370. The complex sentence is formed in French on the same principles as in English : it consists of one or more main clauses showing the same moods as the simple sentence, and of subordinate noun, adjective, or adverb clauses. The latter are introduced by conjunctions or relative pronouns which may not be omitted as so frequently happens in English.

Je sais **qu'**il est là. *I know he is there.*
Je ne doute pas **qu'**il ne réussisse. *I have no doubt he will succeed.*
Voici un livre **que** je n'ai pas lu. *Here is a book I haven't read.*
Voilà le livre **dont** je parlais. *That's the book I was talking of.*

Note.—In a few constructions the relative pronoun is indefinite, and has no expressed antecedent. The adjective clause becomes a noun clause and acts as subject to the main verb.

Qui vivra | verra.
Quiconque flatte ses maîtres | les trahit.

§ 371. Mood of the Subordinate Clause.

The action or state expressed by the verb may be presented:

1. **As a fact,** something which is, has been, or will be, either certainly or probably.

2. As **not a fact,** *i.e.* as an idea, existing only in the mind of the speaker. It may then be:

(*a*) **Possible,** but not yet realized.
(*b*) **Doubtful** or **improbable.**
(*c*) Admittedly **contrary to fact.**
(*d*) **Assumed** (Hypothesis). The assumption may be a possible or an impossible one.
(*e*) **Merely conceded,** with an implication of doubt.

3. **As a fact,** acknowledged as such; **but the acknowledgment of the fact is secondary in importance to the expression of the mental attitude of the speaker toward this fact.**

(*E.g.* compare the two statements: 'I know that he is ill.' 'I am sorry that he is ill.' The former is merely a stronger affirmation of the statement: 'He is ill'; but in the latter, the important statement is my expression of sorrow; that he is ill, is admitted, but is not the main affirmation.)

Case 1 above calls for the **indicative mood.**

Cases 2 and **3** call for the **subjunctive mood.**

§ 372. The following reservations must however be made:

1. **Noun clauses.** Dependent questions always have the indicative mood.

Il demande à quelle heure on **part,** si c'**est** bien vrai.
On ne savait pas où on **allait.**

2. **Adverb clauses.** Assumptions introduced by **si** always **have** the indicative mood.

S'il m'**écrit** je lui **répondrai.**
Si vous m'**aviez écrit** je vous aurais **répondu.**

Note.—But as a literary elegance the subjunctive may in the compound tenses be used in both the 'if' and the 'then' clauses, or in either.

Si vous m'**eussiez** écrit, je vous **eusse** répondu.
Si vous m'**eussiez** écrit, je vous aurais répondu.
Si vous m'aviez écrit, je vous **eusse** répondu.

NOUN CLAUSES

§ 373.

Indicative	*Subjunctive*
Fact certain or probable	*Fact possible, but not certain*
Il est vrai / Il est certain / Je sais / Il est probable } qu'il est là. / qu'il **viendra.** / qu'il **est venu.**	Il est possible / Il se peut } qu'il **vienne.** / qu'il **soit venu.**
	Il craint que vous **ne soyez** fâché.
	Ta mère a peur que tu **sois** marin.
Official commands and decrees: Le Premier Consul ordonne que des crêpes **seront** suspendus à tous les drapeaux. La cour a ordonné que ce témoin **sera entendu.**	Thus after expressions of will (desire, wish, command, permission, advice, prevention, avoidance, prohibition) and of necessity.
J'espère qu'il **viendra.** (Note that espérer implies not only wish, but also probability, so that the dependent noun clause is in the indicative.)	Je veux / Je souhaite / J'ordonne / Je permets / Je defends } qu'il **vienne.**
	Je m'oppose à ce qu'il **vienne.**
	Je tiens à ce que tout **soit** prêt à mon retour.
	Mon ambition serait que mon livre **donnât** la curiosité de lire.
Je suis d'avis qu'il **viendra.** *In my opinion he will come.*	Je suis d'avis qu'il **vienne.** *In my opinion he ought to come.*
	Il faut / Il est nécessaire / Il est urgent } que cela **se fasse.**
	Il avait besoin qu'on lui **témoignât** de l'amitié.
Dites-lui que nous le **ferons.**	Dites-lui qu'il **fasse** vite.
Ils crièrent qu'ils **avaient** faim.	Ils crièrent qu'on les **servît** promptement.
Je vous préviens que je **suis** de mauvaise humeur.	Ils prévinrent qu'on ne **jugeât** pas leur fortune d'après leur apparence.

§ **374.**

Fact certain or probable	*Fact doubtful or improbable*
Je suis sûre que vous m'**aimez**,	mais je ne suis pas sûre que vous m'**aimiez** toujours.
Il est évident que vous **avez** raison.	Il n'est pas évident que vous **ayez** raison.
Je pense qu'il **viendra**.	Je ne pense pas qu'il **vienne**.
A quelle heure pensez-vous qu'il **viendra** ? (The interrogation bears on the time of his coming ; his coming is not in doubt.)	Pensez-vous qu'il **vienne** ? Si vous pensez qu'il **vienne**, nous allons attendre.
Croyez-vous que je **suis** ici pour perdre mon temps ? (Rhetorical question, affective, = Vous savez bien que je ne suis pas ici . . .)	
Il est probable qu'il **viendra**.	Il est peu probable qu'il **vienne**.
On a de la peine à s'imaginer que la terre **est** ronde. (That it is round is admitted.)	On a de la peine à s'imaginer que la nature **accomplisse** de tels miracles.

§ **375.** The dependent statement of an admitted fact may often be either in the indicative, being viewed as a fact, or in the subjunctive, as viewed through the mind of the subject of the head clause (' objective ' and ' subjective ' points of view).

Thus, there is no essential difference in meaning, but merely a difference in point of view, implied by the moods in the following :

Je ne savais pas qu'il **était** de retour.	Je ne savais pas qu'il **fût** de retour.
Elle l'attendit à la poterne, car elle ignorait qu'il **était** au tournoi.	. . . car elle ignorait qu'il **fût** au tournoi.

§ **376.**

	The dependent statement is admittedly contrary to fact
	Je nie que cela **soit** vrai.
Il est **vrai** qu'il l'**a dit**.	Il n'est pas vrai qu'il **ait dit** cela.
	Notre Père qui êtes aux Cieux, de combien il s'en faut que votre volonté **soit** faite !
	Il serait excessif de prétendre que la France **ait marché** toujours, et dans toutes les directions, à la tête des nations.

§ **377.** *Assumption, hypothesis*

The assumption introduced by **si** is in the indicative, otherwise in the subjunctive.

Si son fils **revenait** ! . . .	Supposons qu'il **revienne** en effet.
(Je suppose qu'il **reviendra** demain. = Je pense que . . . This is not an assumption.)	Qu'il **vienne** ou qu'il ne **vienne** pas, cela m'est bien égal.
	Qu'il **vienne** ou **non,** cela m'est égal.

Whenever the dependent noun clause precedes the main clause, it is presented as an assumption.

Il est certain que vous **avez** raison.	Que vous **ayez** raison, c'est certain.
Je crois qu'il a **eu** cette intention.	Qu'il **ait** eu cette intention, je le crois.

§ **378.** *Concession*

Je ne nie pas que **cela (ne) soit** vrai.

§ **379.** *The reality of the fact is acknowledged, but the important statement is that of the effect which it produces on the speaker*

Je regrette que vous **soyez** à Paris pour si peu de temps.
Ça me fait de la peine que tu **sois** fâchée avec papa.
C'est bien heureux qu'on **t'ait** reconnu.
Je suis enchanté que vous **ayez remporté** ce succès.[1]
Il est très naturel que vous **ayez** hâte de partir.
Je comprends que le livre **soit** arrivé à sa troisième édition, mais je m'explique qu'il **ait** mis dix ans pour y arriver.

"Une lettre, père Azan ? — Oui monsieur . . . ça **vient** de Paris."	Il était tout fier que ça **vînt** de Paris, ce brave père Azan.[1]

[1] These are, strictly speaking, adverb clauses, but they may conveniently be dealt with here.

ADJECTIVE CLAUSES

§ 380.

Fact realized or certain	*Possibility not yet realized*
Savez-vous ce que je vous **donnerai** ?	
Il ne sait pas ce que je lui **donnerai.**	
Il a un ami qui lui **dit** toujours la vérité.	Il lui faudrait **un ami** qui **lui dise** la vérité.
Voici un livre qui **est** bien amusant !	Donnez-moi un livre qui **soit** amusant.
	Donnez-moi une chambre **où** l'on n'**entende** pas le piano.

§ 381.

	Fact doubtful or improbable
Voici un élève qui **saura** vous répondre.	Y a-t-il un élève qui **sache** cela ?
Je connais quelqu'un qui **pourra** vous aider.	Si vous connaissez quelqu'un qui **puisse** m'aider, donnez-moi son adresse.

§ 382. A shade of doubt, **or** 'softened affirmation,' is thus introduced into adjective clauses when the antecedent is restricted by an adjective in the superlative or by its equivalent (**le premier, le dernier, le seul, ne . . .** que) ; sometimes also by an adjective in the positive degree ; also by **peu, pas beaucoup.** In all these cases, the indicative *may* be used, to remove any implication of doubt, and it is thus used especially in the past historic and in the future.

C'est le meilleur **ami** que nous **avons.**	C'est le meilleur **ami** que nous **ayons.**
Vous êtes le premier qui **savez** votre leçon.	Vous êtes le premier qui **sachiez** votre leçon.
	Il avait l'air du plus féroce coquin qui se **pût** voir.
Les Français furent les seuls qui **réussirent** dans ce genre d'éloquence.	Les Français sont les seuls qui **aient réussi** dans ce genre d'éloquence.
Je ferai sauter la cervelle au premier qui **parlera** de se rendre.	
Il y a beaucoup de gens qui **savent** cela.	Il y a peu de gens qui **sachent** cela.
	C'est un des **bons** dîners que **j'aie faits.** (Affective stress on **bons**).

Note.—The indicative mood is, of course, always used when **c'est qui, c'est que** are intended merely to emphasize a subject or object (§§ 323, 324).

C'est la plus âgée qui **a** répondu. (=La plus âgée a répondu.)
C'est la plus âgée que nous **préférons**. (=Nous préférons la plus âgée.)

(Cp. 'C'est le meilleur vin que je puisse vous offrir,' which is *not* equivalent to 'Je puis vous offrir le meilleur vin.')

§ 383. The same implication of doubt is contained in the group of concessive constructions:

Qui que tu **sois**,
Quoi que tu **aies** fait,
Quelles que **soient** tes fautes,
Quelques fautes que tu **aies** commises,
Quelque grandes que **soient** tes fautes,
} Dieu te pardonnera.

But **tout . . . que** generally with the indicative:

Toutes grandes que **sont** tes fautes,

Note.—Also in the concessive **que je sache**, in which **que** is a neuter relative pronoun. The antecedent clause is nearly always negative.

Il n'est venu personne, que je **sache**.

§ 384.

Ce n'est pas **lui** qui m'**a dit** cela.
Ce n'est pas cette personne qui **m'a répondu**.

Dependent statement contrary to fact

Il n'y a pas **un élève** qui **sache** cela.
Je ne connais **personne** qui **puisse** vous répondre.
Vous n'allez **rien** apprendre qui vous **soit** agréable.
Plus de corde, plus de pieu, **rien** qui l'**empêchât** de gambader, de brouter à sa guise.

Note.—The subjunctive remains even though two negations destroy each other. Compare Latin usage. The construction is entirely literary.

Tout le monde **sait** bien que la terre est ronde.
N'importe quel prince en France **s'honorerait** de l'épouser.

Il n'y a **personne** qui **ne sache** que la terre est ronde.
Je crois qu'il n'y a **point de prince** en France **qui ne s'honorât** de l'épouser.
Il n'y avait pas jusqu'à compère le Loup et son cousin Maître Renard qui **ne prissent** plaisir à escorter la petite Fleur-des-Blés.

ADVERB CLAUSES

§ **385.**

Fact realized or certain	*Possibility not yet realized*

Time Clauses

Quand, dès que, après que, etc.	**Avant que, en attendant que**
Il se met en colère **quand** on **rit.**	**Avant** qu'il **eût pu** frapper, Jean lui saisit le poignet.
Il est venu à moi **dès qu'il m'a aperçu.**	Je lis **en attendant** qu'on **vienne** me chercher.

jusqu'à ce que

Il dormit **jusqu'à ce** qu'une détonation le **réveilla.**	Je resterai à Paris **jusqu'à ce** qu'on m'**écrive** de revenir.

Clauses of Purpose

	Pour que, afin que, de crainte que ; que (=afin que) . . . after imperative
	Je parle lentement **pour que** vous me **compreniez.**
	Levez le doigt, **que** je **voie** s'il est bien gras.

Consecutive Clauses

De sorte que, de façon que,

tant, si, tel, tellement, que

si bien que, plus, moins, que	**assez, trop, . . . pour que**
Il est sorti sans pardessus, **de sorte** (*or* **si bien**) qu'il **a attrapé** un rhume.	Parlez **de sorte qu'on vous comprenne.**
Il n'arrivait jamais **à** l'heure, **si bien qu'on a fini** par ne plus l'inviter.	
L'auditoire riait **tellement** (*or* **tant**) **qu'on** ne **pouvait** entendre les acteurs.	

Il est **plus** âgé, **moins** âgé, **que** vous ne **pensez.**

Vous êtes **assez** grand **pour qu'on puisse** vous traiter en homme.

§ **386.** *Fact doubtful or improbable*

Il est **tellement** (*or* **si**) fatigué **qu'il** ne **peut** nous accompagner.

Êtes-vous **tellement** fatigué **que** vous ne **puissiez** nous accompagner ?

§ **387.** *Dependent statement contrary to fact*

Il a une autorité **telle qu'il est** sûr d'être obéi.

Il n'a pas une autorité **telle qu'il soit** sûr d'être obéi.

Il ne demeure pas **à si** grande distance **que** vous ne **puissiez** courir chez lui (§§ 274.2.*a* ; 384, note).

Vous êtes **trop** grand **pour qu'on puisse** vous traiter en enfant.

Restrictive Clauses

Non (pas) **que, sans que, loin que**

Nous le connaissons, **non** (pas) **que** nous le **voyions** souvent.

Sortez **sans qu'on** vous **entende.**

§ **388.** *Assumption*

En cas que, à moins que, pourvu que, supposé que, en supposant que

Venez avec nous, **à moins que** vous ne **soyez** trop fatigué.

Nous sortirons **pourvu qu'il fasse** beau.

Que . . . ou que, que . . . ou non

Qu'il vienne ou qu'il ne **vienne** pas, je partirai demain.

Que le fait **soit** exact **ou non,** il paraît vraisemblable.

Asyndetic assumptive constructions

Vienne un peu de soleil, toutes ces fleurs s'épanouiront.

Je garderai mes bêtes, le roi les voulût-il.

Que le ciel demeurât couvert pendant six jours, et il faudrait remettre l'observation à une autre année.

'If' clauses

An assumption introduced by **si** is in the indicative ; introduced by **que** replacing **si** it is in the subjunctive.

S'il fait beau et **qu'il** ne **fasse** pas trop de vent, nous ferons une promenade en bateau.

Note.—An assumption and its consequence are both expressed in the future in the past tenses, in the following 'even though' constructions :

Me donnerait-on cent mille francs, je ne **tenterais** pas l'aventure.
On me **donnerait** cent mille francs que je ne **tenterais** pas l'aventure.
Quand on me **donnerait** (Lors même qu'on me **donnerait**) cent mille francs, je ne **tenterais** pas l'aventure.

In the compound tenses the subjunctive may be used (literary construction).

On m'**aurait** (m'eût) donné cent mille francs que je **n'aurais** (n'eusse) pas tenté l'aventure.
Quand on m'**aurait** (m'eût) donné cent mille francs, je **n'aurais** (n'eusse) pas tenté l'aventure.

§ 389 *Concession*

Quoique, bien que

Attendons encore, **quoique** nous **soyons** déjà en retard.

§ **390.** A clause dependent on a clause in the subjunctive is usually also in the subjunctive, as sharing the doubt, contrariness to fact, etc., implied in its head dependent clause.

Le colonel trouva singulier qu'il y **eût** en Corse des familles où l'on **fût** ainsi caporal de père en fils.
Ainsi vous ne pensez pas qu'il soit certain qu'il **ait** reçu ma lettre ?

But the sense may demand the indicative.

Il n'y a personne qui ne sache que la terre **est** ronde.
Croyez-vous que le baron se soit aperçu que nous ne l'**avons** pas salué ?

§ **391.** The subjunctive has never been widely used in colloquial French, apart from a few of the commoner constructions, such as the subjunctives of desire and necessity, *e.g.*

Je **veux** qu'il me le **dise.** Il **faudra** bien qu'il le **fasse.**
Que le bon Dieu vous **bénisse !** (To a person who has sneezed.)

Other constructions constantly take its place. Thus :

Il est possible qu'il vienne.	Peut-être qu'il viendra.
Je lui écrirai qu'il vienne.	Je lui écrirai de venir.
Je nie que cela soit vrai.	Je vous dis que ça n'est pas vrai !
Que vous ayez raison, c'est certain.	Mais vous **avez** raison, c'est certain !
Rien qui l'empêchât de gambader.	Rien **pour l'empêcher** de gambader.
Sortez sans qu'on vous entende.	Sortez sans **faire** de **bruit.**
A moins que vous ne soyez fatigué.	Si vous n'êtes pas fatigué.

§ **392.** Even in written and literary French the subjunctive is losing ground, and in modern works the student will frequently observe infractions to the rules given above.

Êtes-vous bien certain que vous ne vous livrez pas à des craintes exagérées ?—*H. Bataille.* (Cp. § 374.)
Certes, on ne peut pas dire qu'ils sont jolis, jolis.—*A. Dauzat.* (Cp. § 376.)
Il est possible que l'idée de faire cueillir des lauriers au Kronprinz **a fait** décider l'attaque.—*Le Temps.* (Cp. § 373.)

The past tenses in **-asse, -usse,** etc., are in especial disfavour.

Un mois tout entier se passa sans qu'elle ni moi nous nous **donnâmes** signe de vie.—*Courteline.* (Cp. § 387 ; the 'correct' form would be **donnassions** or **fussions donné.**)
En supposant que les apparitions **venaient** de mauvais esprits, Jeanne ne devait pas être considérée comme hérétique.—*L. Boucher.* (Cp. § 377 ; the rule calls for **vinssent.**)

See also § 396.

§ **393.** After indirectly transitive verbs, taking a noun object governed by **de** or **à,** the noun clause should be introduced by **de ce que, à ce que.** So also with clauses adverbial to an adjective.

{ J'ai profité **de** l'occasion.
{ Robert était d'une malice de singe ; il profitait toujours **de ce que** Christophe avait Ernst sur les bras pour faire derrière son dos toutes les malices possibles.

{ On se plaint **de** votre conduite.
{ On se plaint **de ce que** les plus belles tragédies de Voltaire **sont** fondées sur des malentendus (*misunderstandings*).

{ Je consens **à** cet arrangement.
{ Je consens **à ce que** vous vous **arrangiez** ainsi.

Furieux de ce qu'elle leur échappait, ils se précipitèrent sur moi.

But the noun object governed by **de** may often be replaced either by a noun clause in the indicative, introduced by **de ce que**, or by a clause introduced simply by **que**, if the latter calls for the subjunctive.

Vous vous étonnez **de ce que** je suis encore en vie.
Vous vous étonnez **que** je sois encore en vie.

And **de ce que** is occasionally found introducing a subjunctive.

Je me plains **de ce** qu'il ne soit pas venu.
Félicitons-nous **de ce que** ces heureux résultats n'aient pas été retardés.

§ **394.** Ellipsis in subordinate clauses. The following are common cases:

1. In comparisons, the subordinate clause is most frequently reduced to the second term of comparison.

Henri est plus grand **que** Paul (=que Paul n'est grand).
J'aime mieux Paul **que** Henri (=que je n'aime Henri).

2. Thus also with **comme**.

Elle était **comme** anéantie (=comme si elle était anéantie).
Je m'assis en m'appuyant au tilleul, **comme** autrefois **M. le curé.**

3. Ellipsis is frequent after **quoique**, if both clauses have the same subject.

Il est vigoureux, **quoique** petit (=quoiqu'il soit petit).
Quoique peu **robuste,** il maniait assez bien le fleuret.

And occurs after **parce que, puisque,** etc.

Je suis heureux, **quoique** garçon (*a bachelor*) ou **parce que** garçon.

Note.—On the other hand, there is no ellipsis in French after **quand, lorsque.**

When in London, *I shall get you some.* Quand je me trouverai à Londres, je vous en procurerai.
When a child, *I often had this dream.* Lorsque j'étais enfant, je faisais souvent ce rêve.

Nor after **comme si.**

The sky grew dark, as if obscured *by a cloud.* Le ciel s'assombrit, comme s'il eût été obscurci par un nuage.

4. There is ellipsis of a conjunction que ('haplology') when a clause introduced by que follows immediately on que introducing a second term of comparison, or on ne plus que.

Je ne demande pas mieux que cela soit (= Je ne demande pas mieux que que cela soit). *I ask for nothing better* than that *it should be so.*
Je ne demandais pas mieux qu'il fût mon ami.
Si cet enfant est à elle, quoi de plus simple qu'elle l'ait pris ?
Il **ne** manquerait plus **que** M. Fège imitât son exemple !

TENSE SEQUENCE

§ 395. The tense sequences in the complex sentence vary according to the relation between the dependent and the main clauses, but usually conform to one or other of the following types.

Dependent Clause in the Indicative Mood

1. The commonest sequence is as follows:

Head clause		Dependent clause	
Il affirme Il affirmera Il affirmerait	qu'il	le voit le voyait	(1)
		le vit l'a vu	(2)
		le verra le verrait	(3)
		l'aura vu l'aurait vu	(4)

When the head clause passes into the past tenses, including the present perfect (=conversational past) and the future perfect, the tenses in the dependent clause bracketed in pairs above, fall together as follows:

Head clause		Dependent clause
Il affirmait Il affirma Il a affirmé Il avait affirmé Il aura affirmé Il aurait affirmé	qu'il	le voyait (1) l'avait vu (2) le verrait (3) l'aurait vu (4)

Note.—There is, of course, no absolute and mechanical rule. A head clause in the past may require a dependent clause in the present.

Il sait que la terre est ronde.
Il savait, il apprit, que la terre est ronde.

2. Between a head clause and a dependent time clause, expressing actions simultaneous or in sequence, there is a strict parallelism in the tenses, which stands in contrast with the much simplified English sequence. Thus:

Je sors	quand il fait beau	*when it* is *fine*
Je sortais	quand il faisait beau	*when it* was *fine*
Je sortis	quand il fit beau	*when it* was *fine*
Je suis sorti	quand il a fait beau	*when it* was *fine*
J'étais sorti	quand il avait fait beau	*when it* was *fine*
Je sortirai	quand il fera beau	*when it* is *fine*
Je sortirais	quand il ferait beau	*when it* was *fine*
Il sera sorti	quand il aura fait beau	*when it* was *fine*
Je serais sorti	quand il aurait fait beau	*when it* was *fine*

Or let the dependent clause be originally in the perfect tense :

Il sort	quand il a dîné	*when he* has *dined*
Il sortait	quand il avait dîné	*when he* had *dined*
Il sortit	quand il eut dîné	*when he* had *dined*
Il est sorti	quand il a eu dîné (1)	*when he* had *dined*
Il était sorti	quand il avait eu dîné (2)	*when he* had *dined*
Il sortira	quand il aura dîné	*when he* has *dined*
Il sortirait	quand il aurait dîné	*when he* had *dined*
Il sera sorti	quand il aura eu dîné (3)	*when he* had *dined*
Il serait sorti	quand il aurait eu dîné (4)	*when he* had *dined*

In this exact parallelism of tenses lies the origin and the explanation of the 'temps surcomposés' (1, 2, 3, 4 above) already referred to in § 82.

The same sequences occur with a dependent **adjective** clause.

Ceux qui perdent paient.
Ceux qui perdaient payaient.
Ceux qui perdirent payèrent.
Ceux qui ont perdu ont payé.
Ceux qui perdront paieront.
Etc.

Ceux qui **ont fini** les premiers **partent.**
Ceux qui **avaient fini** les premiers **partaient.**
Ceux qui **eurent fini** les premiers **partirent.**
Ceux qui **ont eu fini** les premiers **sont partis.**
Etc.

Notes.—1. The above sequence does not hold, of course, if one of the verbs is descriptive. In this case sequence 1 reasserts itself.

Il faisait beau { quand je sortis. / quand je suis sorti. / quand j'étais sorti. }

Ceux qui avaient fini { partirent. / sont partis. }

Et quand il fut sorti, il ne pouvait leur parler. *Luke* i. 22.
Quand le bois fut consumé, la viande était cuite à point.

2. The past historic tenses may occur in the dependent clause, although the head clause stands

(*a*) In the present historic (§ 73.5).

Quand il fut à l'échelle, il monte, son couteau entre les dents.

(*b*) Or in the past descriptive = past historic (§ 77.5).

Un beau matin, lorsqu'il eut atteint ses vingt ans, il déclarait à son père furieux et stupéfait qu'il voulait se faire comédien.

3. In literary French, the 'temps surcomposé' is frequently avoided, the second past perfect taking its place.

> Dès que nous eûmes mis le pied sur cette terre, **nous avons été pris**, . . . emportés dans un tourbillon.

Conversational past and past historic are also frequently found in sequence.

> Quand M. de Talleyrand apparut pour la première fois dans ma carrière politique, j'ai dit quelques mots sur lui.

3. The dependent clause is an **assumption** introduced by **si.** The following are the usual combinations (note that the 'if' clause is never in the future tenses):

Je sors
Je sortirai } s'il **fait** beau, si la pluie **a cessé.**

Je sortais
Je sortirais } s'il **faisait** beau, si la pluie **avait cessé.**

Je serais sorti { s'il **avait fait** beau, si la pluie **avait cessé.**
s'il **eût fait** beau, si la pluie **eût cessé.**

Note.—This sequence does not apply to **concessive** clauses introduced by **si,** which may be in any tense required by the sense. But since the 'if' clause concedes a fact accepted as such, **the subjunctive mood can never take the place of the indicative.**

> S'il **écrit** mal, il se **fait** comprendre. *Although he writes badly . . .*
> S'il **écrivait** mal, il se **faisait** comprendre.
> S'il **écrivit** mal, il se **fit** comprendre.
> S'il **a écrit** mal, il **s'est fait** comprendre.

Since in this use the 'if' clause concedes an accepted fact, the future tenses seldom occur, but are not in any way ruled out.

> De patients chercheurs sauraient trouver d'autres poètes français d'Angleterre que ceux que je me propose de rapporter ici. Si l'on n'en **pourrait** point trouver de meilleurs, il est à croire que l'on en rencontrerait dont la simple habileté, à défaut de talent même, pourrait fournir un sujet d'étonnement.—*Mercure de France*, 1.5.18.

Here we have the future in the past, but the sentence might equally well have been written:

> De patients chercheurs sauront trouver. . . . Si l'on n'en **pourra** point trouver de meilleurs, il est à croire que l'on en rencontrera . . .

4. In the construction **c'est . . . qui, que, c'est** may either remain in the present tense, or stand in tense correlation with the dependent clause. The compound tenses, however, are never used.

> Puisqu'elle court si fort, **c'est** qu'il y a du danger.
> Puisqu'elle courait si fort, **c'est** (*or* **c'était**) qu'il y avait du danger.

Ce **n'est** pas (*or* Ce ne **fut** pas) Madeleine qu'il **épousa**, mais une de ses sœurs.

Ce n'est pas (*or rarely* Ce ne **sera** pas) Madeleine qu'il **épousera**, mais une de ses sœurs.

C'est (*or* **C'était**, *but not* Ç'avait été) à Strasbourg qu'ils avaient enterré leurs vieux parents.

Note.—Thus also : **C'est** (*or* C'était) à peine si l'on voyait l'eau.

Dependent Clause in the Subjunctive Mood

5. Let the dislocation:

Le **sait**-il ? Je ne l'**affirme** pas.

be put in the normal form:

Je n'**affirme** pas qu'il le **sache.**

Then we have the following correspondences between the tenses of the indicative and of the subjunctive:

Le sait-il ?		qu'il le **sache**	
Le savait-il ?		qu'il le **sût**	
Le sut-il ?	Je n'**affirme** pas	qu'il l'**ait su**	
L'a-t-il su ?	Je n'**affirmerai** pas	qu'il l'**ait su**	
L'avait-il su ?	N'**affirmez** pas	qu'il l'**eût su**	
Le saura-t-il ?	Je n'**affirmerais** pas	qu'il le **sache**	(*But see*
Le saurait-il ?	Je n'**ai** pas **affirmé**	qu'il le **sût**	*note.*)
L'aura-t-il su ?		qu'il l'**ait su**	
L'aurait-il su ?		qu'il l'**eût su**	

In the above, **je n'affirmerais pas** ranks as a 'softened' affirmation, equivalent to a present tense (§ **84.2**), and **je n'ai pas affirmé** as a present perfect. These tenses reappear below with their value as past tenses.

Le savait-il ?	Je n'**affirmais** pas	qu'il le **sût**
L'avait-il su ?	Je n'**affirmai** pas Je n'**ai** pas **affirmé**	qu'il l'**eût su**
Le saurait-il ?	Je n'**avais** pas **affirmé** Je n'**affirmerais** pas	qu'il le **sût**
L'aurait-il su ?	Je n'**aurais** pas **affirmé**	qu'il l'**eût su**

Note.—It may be necessary to distinguish the future from the present meaning in the dependent clause. **Devoir** is then used as an auxiliary, to form a future subjunctive (§ 86.3).

{Nous suivra-t-il ? Je ne l'affirme pas.
{Je n'affirme pas qu'il **doive** nous suivre.

{Nous suivrait-il ? Je ne l'affirmais pas.
{Je n'affirmais pas qu'il **dût** nous suivre.

§ 396. The tendency to avoid the past and past perfect tenses of the subjunctive has already been referred to in § 392, where it was shown that it often leads to the use of the indicative where the subjunctive would be expected. Still more frequently it leads to disregard of the sequences shown above, the present and present perfect being used instead of the past tenses, not only in homely speech or narrative, but to an increasing extent in literary style. Thus:

Les voyageurs étaient tous descendus de la voiture pour que les chevaux **aient** moins de mal. Tous les jours ensuite, dans la crainte que je **tombe,** elle m'avertissait quand nous étions devant la maison des morts. J'allais rentrer dans l'église, en attendant que Martine **vienne** me chercher. Elle voulait que je l'**appelle** tout simplement Pauline. Colette ne comprenait pas que je ne **sois** pas encore mariée.

Ils pourraient certainement traverser l'Atlantique, . . . à condition que l'état atmosphérique leur **soit** favorable.

('Pourraient' is not a 'softened' affirmation here; the strict sequence would be . . . leur **fût** favorable.)

MULTIPLE SENTENCES

§ 397. Co-ordination takes place in French much as in English, and calls for few remarks beyond what has been said in the sections on conjunctions (§§ 310, 311).

Co-ordination in multiple sentences is the rule, asyndetic constructions being characteristic of a certain emotional literary style ('style brisé,' 'style haché') which came into vogue with the Romantic School.

Quel spectre que cette voile qui s'en va! Il la regarde, il la regarde frénétiquement. Elle s'éloigne, elle blêmit, elle s'en va. Il était là tout à l'heure, il était de l'équipage, il allait et venait sur le pont avec les autres, il avait sa part de respiration et de soleil, il était un vivant. Maintenant, que s'est-il donc passé? Il a glissé, il est tombé, c'est fini!—*V. Hugo*, "*Les Misérables*."

§ 398. In **co-ordinated subordinate clauses,** the following constructions are possible:

1. The subordinating conjunction is not repeated.

S'il entre et me trouve ici,
Quand il entrera et me trouvera ici, } que dira-t-il?

This construction is rare.

2. The subordinating conjunction is repeated.

S'il entre, s'il me trouve ici,
Quand il entrera, quand il me trouvera ici, } que dira-t-il?

This is usual when the clauses are not joined by a co-ordinating conjunction.

3. The subordinate clauses are joined by the conjunctions **et, ou, mais** : subordination of the second clause is then indicated merely by **que**. This is the normal construction.

> **Quand** il entrera et **qu'il** me trouvera ici, que dira-t-il ?
> **Comme** il faisait beau et **que** tout le monde se sentait dispos, on fit une longue promenade.
> **Lors** même **qu'il** le permettrait ou **qu'il** le souffrirait, ce ne serait pas une chose à faire.
> **Avant que** nous soyons rentrés et **que** nous puissions dîner, il sera fort tard.
> Venez avec moi, **puisque** vous êtes libre et **que** cela vous intéressera.

§ **399.** The mood in the second subordinate clause is the same as in the first in all cases except when **que** replaces **si, comme si** (§ 388).

> **S'il** revenait et **qu'il fît** une réclamation, vous seriez fort embarrassé.
> Hermann ! s'écria-t-il, **comme s'il** ne pouvait se contenir, et **que** son secret lui **échappât**.

Note.—**Que** + **subjunctive** may only replace **si** in **assumptive** adverbial clauses. The substitution never takes place

1. If **si** introduces **concessive clauses** (of admitted facts).
   S'il est **malheureux** et **s'il** a des ennemis, c'est **entièrement de** sa **faute**.

2. If **si** introduces **noun** clauses (indirect questions).
   Je lui demandai s'il était marié, et si ses parents vivaient encore.

§ **400.** An adjective clause is often found co-ordinated with an adjective.

> Voici trois choses **incroyables et qui néanmoins sont arrivées.**

And **a noun** clause is occasionally found co-ordinated with a noun.

> Rappelez-vous **les difficultés** de l'entreprise, et **qu'il** les **surmonta toutes** !
> **J'ai** appris votre belle **conduite**, et **quelle admiration elle a inspirée.**

§ **401.** In colloquial French, simple statements often take the form of a subordinate clause dependent on an adverb.

> **Certainement qu'il** viendra ! **Heureusement qu'il était là.**
> **Peut-être qu'il** est malade.
> "Si tu crois être sur la terre pour t'amuser ?" **Oui donc ! que je le croyais.**

DEPENDENT INFINITIVE CLAUSES

§ **402.** If the subject of a dependent noun clause is already contained in the head clause, either (*a*) as subject, or (*b*) as object, the dependent clause is usually in the infinitive mood, and not in a finite mood introduced by **que.**

Whether the infinitive is or is not preceded by a preposition, depends on the governing verb (§§ 92–112).

(*a*) Je voudrais vous **aider.**
Je pourrai **partir** demain.
Je me suis hâté **de partir.**

Je tâcherai qu'on vous vienne en aide.	Je tâcherai **de vous venir** en aide.
Elle est tout étonnée que je n'y aie pas encore songé.	Elle est tout étonnée **de** n'y **avoir** pas encore songé.
Je suis heureux que vous puissiez m'aider.	Je suis heureux **de pouvoir** vous aider.
Je demande qu'il parle.	Je demande **à parler.**

(*b*) Laissez-**moi écrire** une lettre.
A mesure que je monte, je vois **l'horizon s'élargir.**
Je **lui** demanderai **de venir.**
Voici la personne **à qui** vous avez écrit **de venir.**
Priez-**la de s'asseoir.**
Je l'ai invité **à passer** les vacances chez nous.
Elle **me** forçait **à rire** par quelques remarques plaisantes.

If the subject of the dependent clause is not contained in the head clause, the infinitive construction is not used. Thus 'I want *you to help* me' must take the form

Je voudrais **que vous m'aidiez.**

§ **403.** Dependent on verbs of 'saying' and 'believing' (§ 96), the infinitive is a literary construction; colloquial, and indeed normal French prefer the dependent clause introduced by **que.**

J'affirme **que je l'ai vu.**	J'affirme **l'avoir vu.**
Je crois **que je vous en ai déjà parlé.**	Je crois **vous en avoir déjà parlé.**

Pendant un instant, je crus **que je rêvais** encore.

But if the head verb has a relative pronoun as object, the dependent infinitive is always used, and may have as subject either (*a*) the subject of the head clause, or (*b*) the antecedent to the relative pronoun.

(*a*) C'est une chose **qu'il** affirme **avoir vue.**
(*b*) C'est une chose **qu'il** affirme **être vraie.**

This is to avoid the very heavy 'qu'il affirme qu'il a vue,' '**qu'il affirme qui est vraie.**'

§ **404.** Dependent on impersonal constructions, and on '**c'est . . . de,**' the infinitive may be used when the subject (*a*) remains indefinite, or is plainly indicated by the context, or (*b*) is contained as an object in the head clause.

(*a*)	Il vaut mieux qu'on le lui dise. Il vaut mieux que vous le lui disiez.	Il vaut mieux le lui **dire.**
	Il faut qu'on le fasse. Il faut que vous le fassiez.	Il faut le **faire.**
	C'est déjà trop que je vous écoute.	**C'est** déjà trop **de** vous **écouter.**
	La première condition pour écrire, **c'est de** se **connaître,** et pour cela, **de s'examiner, de s'étudier.**	
(*b*)	Il arrive parfois qu'il se trompe.	Il **lui** arrive parfois **de se tromper.**

Note.—**Falloir** may have an unstressed dative pronoun object,

Il **lui** faudra faire les achats nécessaires,

but this construction is used only in literary style and 'careful' speech ; normally the subjunctive is preferred :

Il faudra qu'**il fasse** les achats nécessaires.

§ **405.** A dependent adverb clause is replaced by an infinitive clause when the two clauses have the same subject, and if to the conjunction there is a corresponding preposition or prepositional phrase. Thus :

après que **pour que** **sans que**	are replaced by	**après** **pour** **sans**
avant que **afin que** **à moins que** **loin que** **à condition que** **de peur que** **de crainte que** **au lieu que** **en attendant que**	are replaced by	**avant de** **afin de** **à moins de** **loin de** **à condition de** **de peur de** **de crainte de** **au lieu de** **en attendant de**
de manière que **de façon que**	are replaced by	**de manière à** **de façon à.**

Après que j'eus parcouru la lettre, il la reprit.	**Après avoir** parcouru la lettre, je la lui rendis.
Je ne viens pas pour qu'on me félicite.	Je ne viens pas **pour recevoir** des félicitations.
Il sort sans qu'on l'entende.	Il sort **sans faire** de **bruit.**

Allez le voir avant qu'il soit trop tard.	Allez le voir **avant de partir.**
Je vous apporte ce livre afin que vous le consultiez.	J'ai emprunté ce livre **afin de le consulter.**
Loin qu'on me remercie, je m'attire des injures.	**Loin de me remercier,** on m'a dit des injures.
Je vous donne cette somme à condition que vous partiez sur-le-champ.	Vous recevrez cette somme **à condition de partir** sur le champ.
Il ne sort jamais seul, de peur qu'on l'attaque.	Il ne sort jamais seul, **de peur d'être attaqué.**
Lui détruit, au lieu qu'eux édifient (*build*).	Il détruit **au lieu d'édifier.**
Il a répondu de manière que tout le monde s'est trouvé content.	Il a répondu **de manière à contenter** tout le monde.

§ **406.** There are, of course, many conjunctions which have no corresponding prepositional form allowing of the use of the infinitive. The dependent clause must then in all cases stand in a finite mood. Thus with

quand, aussitôt que, depuis que, bien que, parce que.

Quand j'ai chaud je bois du thé.
J'ai beaucoup appris depuis que je suis ici.
Il écrit beaucoup, bien qu'il ait peu de talent.
Je le sais parce que je l'ai vu.

Note.—**Pour + infinitive** has often a causal meaning, and the last example might be expressed :

Je le sais **pour l'avoir vu.**

§ **407.** An infinitive may be more loosely related than is set forth in the rules given above, when no ambiguity can arise.

Nos chaussures, enveloppées de laine **afin de pouvoir** marcher sans glisser, ne faisaient aucun bruit.—*Maupassant.*

The subject is really contained in the possessive **nos,** and the reference is sufficiently clear. The alternative would be "afin que nous pussions," which is hardly tolerated.

Le petit regarde, agite ses ailes. . . . Tout cela se fait dans le nid. . . . La difficulté commence **pour se hasarder** d'en sortir.—*Michelet.*

Quite as clear as " pour qu'il se hasarde d'en sortir."

" **Elle lui proposa de les acheter** " is ambiguous, since **acheter** may have for subject either **elle** or **lui.** But there is no ambiguity in

La veuve ramassa les œufs et elle les porta à un marchand d'œufs **en lui proposant de les acheter.**

PARTICIPLE AND GERUND CLAUSES

§ **408.** Participle clauses may qualify either the **subject or an object** of the head clause. They are for the most part

1. Equivalent to a **relative clause.**

   J'ai parcouru le parc, où de rares promeneurs **osant** braver l'humidité parcouraient les allées. (=qui osaient.)

   Le curé vivait obscurément, pour ne pas attirer sur lui les vexations **menaçant** à cette époque les prêtres.

   Il s'adressa à un collègue **arrivé** avant lui. (=qui était arrivé.)

2. Equivalent to a **time clause.**

   Arrivé sur le pont, notre cavalier se trouva arrêté par un groupe de curieux. (=Lorsqu'il fut arrivé.)

3. **Causal.**

   Ayant beaucoup à faire, je ne peux vous accorder que dix minutes. (=Comme j'ai beaucoup à faire.)

   Ne **pouvant** plus rester en place, il se leva brusquement, alla à la fenêtre. (=Comme il ne pouvait plus.)

   Croyant qu'elle avait besoin de mes services, j'accourus.

4. **Concessive.**

   Quiconque, le **pouvant,** ne nourrit pas son frère qui a faim, est un meurtrier. (=bien qu'il le puisse.)

5. Clauses of **attendant circumstances.**

   Elle courait dans tous les sens, **sautant** sur les bancs et **montant** sur les tables.

§ **409.** The participles are much used to form 'absolute' adverbial clauses, containing their own subject, and not formally related to the head clause (*cf.* § 178.2). These may be

1. Equivalent to a **time clause.**

   La porte ouverte, je voulus entrer. (=Lorsque la porte fut ouverte.)

   La journée finie, il partait en avant pour arriver plus vite à la maison. (=Quand la journée était finie.)

   Une fois traversé le dernier village de la vallée, on ne trouve plus de lieu habité. (=Quand une fois on a traversé.)

2. **Causal.**

   Le pied ne remplissant pas la chaussure, on garnissait le vide avec du foin. (=Comme le pied ne remplissait pas.)

   Son oncle l'ayant exercé de bonne heure au maniement des armes, il fut bientôt prêt à rejoindre le régiment.

3. **Assumptive.**

Dieu aidant, je réussirai. (= Si Dieu m'aide.)
Un triangle quelconque étant donné, y inscrire un cercle.

§ **410.** Gerund clauses usually have for their subject the subject of the head clause. They indicate for the most part

1. The **manner** of doing a thing.

Il n'y a que les Français qui se battent **en riant.**

2. The **means** by which a thing is done.

On ne fait son bonheur qu'**en s'occupant** de celui des autres.
Si les princes acquièrent quelques-uns de leurs sujets **en les achetant,** ils en perdent une infinité d'autres **en les appauvrissant.**

3. **Time.**

En arrivant chez lui, il s'aperçut qu'il avait oublié sa clef. (= Lorsqu'il arriva.)
Ils causaient joyeusement **tout en buvant.** (= pendant qu'ils buvaient.)

4. **Concession.**

Tout en condamnant leur conduite, il ne voulut pas les punir. (= Bien qu'il condamnât.)

5. **Attendant circumstances.**

Il sortit **en toussant.**
Elle me donna une bonne gifle (*slap*), **en m'appelant** petite brute.

§ **411.** The gerund not infrequently refers to an object of the head clause, or remains unrelated, when no ambiguity can arise.

Je **la** vis venir vers moi **en se dandinant** (*swaying her hips*).

Se makes the reference to la quite clear. But even the pronoun se is hardly necessary for lucidity.

Je **le** vis venir vers moi **en trébuchant** (*staggering toward me*).

It is quite clear that he, and not I, was staggering.

L'appétit vient **en mangeant.**
Tout en nous chauffant, il me chantait la chanson de l'Eau et du Vin (*While we warmed ourselves* . . .).
Madeleine devait surveiller notre recueillement (*pious meditation*), mais il **lui** arriva plus d'une fois de le troubler **en se disputant** avec l'une ou l'autre.

The gerund refers to the object **lui** contained in the impersonal head clause. Cp. the use of the infinitive in § 407.

THE CONCORDS

Concord of the Adjuncts of the Noun.

§ **412.** **Adjectives,** including the **articles,** agree in gender and number with their head noun.

> **Un** homme et **une** femme. **Le** père, **la** mère et **les** enfants.
> **Mon** frère et **ma** sœur. **Du** pain, **de la** salade et **des** œufs.
> **Ce** paquet et **cette** lettre sont arrivés ce matin.
> **Quel** espoir, **quelle** espérance avez-vous ?
> **Tel** maître, **telle** maison.
> Il était en **grande** tenue, chapeau **noir,** cravate **blanche,** gants **blancs.**

§ **413.** An adjective qualifying several nouns stands in the plural, and in the masculine if the nouns differ in gender.

> Il nous expliquait les événements avec une précision et une clarté **surprenantes.**
> Appartements et chambres **meublés.**
> On demande un homme ou une femme **âgés.**

But the adjective following several nouns showing a gradation in meaning may agree with the last noun only.

> L'aigle fend les airs avec une vitesse, une rapidité **prodigieuse.**

§ **414.** A plural article or possessive adjective may determine two or more nouns, when the latter form one idea.

> **Les** parents et amis du défunt. **Tes** père et mère honoreras.
> **Vos** nom et prénoms ?

§ **415.** The head noun may be in the plural, and qualified by two or more singular adjectives in such groupings as the following :

> Les langues **anglaise** et **française,** *or* La langue anglaise et la française.
> Les **onzième** et **douzième** siècles, *or* Le onzième et le douzième siècles.
> Le capitaine Guynemer a dans la même journée descendu **son 17e et 18e** avions.
> La Grèce est baignée par les mers **Adriatique** et **Ionienne,** *or* . . . par la mer Adriatique et la mer Ionienne.
> Ce musée possède des tableaux des écoles **espagnole, italienne,** et **flamande.**

§ **416.** The adjectives **demi, nu,** preceding the noun, form compound expressions in which they usually remain invariable.

Une **demi-heure.** Une **demi-livre** de beurre.

(But: Une heure et demie.)

Il courait **nu-pieds, nu-tête,** *or* pieds **nus,** tête **nue.**

Note.—Thus also: **Feu** la reine, *or* La **feue** reine. *The late queen.*

§ **417.** In a compound of two adjectives, both parts **vary,**

Une enfant **sourde-muette**; des cerises **aigres-douces,**

unless the first adjective has the force of an adverb qualifying the second one, when it should remain invariable:

Elles allaient **court-vêtues.** On la retrouva **demi-morte.**
Des arbres **clair-semés** (*or* **clairsemés**).

But this rule, which follows the dictates of logic, is transgressed in a number of expressions dating back to an earlier stage of the language:

La fenêtre était **grande ouverte.** La **nouvelle-mariée** portait un bouquet de fleurs **fraîches-écloses.** Je m'adressai aux **nouveaux-venus.**

§ **418. Tout,** adverbial (='quite,' § 247.3), should also remain invariable, but the people have never made the subtle distinction between the adjective and adverb functions, and **tout** has always agreed in **sound** with the following adjective.

Elle était **toute** petite.

Grammar has been compelled to accept the *fait accompli,* and to enact that adverbial **tout** shall vary before a feminine adjective beginning with a consonant or 'aspirate' **h.**

Je traversai la cour **toute** seule. Elles sont **toutes** tristes.
Elle est **toute** honteuse de ce qui lui arrive.

In other cases adverbial **tout** is supposed not to **vary.**

Ses cheveux sont **tout** blancs.
Je me dressai sur le lit, **tout** étonnée d'être couchée en plein jour.
Les exercices du corps sont **tout** aussi utiles que ceux de l'esprit et contribuent **tout** autant à former la volonté.

But the rule is often transgressed before an adjective.

Elle en était **toute** étonnée.

§ **419.** The adjectives **haut** and **plein** have adverbial function, and are invariable, in the phrases **haut la main, plein les poches, plein la bouche,** etc.

> Il remportera le prix **haut la main.** *He will carry off the prize easily;* literally *'win in a canter.'*
> Il avait de l'argent **plein** ses poches.

Note.—The adjective is, of course, invariable in the adverbial function studied in § 153.

Also the points of the compass, in their adjectival use.

> Les côtes **ouest** de la France.

§ **420.** Compound adjectives of colour, such as **bleu foncé, rose pâle,** do not vary.

> Elle portait une robe **bleu foncé,** ornée de rubans **bleu pâle.**
> Les uniformes **bleu horizon** des troupes françaises.
> Des paons **vert et or.** Des marins aux visages **rouge brique.**

(The construction is elliptical, and still felt as a contraction of **une robe d'un bleu foncé,** in which **bleu** has noun function.)

Similarly, nouns used as adjectives of colour are invariable, when still felt as nouns.

> Des rubans **pivoine, citron, olive** ; une robe **marron.** (=Des rubans de la couleur d'une pivoine, etc.)

In a few cases the noun has become a real adjective, and varies.

> Des rubans **roses.** Des étoffes **pourpres.**

§ **421.** Attributive adjectives preceding the collective **gens,** which was originally feminine, still take the feminine form.

> Ces **bonnes** gens. Des **petites** gens (*People in a modest position*).

The compounds thus formed are, however, felt as masculine; following attributive adjectives, and also predicative adjectives, are usually in the masculine.

> **Heureux** les **petites** gens **éloignés** des grandeurs !

Note.—**Quels** sont ces gens ? **Quels** or **Quelles** sont ces **bonnes** gens ?
Tous ces **pauvres** gens ne savaient que faire.
Toutes ces **bonnes** gens m'adoraient.

§ **422.** The **cardinal** numbers are invariable, except **un, vingt,** and **cent.**

Un agrees in gender with the noun.

> Nous avons lu vingt et **une** pages.

Vingt and **cent** take a plural s when multiplied by a preceding numeral and not followed by another numeral.

J'ai collectionné plus de quatre-**vingts** timbres-poste, et mon frère en a près de trois **cents**.
Vous me devez en tout deux mille quatre **cent** quatre-**vingt**-dix francs.

But **un, vingt, cent** never vary if used with ordinal functions (§ 260).

Ouvrez vos livres à la page vingt et **un**, à la page quatre-**vingt**, à la page trois **cent**. Je suis né en l'année dix-neuf **cent**.

§ **423. Pronouns,** when they stand for a noun, agree in gender and number with their head-noun.

Marie est-**elle** là ? — Oui, **la** voilà.
Ils sont gentils, vos enfants.
Vos amis et **les miens** ne se voient jamais.
Ces livres-là ne sont guère intéressants ; lisez plutôt **ceux-ci.**

§ **424.** In colloquial and familiar style, and in dislocations generally, the neuter pronouns **ce** and **cela** (**ça**) often stand instead of the masculine or the feminine.

Ce is thus regularly used with **être** and a predicative complement noun or pronoun.

L'école **c'est** le monde en petit.
C'est moi. **Ce sont** mes amis.
(Colloq.) **C'est** gentil, cette petite fête en plein soleil.
(Colloq.) Les cigares, je n'aime pas **ça** (§ 324.1).

§ **425. Predication and Apposition.** Predicative and appositive nouns, adjectives, and pronouns agree in number and gender with their head-noun or pronoun.

Il est **acteur.** **Elle** est **actrice.**

(Adjectival use of the noun. The alternative construction is C'est un acteur ; C'est une actrice. § 196.2.)

La raison du plus fort est toujours **la meilleure.**
Vous êtes aussi **grande** que moi.
Elle se sent **fatiguée.** Je **la** trouve **jolie.**
On **la** traita de **petite sotte.**
Encore **vaillante,** malgré son âge, **la grand'mère** travaille au jardin.
Elle restait debout, **hésitante.**

But a predicative or appositive noun or pronoun often necessarily differs in gender or number from its head-word.

> **Elle** était **le véritable chef** de l'entreprise.
> On traita **le pauvre garçon** de **poule mouillée** (*milksop*).
> **Ce soldat** est **une recrue.**
> **Les consolations** sont **un secours** que l'on se prête, et dont, tôt ou tard, chaque homme a besoin.
> **Mme de Staël, le célèbre auteur** de Corinne.
> **L'humanité** est devenue **ce que** nous **la** voyons.
> **La** voilà devenue **quelqu'un.**

Note.—For the concords with **nous** and **vous**, see §§ 214, 215.

§ 426. After **avoir l'air**, = **sembler, paraître**, the adjective may be treated as predicative either to **air** or to the subject.

> Elle **a l'air intelligent** or **intelligente, doux** or **douce.**

If the subject is a 'thing' (as opposed to a person), the adjective is usually predicative to the subject.

> Cette viande **n'a** pas **l'air fraîche.**

Concord of the Verbs.

Simple Subject.

§ 427. Verbs in a finite mood agree in person and number with their subject.

> **Le général commande, les soldats obéissent.**
> **Je** vous **parle, écoutez-vous ?**
> **Les États-Unis étaient** une colonie anglaise. *The United States* was *a British Colony.*

§ 428. When the subject is a relative pronoun, the verb agrees with the antecedent.

> Nous y étions, **nous** qui vous **parlons.**
> Il n'y a que **nous deux** qui **sachions** cela.
> C'est **vous** qui me **l'avez** dit.
> C'est **moi** qui **serai** leur protecteur.

But when there is a predicative or other complement, the latter may be taken as antecedent, and thus two different concords are possible.

> { **Vous** êtes les seuls qui **m'avez** (*or* **m'ayez**) répondu.
> { Vous êtes **les seuls** qui **m'ont** répondu.
> { **Un** des romans qui **m'a** le plus intéressé, c'est *Colomba.*
> { Un **des romans** qui **m'ont** le plus intéressé, c'est *Colomba.*

§ **429.** A singular collective noun requires the verb, and also pronominal references, in the singular, the loose concords found in English not being tolerated.

> **Le conseil** n'a pas encore discuté l'affaire. *The council* have *not yet . . .*
> **La cavalerie** se **montait à** deux mille hommes. *The cavalry* were *two thousand.*
> Quand **la compagnie eut atteint** le bois, **elle** se répandit de tous côtés. . . . they *spread in all directions.*
> **La famille prenait** le thé dans le jardin. . . . was *or* were *having tea.*
> **Le parti libéral s'intéresse** à la question. *The Liberal party* is *or* are *interested in the question.*

§ **430.** But if the singular collective is followed by a partitive noun in the plural, the verb may be either in the singular or the plural, the tendency being to use the plural.

> Le reste des naufragés **ont** or **a** péri.
> Une foule de gens **pensent** ainsi.
> Il fallut attendre qu'une demi-douzaine de spectateurs **eussent** payé.
> Des montagnes de la Suisse **descendent** une infinité de cours d'eau.
> Une nuée de flèches **transpercèrent** les chevaliers.

Occasionally the collective noun is obviously the real subject, with which the verb must agree.

> Une nuée de flèches **obscurcit** l'air.

§ **431.** If the partitive noun in the plural is dependent on an adverbial expression of quantity, the verb is, of course, in the plural.

> Beaucoup de gens, pas mal de gens, nombre de gens, la plupart des gens, **pensent** ainsi.

And the verb is still in the plural though the partitive noun be understood.

> Beaucoup, la plupart, **pensent** ainsi.

Notes.—(*a*) After **chacun** the verb is always in the singular.

> Chacun (*or* Chacun de ces élèves) **sera** puni.

(*b*) After **plus d'un** the verb is either singular or plural.

> Plus d'un de ces hommes **était blessé** or **étaient blessés**.

§ **432.** **C'est** followed by a logical subject is in normal French attracted to the number of the latter in the third person plural; in familiar speech or writing it remains in the singular.

> C'est moi. C'est nous. **Ce sont eux** *or* **C'est eux.**
> **Ce sont des artichauts** dont vous déjeunez là ?
> **Ce** ne **sont** pas les **places** qui honorent les hommes, c'est nous qui devons honorer les places.
> **Ce** n'**étaient** pas là **de vaines paroles.**
> **Ce furent les troupes anglaises** qui soutinrent l'assaut.

Notes.—(*a*) Thus also: On sonne. **Ce doivent être** (*or* **Ce doit être**) **mes amis.**

(*b*) But forms such as **seront-ce, furent-ce, fussent-ce,** are always avoided, and even **sont-ce** is rare.

> **Est-ce** mes amis qui vous ont dit cela ?
> Écrivez-moi, ne **fût-ce** que quelques lignes.

(*c*) The expression **si ce n'est** is invariable.

> Aucun peuple de l'antiquité, **si ce n'est** les Phéniciens, ne connaissait la côte occidentale de l'Afrique.

§ **433.** In the impersonal form the verb always remains in the singular, even when followed by a logical subject in the plural.

> **Il est** trois heures. **Il y a là** deux **messieurs** qui vous demandent.
> **Il est venu** plusieurs personnes.

Multiple Subject.

§ **434.** If the subjects are of different persons, the verb is always in the plural, and in the first person rather than in the second or third, in the second rather than in the third.

> Ton frère et toi **êtes** invités. Ni toi ni ton frère n'êtes invités.
> Vous ou moi lui **parlerons.**

It is usual, however, to sum up the subjects joined by **et** or **ou** in an unstressed pronoun.

> Ton frère et toi, **vous** êtes invités.
> **Vous** êtes invités, ton frère et toi.
> Vous ou moi, **nous** lui **parlerons.**

With two or more subjects of the third person, joined by et, the verb is in the plural.

> Henri et son frère **sont** invités.
> **Lui** et son frère **sont** invités.

§ **435.** When the subjects are joined by **ni, avec, ou,** the verb may stand either in the singular or in the plural ; the tendency is to use the plural unless the sense points clearly to the use of the singular.

Ni Henri ni son frère ne **sont** invités *or* n'est invité.
Ni Henri ni son frère ne **remportera** le prix. (Subjects mutually exclusive, as there is only one prize.)
On ne savait pas encore si à Marie Tudor **succéderait** Marie Stuart ou Élisabeth. (Subjects mutually exclusive.)

§ **436. L'un ou l'autre** consists of two subjects that are always mutually exclusive, and the verb is always in the singular.

L'une ou l'autre **devait** forcément monter sur le trône.

But **l'un et l'autre, ni l'un ni l'autre,** take the verb either in the singular or in the plural.

L'un et l'autre se **dit** *or* se **disent.**
Ni l'un ni l'autre n'**est venu** *or* ne **sont venus.**

§ **437.** A multiple subject is often summed up by one of the pronouns **tout, le tout, rien, tout le monde, chacun, personne, aucun, nul,** after which the verb is in the singular.

Habitants, animaux, maisons, **tout fut** entraîné par les eaux.
Menaces, promesses, flatteries, **rien** ne **servit.**

Concord of the Participles.

§ **438.** The verbal form in **-ant,** used as a **present participle,** as a **gerund,** or as a **preposition,** is **invariable.** For examples, see §§ **113.**1, 3 ; **300.**

Used as a **verbal adjective** or as a **noun,** it varies like other adjectives and nouns. See § **113.**2, and note *a*.

§ **439.** The **past participle** used as an **adjective** or as a **noun,** varies like other adjectives and nouns.

§ **440.** Used as a **preposition,** it is **invariable.**

Passé neuf heures, la grille est fermée.
Supposé cette circonstance, tout s'explique facilement.
Y compris votre famille nous serons dix à table.

(See also § **116**, note *b*.)

§ **441.** Used with the auxiliary **être** to form (*a*) the compound tenses of certain **intransitive** verbs (§ 63), and (*b*) the **passive voice of the** verb (§ 65), the past participle agrees with the subject.

(*a*) **Elle est venue** hier.
Où **êtes-vous allés**, mes garçons ?
Où **êtes-vous allé**, mon garçon ?
(*b*) **Ils sont respectés** de tous.
Elle a été aidée par sa sœur.

§ **442.** Used with the auxiliary **avoir**, the past participle is **invariable,**

Il nous a **raconté** une histoire,
Elle m'a **écrit** une lettre,

unless it is preceded by a direct object, in which case **it agrees in gender and number with the direct object.**

The following are the constructions in which this may occur :

(***a***) **Interrogation.**

Quelle histoire vous a-t-on **racontée** ?
Lequel de ces livres avez-vous **lu** ?
Lesquels de ces livres avez-vous **lus** ?
Combien de lettres avez-vous **écrites** ?

(*b*) **Exclamation.**

Quelle belle journée nous avons **passée** !
Que de (*or* **Combien de**) **misères** nous avons **endurées** !

(*c*) The direct object is **an unstressed personal pronoun.**

Il **nous** a **encouragés** de ses conseils.
Je **vous** ai **entendue,** mademoiselle !
Cette lettre, je **l'**ai **écrite** hier.
Avez-vous parlé à mes parents ? — Oui, je **les** ai **vus** ce matin.

(*d*) The direct object is **a relative pronoun** ; the concord is with the **antecedent.**

Voici **la lettre qu'**il m'a **écrite.**
C'est **nous qu'**on a **punis.**

Notes.—(*a*) It follows that the past participles of indirectly transitive verbs, and of intransitive verbs other than those conjugated with être, are always invariable.

Ils nous ont **parlé.**
On ne nous a pas **obéi.**
Nous avons bien **ri** !

(*b*) Although the past participle agrees with a preceding partitive noun, it does not agree with partitive **en** and **dont**, which are considered as genitives, even when partitive.

> Combien de gâteaux avez-vous achetés ? — J'en ai acheté deux.
> Voici la liqueur dont nous avons bu.

But the participle *may* agree with **combien**.

> Je vous ai écrit trois lettres ; combien en avez-vous reçu *or* reçues ?

The strict application of the rule that the past participle agrees with a preceding direct object involves consideration of the following special cases:

§ 443. Voir, regarder, entendre, écouter, laisser, sentir, + infinitive + object. Consider the following groups of sentences:

(*a*) J'ai vu bâtir cette maison.
J'ai déjà entendu jouer cette mélodie.
Il a laissé punir sa petite sœur.

(*b*) J'ai vu sortir les enfants.
J'ai entendu chanter mademoiselle votre sœur.
Il a laissé entrer tout le monde.

In sentences (*a*) the noun is the object, not of **voir, entendre, laisser,** but of the dependent infinitive.

In sentences (*b*) the noun is the object of **voir, entendre, laisser,** and is the subject of the dependent infinitive.

And the participial concord should conform to this analysis. Therefore:

(*a*) No agreement in

> Cette maison, je l'ai **vu** bâtir.
> Quelle maison avez-vous **vu** bâtir ?
> Voilà la mélodie que j'ai **entendu** jouer.
> Sa petite sœur, il l'a **laissé** punir.

(*b*) The participle agrees in

> Les enfants, je **les** ai **vus** sortir.
> Est-ce votre **fille que** j'ai **entendue** chanter ?
> Ces personnes, pourquoi **les** avez-vous **laissées** entrer ?

But this nice point of grammar is seldom remembered, or even understood, and false concords are committed even by members of the Académie. To-day the agreement or non-agreement of the past participle are officially 'tolerated' in both (*a*) and (*b*).

> Sa petite sœur, il l'a **laissée** punir.
> Est-ce votre fille que j'ai **entendu** chanter ?

§ **444. Faire + infinitive** = factitive verb (§ 92).

The past participle of **faire** never varies in this construction.

Il nous a **fait** venir.
Je vous félicite des progrès que vous lui avez **fait** faire.
Je n'ai pas encore vu la maison qu'il a **fait** bâtir.

§ **445. Croire, vouloir, pouvoir, + infinitive + noun.**

Il a cru entendre des chuchotements.
Il a voulu revoir son ancienne demeure.
Il a pu faire encore quelques efforts.

The object to **croire, etc.,** is the dependent infinitive, not the noun. Therefore :

J'ai été averti par certains chuchotements que j'ai **cru** entendre.
Il me conduisit à son ancienne demeure, qu'il avait **voulu** revoir.
J'ai fait tous les efforts que j'ai **pu** (= que j'ai pu faire).
Il a fait toutes les promesses qu'on a **voulu** (= qu'on a voulu qu'il fît).

§ **446. Marcher, courir, valoir, coûter, dormir, vivre, durer, etc.** Consider the following groups of sentences :

(*a*) J'ai dormi **deux heures.** J'ai couru **deux lieues.**
Ce cheval a coûté (valu) **trois mille francs** autrefois.
Il a vécu **dix ans** à l'étranger.
Sa splendeur avait duré **deux ou trois mois.**

(*b*) Mon discours m'a coûté **plusieurs heures** de travail, mais il m'a valu **des félicitations** unanimes.
Il a couru **de grands dangers.**

In (*a*) the verbs are followed, not by an object, but by an adverbial extension of time, measure, etc. (§ **126**, note).

In (*b*), **heures, félicitations, dangers,** are considered as the objects of the verb. Therefore :

(*a*) No agreement in

On me reproche les deux heures que j'ai **dormi.**
On ne me tient pas compte des deux lieues que j'ai **couru.**
Trois mille francs, ce cheval les a **valu** (**coûté**) autrefois, mais il ne les vaut plus aujourd'hui.
Les dix ans qu'il a **vécu** à l'étranger lui ont élargi l'esprit.
Pendant les deux ou trois mois qu'avait **duré** sa splendeur, il avait fait une foule de connaissances.

(*b*) The participle agrees in

Vous savez **les heures de travail que** ce discours m'a **coûtées**, mais j'en ai été récompensé par **les félicitations qu'**il m'a **values.**
Si vous saviez **les dangers qu'**il a **courus !**

§ 447. Impersonal Verbs.

(*a*) Il est **tombé** beaucoup de pluie.
Il est **arrivé** de bonnes nouvelles.
Combien de voyageurs est-il **arrivé** ce matin ?

The past participle does not agree with the logical subject.

(*b*) Il lui a fallu une forte somme.
Il a fallu de grands efforts pour les sauver.
Il a fait hier une grande chaleur.
Il y a eu une révolte à bord (*a mutiny on board*).

In these sentences, the noun following the impersonal verb is rightly or wrongly considered as the **logical subject**, not as the object (§ 98). Therefore, there is no agreement in the corresponding adjective clauses.

Savez-vous la somme qu'il lui a **fallu** pour cette entreprise ?
Vous n'imaginez pas quels efforts il a **fallu** pour les sauver.
Les grandes chaleurs qu'il a **fait** nous ont ôté toute énergie.
Le public ne se douta pas de la révolte qu'il y avait **eu** à bord.

Hence the rule : **The past participle of an impersonal verb is invariable.**

Pronominal Verbs.

§ 448. The verbs of groups 1 and 2 in § 70, although conjugated with **être**, have the same participial concords as the verbs conjugated with **avoir** : the past participle agrees with the preceding direct object, if there be one ; the direct object may or may not be the unstressed object pronoun.

1. Marie s'est **coupée** au doigt.
Marie s'est **coupé le doigt.**
Ils se sont **nui** par leur inexactitude. (Nuire à qqn.)
En deux ans, trois rois s'étaient **succédé** sur le trône. (Succéder à qqn.)
Nous nous sommes **donné** une poignée de mains.
Elle m'a montré **les gants qu**'elle s'était **achetés.**
Comment se sont-ils **arrogé ce droit.**
Je ne lui reconnais par **les droits qu**'il s'est **arrogés.**
Ils se sont **laissé** (*or* **laissés,** cf. § 443) éblouir par ces belles promesses.

2. Les deux chiens se sont **montré** les dents.
Elles se sont saluées, mais ne se sont **pas parlé.**

§ **449.** In the verbs of group 3 (*a*, *b*, *c*), the past participle may be said to agree with the subject.

(*a*) **Ils se sont moqués de vous.**
Elle s'est repentie de sa faute.
Vous êtes-vous souvenue de mes recommandations ?

(*b*) **Nous nous sommes aperçus de notre erreur.**
Nous ne nous étions jamais doutés de la valeur de ce document.
Elles s'en sont allées.

(*c*) **Ces articles se sont bien vendus.**

Note.—Under (*b*) there are a few verbs the past participle of which is supposed never to vary, *e.g.* **se rire** and **se plaire.** It is alleged that **se** is in the dative, these verbs being indirectly transitive (**rire à qqn.**, **plaire à qqn.**). Thus:

Ils se sont ri de nos menaces.
Elles se sont plu à nous tourmenter.

But the relationship between the constructions of the simple and the pronominal forms of the verb has long ceased to be felt, and the tendency to-day is to write

Ils se sont plus à nous tourmenter.

INDEX

The references are to sections